Monsieur de Saint-George

Monsieur de Saint-George

VIRTUOSO, SWORDSMAN,
REVOLUTIONARY

A Legendary Life Rediscovered

Alain Guédé

Translated from the French by
Gilda M. Roberts

PICADOR

NEW YORK

Picador® is a U.S. registered trademark and is used by
St. Martin's Press
under license from Pan Books Limited.

www.picadorusa.com

Book design by Kathryn Parise

The publisher gratefully acknowledges the assistance of the
French Ministry of Culture—*Centre national du livre.*

LIBRARY OF CONGRESS CATALOGING-IN-PUBLICATION DATA

Guédé, Alain.
[Monsieur de Saint-George. English]
Monsieur de Saint-George : Virtuoso, Swordsman, Revolutionary /
A Legendary Life Rediscovered / Alan Guédé, translated from
the French by Gilda M. Roberts.
p. cm.
Includes bibliographical references (p. 279) and index (p. 238).
ISBN 0-312-30927-9
1. Saint-Georges, Joseph Boulogne, chevalier de, d. 1799. 2. Nobility—France
Biography. 3. Musicians—France—Biography. 4. Racially mixed people—
France—Biography. I. Title.

DC137.5.S35G8413 2003
944'.00496'0092—dc21
[B]
2003049888

First published in France under the title *Monsieur de Saint-George:
Le Nègre des lumières* by Editions Actes Sud

First U.S. Edition: December 2003

10   9   8   7   6   5   4   3   2   1

Music is an act of resistance.

—ARTURO TOSCANINI

CONTENTS

Contents

Detail showing the Place Royale and the Bastille, from the *Plan de Turgot*, started in 1734 and completed in 1739 under the direction of Michel-Etienne Turgot. COURTESY OF THE AVERY LIBRARY, COLUMBIA UNIVERSITY

Monsieur de Saint-George

I

Nanon

Lesser Antilles, Christmas Day, 1739. Cool trade winds caressed the colonnaded mansion, but in an upstairs bedroom, its windows tightly shuttered, the atmosphere was stifling. A green haze enveloped the room, produced by smoke from burning cactus sticks. Barely visible in the gloom were dark European furnishings, the most striking of them an elegant dresser, over which hung a faded mirror, and a bed, on which lay a woman in labor.

"Stiffen up now. Don' you let up. Stiffen up now. Don' you let up," a midwife urged the woman in labor, whose name was Nanon.

Squealing children chased one another around her bed, avoiding the swats of their scolding mothers, who were bustling about in the room.

"Now don' you let up!"

The sound of chanting and singing drifted over from the sugar factory a few hundred yards down from the mansion, hidden behind a thick curtain of trees. There was also the pounding of drums and the beating of sticks against the trunk of a cedar tree. That morning these same musicians, slaves, had been herded to a mass celebrated by a

Capuchin priest named Father Casimir.[1] The sanctioning of the slave trade by the Church over a century earlier, in 1612, had not come without strings; in exchange for its blessing, the Church had been given greater opportunities to evangelize among the slaves, who were henceforth released from work on Sundays and feast days. For his part, Father Casimir had devised an efficient stratagem for ensuring control over souls as well as for preserving certain commercial interests that had recently been damaged by interfering Jesuits: Every slave visiting his confessional received a coin, which he was then free to go off and spend at the tavern.

No sooner were their churchly obligations fulfilled, however, than the slaves turned to pursuits that were decidedly un-Christian. Couples paired off to dance the *calenda*; the rhythm of the drums grew ever wilder. More and more deafening, the music spread the length of the rue Case-nègre—roughly, Slave Cabin Street—until there wasn't a room in the big house up on the bluff not bombarded by the din of drums.

"Don' you let up now!"

In the room next door, a small group of Frenchmen were nervously chewing tobacco leaves and sipping beakers of rum. Among them was Monsieur Plato, a former customs officer from Bercy, near Paris.[2] Plato—no one knew if such was his real name or a nickname given him by the slaves—acted as the sugar plantation's steward; he balanced the books with almost obsessive care. Also present was Georges Bologne "de Saint-Georges," as he styled himself, the descendant of a line of slave-owning planters who worked one of the most prosperous estates on Guadeloupe. Between the two sat the most anxious of them all, the father of the baby due at any moment, Guillaume-Pierre Tavernier de Boullongne. In contrast to that of Georges Bologne, the "de" in Guillaume-Pierre's name denoted the real thing—legitimate aristocratic descent

"Don' you let up!"

Steam from the calabashes of boiling water that had been carried in by Clairon, a mixed-race woman in her twenties, swirled in the air and mingled with fumes from the burning cactus sticks, which, when lit, were thought to keep away insects. With a final, supreme effort, Nanon was delivered of a baby, a boy. The midwife exulted.

Ti moune la ça, si Bon Dié baille vie santé en peu di y ke grand missié!

"If the good Lord gives him life and health, your baby be a *fine* gentleman!" Then she ventured a prophecy. "One day this boy meet the king of France!"

Nanon, by general acknowledgment the most beautiful woman on the island of Guadeloupe, had just presented Guillaume-Pierre with a son. For Father Casimir, it was one more baptism to celebrate in a parish already growing by leaps and bounds; in a few months he would place the first stone in what would become Saint-François church. As this was Christmas Day, he decreed that the name "Joseph" was imperative. The name was all the more appropriate given that the patron saint of carpenters was also that of the so-called *nègres à talent*, "skilled Negroes"—those who by dint of industry and expertise in some area had managed to free themselves from the driver's whip. Nonetheless, Joseph's name would not be listed on the registry kept by the curate of nearby Le Baillif. His father might be a French nobleman, but Nanon was a slave, and the children of slaves were not recognized by the Church.

Only a year and some before, this youngest son of the Tavernier de Boullongne family line had been miles away from the Lesser Antilles, fighting grim battles against the Austrians and Prussians in the mud and drizzle of Flanders. But all that was in the past. Today, everything seemed to have turned out splendidly for twenty-nine-year-old Guillaume-Pierre, who had come to Guadeloupe vowing to earn his fortune and thereby to restore to his ennobled family's name a luster somewhat lost over the course of several generations. The Boullongnes were among the oldest families of French Flanders. They had had their ups and downs, however. At the beginning of the seventeenth century, for example, Louis de Boullongne was pursued by creditors, forced to flee the family seat, and set himself up in the town of Beauvais, north of Paris. Thinking it prudent, he had concealed his noble title, calling himself simply "Tavernier." The ruse was a necessity for only a brief time; once the moneylenders' threats had passed, Louis immediately began to display openly his title and coat of arms.

Doing so was more than a mere matter of pride. In France during this period, the rising bourgeoisie was engaged in a frantic quest for prestige; in their eyes, that aristocratic "de" in Louis's name was a real prize. He managed to marry off his son, Charles, to a nouveau riche's daughter, whose dowry, in turn, enabled her husband to buy the position of "personal lieutenant." Though most certainly not up to the level of what it would have been had it taken place in Versailles, the marriage ceremony had been celebrated by no less a personage than the bishop of Senlis. The same procedure was followed in due course by the grandson, Guillaume—Guillaume-Pierre's father—who made equally clever use of his wife's dowry in 1708 by buying, admittedly at an extremely elevated price, the lucrative post of director of the salt tax in the town of Orléans.

While the upper-echelon aristocracy was parading around at court, looking down their noses at petty provincial nobles who, in their view, were debasing themselves by consenting to work, others had understood the direction in which the winds of change were blowing: money. At Versailles, dukes and barons were bankrupting themselves buying places among the front rank at the king's levee, the king's supper, or even the royal defecation. Meanwhile, in Paris, viscounts and petty marquises engaged in all kinds of speculation on the rue Saint-Honoré and around the newly created place des Victoires, which was becoming a busy center of financial activity.

Moreover, the line between the petty nobles with money and the aristocrats attached to the court could often prove quite porous. Indeed, a distant cousin from the provinces might be welcomed at Versailles, particularly if he possessed some hard cash or an impressive title. This the Tavernier de Boullongne family perfectly grasped when, around 1660, they imposed themselves upon the world of the Versailles Boullongnes, who were court painters of some renown but not themselves of the nobility. The darlings of Louis XIV, admired by his powerful minister Jean-Baptiste Colbert, Louis "the elder" Boullongne and after him his children—Louis, Bon, and their four sisters (two of whom were, very unusually, admitted to the Académie des Beaux-Arts)—had at first adorned with representations of cherubs, Dianas, and Jupiters the most illustrious ceilings and walls of France, including the Hall of Mirrors at Versailles, the Louvre, the chapel in Val-de-Grâce, and so on. Louis junior's son Jean—born in 1690—had, for his part, taken the opposite tack and turned to making not art but money. Jean Boullongne became one of the king's eight finance *intendants,* or administrators. Far from inconveniencing him, the increasingly frequent visits from his ennobled country cousins were a godsend. What the Taverniers offered this—from all accounts—affable and witty individual was the aristocratic claim he lacked in order to compete with the king's other counselors, most of them nobles of ancient lineage. The Boullongne painters were finally ennobled in 1721. In Jean's ambitious race to power, such a late date was of course not quite a match for an ancient title. But it was something. Soon the interests of all the Boullongnes—painters and country gentry—were inextricably intertwined: The provincials brought with them the legitimacy of blood; the worldly Parisian offered financial savvy and counsel.

What united them was the seeking of fortune. For Guillaume-Pierre and his brother, Philippe-Guillaume Tavernier de Boullongne, joining the military seemed the only recourse. Cousin Jean managed to persuade them that there were far better things to do in the army than die in combat. Given that they had chosen to wear a uniform, he advised they use it to make a profit. Thus, with the help of the *intendant,* the Tavernier brothers were appointed supply officers to the maréchal Maurice de Saxe.

At thirty-five, Maurice de Saxe, who would become famous in the world of the eighteenth century as the so-called "conqueror of Fontenoy," was the last of the aristocratic warriors. The natural son of the Elector of Saxony (later king of Poland), he had been merely twelve years old when his father sent him off to learn soldiering at the siege of the city of Lille. Two years later, in 1710, he completed his apprenticeship through brutal combat in frigid temperatures against Peter the Great's Cossacks. Maurice de Saxe swept through every European battlefield during sieges and civil wars with the roving militia his father had helped him recruit and generously maintain. Whenever he was forced by inactivity to return home to Dresden, this living legend and lover of the good life fought idleness by indiscriminately bedding chambermaids and duchesses. Anxious to see him settled down, his mother, Aurora von Königsmark, succeeded in getting him married off to an aristocrat with money. However, the warrior soon felt constricted by his wife, apparently a pathologically jealous woman. In 1720, he crossed the French frontier at the head of an army of seasoned veterans, duly paid for by his father, and put himself and his services at the disposal of the regent, the duc d'Orléans.

The duke immediately saw the advantages he could reap from this warlord and his formidable army of mercenaries. Maurice de Saxe was, in fact, the first military leader to rigorously systematize peacetime training and maneuvers. Outfitting the army was next on the agenda, and here the Tavernier brothers would play their part. At the time, supply officers were responsible for provisioning the whole regiment. Gold soon started to flow their way. Regulations during the *ancien régime* were particularly favorable to war profiteers. Benefiting from a virtual monopoly on goods and services—and from collusion with foundry- and saltpeter-works owners, butchers and bakers, and tailors and saddlers, all of whom swarmed around the regiment—the supply officers acted as middlemen, essentially dictating their prices to the warlord. The allowance paid out by the Prince-Elector of Saxony quickly proved insufficient to cover his son's militia's huge expenses, and the French coffers were soon empty. Undeterred, de

Saxe sought assistance from his beautiful mistress, another legend in her own right, the *tragédienne* Adrienne Lecouvreur. Lecouvreur sold off her diamonds and had her silver plate melted down—all to support her dashing lover's military campaign (he was, just then, conducting a siege in Jelgava, in Latvia). Alas, her sacrifice was to no avail. Most of what she gave him soon vanished into the war profiteers' pockets. (Lecouvreur's life was tragic in other ways. Two centuries later, in 1902, Francesco Cilea wrote an opera based on the actress's life in which it is clear he subscribes to the theory that she had been poisoned by a rival for the love of Maurice de Saxe.)

When they left de Saxe's service in early 1738, Guillaume-Pierre and Philippe-Guillaume found themselves in possession of a comfortable sum of around 100,000 *livres* each. Philippe-Guillaume decided to stay in Paris, and there saw his small fortune grow, thanks in part to the help of good cousin Jean de Boullongne. Guillaume-Pierre decided to seek adventure in the wider world. He went to Guadeloupe, one of the pearls of France's colonies in the West Indies.

The most devastating hurricane in more than half a century had just ravaged the island. Sugarcane plantations had been ripped apart, sugar mills blown off the face of the earth, shanties and cabins swept away, the slave population decimated. The aftermath resembled those after-battle scenes in which the supply officer surveys the field to note down the casualties. In all, half the plantations had been ruined and many others badly damaged; no fewer than twenty ships had been destroyed at anchor. It was, in other words, a most opportune moment to do some very good business. The money he amassed in de Saxe's regiment allowed Guillaume-Pierre to set himself up in what had once been a magnificent sugar plantation near Le Baillif, in the province of Basse-Terre, for a mere fraction of its previous value. Situated in the foothills of the majestic La Soufrière volcano, and bounded on one side by the Pères River and on the other by a property known as Le Thillac, the plantation offered a magnificent view of the Caribbean, the brilliant blue waters contrasting so vividly with the gray of his native Picardy.[3] The plantation was, it should be said, in rather pitiful condition, the recent hurricane having been preceded two years before by an earthquake that had caused considerable devastation. The moment he set eyes on it, however, Guillaume-Pierre sensed the plantation's potential, particularly given the river's proximity (his uncle, another protégé of Jean de Boullongne, was an eminent hydrologist; he had recently perfected a method that enabled boats to navigate up the Seine). Once harnessed, the hydraulic energy would save him the considerable expense of buying draft animals to work the sugar mill.

Fortune again smiled on the ambitious planter. His property was wedged between the estates owned by Samuel Bologne and his nephew, the aforementioned Georges Bologne de Saint-Georges. The Bolognes felt very much at home in Guadeloupe. Their ancestors had come over in the previous century in the first boats from Dieppe and survived famine, sickness, and hurricanes. By 1671 they had already become fairly affluent.[4] At that time, the multiple heirs of the great colonial families had taken to differentiating themselves by adding a "de" to their name, followed by the cadastral name of their property. The richest among them would then endeavor to have this fake aristocratic title validated by the island's grand consul. This called for persistence as well as a significant outlay of cash; over the years, the consul had become exceedingly restrictive about granting such titles. Persevering would pay, however. Ennobled nouveaux riches were not treated as upstarts and outsiders when they made visits to the home country, which they did fairly often. Whereas the rest of his family was content to be a "Bologne," or a "de Bologne," Georges was the only one to call himself "de Saint-Georges." (His neighbor, Le Vanier, adopted the name "Le Vanier de Saint-Robert," after the bluffs of the same name on which his property stood. Yet one would be hard-pressed to find one ounce of nobility in this boorish individual.) With five hundred acres of land and more than two hundred slaves, the Bologne plantation was at the time among the most prosperous in Basse-Terre.

Located a short distance from Georges's plantation, and on the other side of the Baillif River, the plantation belonging to Uncle Samuel and Cousin Joseph seemed, by comparison, somewhat unkempt. Samuel led an epicurean life. He was one of the handful of planters on the island to apply the provision of the so-called *code noir*—or "black code"—that, in theory, obligated every planter to devote part of his lands to the cultivation of food crops for feeding his slaves. And, in contrast to the lavish parties of the other whites, his favorite pastime was bringing together fiddlers, flutists, and musette (a sort of bagpipe) players every Sunday, so that his friends could dance in the courtyard with the most attractive female slaves (thus earning him the hearty disgust of his neighbors' wives). Harvesting the sugarcane and negotiating its sale brought him less than it did the other colonists, but Samuel was the proud owner of the *Felicity—La Félicité*—a vessel of some twelve tons that saved him a lot of money when trading among the Windward Islands, especially booming Saint-Domingue (now Haiti).

The Bolognes (who in this period of highly idiosyncratic spelling sometimes signed themselves "Boulogne") observed with amused interest this new "Boullongne" (whose relatives, just to confuse matters, were also wont to sign themselves "Boulogne") who swam into their ken. Could he be, they wondered, a distant cousin of their ancestors who had sailed from Picardy a century earlier? Whether or not this was the case, Guillaume-Pierre was welcomed as if it were. And, having just landed in unknown territory, he was not one to question, let alone spurn, putative but potentially useful family ties. For one thing, upon arrival he had an urgent need for slaves to fill in the dikes of the Pères River, which had powered the water mill before the 1736 earthquake, to rebuild structures razed by the hurricane, and to replant the sugarcane fields. Yet for several decades now, few slave ships had put in at Basse-Terre. Virtually all the ships of the French royal fleet, in fact, remained massed off Martinique to protect the Windward Islands government, leaving the Guadeloupe route exposed to pirates' raids and English whims. In addition, until the marshes bordering the Pointe-à-Pitre harbor roads were drained, sailors were loath to put into port at Basse-Terre, which was also vulnerable to squalls. The only visitors to the island were the rare slave ships that had not managed to unload all their cargo on Martinique or Saint-Domingue. That meant the Basse-Terre colonists were forced to be content with merchandise taken from "the bottom of the barrel." Sometimes no slave ship appeared on the horizon for months on end. In 1731, seven years before Guillaume-Pierre settled on the island, the shortage of slaves had grown so acute that the governor of Guadeloupe, a man named Dupoyer, had had to warn the minister for the colonies in Paris: "No slave ships are coming here. For three years only a small one has put in with but 136 Negroes."[5]

The need for slaves was pressing. In Europe demand for sugar had skyrocketed. To meet it, the number of sugar plantations had doubled in the decades prior to Guillaume-Pierre's arrival. Next, the 1736 revolt of the *marrons,* as runaway slaves were called, had been bloody in the extreme. (However, unlike elsewhere, large-scale executions tended to be the exception on Guadeloupe due to the relative scarcity of slaves.) On July 10, 1739, only a few months after the new plantation owner had settled in, the governor general of Martinique and his *intendant* sent a warning to the minister of the navy. "We cannot," they wrote, "but reiterate our complaints and protestations regarding our present state of neglect by the French slave ships."[6] The result was that, in spite of the formal prohibition of contraband because of the ever-present tension with England, planters able to do so supplied themselves with slaves in Saint-Domingue. A certain skill was called for. The danger came not so much from the French tax collectors—as rare as they were lax in Guadeloupe—as from the English ships and especially the buccaneers who fanned out around the nearby island of Tortuga. Joseph, Georges Bologne's cousin and a neighbor of Guillaume-Pierre's, came up with an effective way of appeasing the pirates. Before each trip to Saint-Domingue, he would swing around toward the point of Antigua, where the wine depots were concentrated. This sensible precaution, first taken to meet the needs of his dissolute father, Samuel, allowed him as the years went by to smooth relations with the buccaneer chiefs. Whole casks were offered in payment for the right of passage granted by the pirates. It also got him arrested and thrown into jail in 1755.[7]

The *Félicité* would thus make numerous voyages as far as Cape François, the main port of Saint-Domingue. It was here, in the vast wooden warehouses with their intermingling fragrances of rare perfumes and spices, odors of tar, and the stench of rotting fruit and sweat, that the finest slaves were sold, often for huge sums. On a single trip, Samuel and Joseph would bring back some thirty slaves for their Boulogne-Boullongne "cousin."

Once relieved of his concerns over slave labor, Guillaume-Pierre was able to explore his new domain a bit more, draw up plans for improvement, and undertake construction work. He could also permit himself to let his gaze rest on the island women. To the European eye, Basse-Terre offered an enticing mélange of female inhabitants. First of all, there were the daughters of the old ruined provincial nobility who proudly affected manners that were perhaps a little out-of-date. Their fathers had sent them to the colonies under various pretexts, praying they would somehow land a wealthy planter. Conversely, the most prosperous colonials all dreamed of seeing their daughter marry a nobleman. When a ship of the French royal fleet dropped anchor in the bay, the officers were systematically invited to the plantations, where their potential as sons-in-law was immediately sized up. In this way, one of Georges Bologne de Saint-Georges's sisters had a certain Galard de Béarn for her first husband, the vicomte de Servanche for her second, and, for her third, one Cazaud du Breuil, who judiciously used his betrothed's dowry toward the purchase of a post as "counselor" to the Bordeaux parliament. Several colonists would have been delighted to see one of their daughters wed to Guillaume-Pierre.

The neighborhood around the port swarmed with groups of

orphans, girls who had been forced to embark to the colonies by
the nuns, with the king's blessing, in order that they might practice
"the reproductive profession," as it was called. Their presence was
designed to encourage the colony of *petits Blancs*, or "little whites"—
civil servants, craftsmen, and tradesmen—so indispensable to the
development of commerce on the island, to settle there. These girls
could practice skills learned in the convent, and might find work as
dressmakers or cooks; they also learned to spin or twist tobacco.[8]
Guillaume-Pierre was amused by the pretense of it all, even as he
pitied these poor girls who, barely an hour after disembarkation,
would be married essentially by lottery.

Guadeloupe was also the place of exile of those so-called women
of easy virtue, who had been shoved on board ships in the hope that
they would make the *petits Blancs* good wives. Thieves, prostitutes,
and beggars made up the regular human cargo of the ships that traded
with the islands directly—ships of *droiture*—without first having to
make a detour around the African coast. Roger de Bussy-Rabutin
commemorated their voyages in song:

> *Farewell Pont-Neuf, Samaritaine,*
> *Butte Saint-Roch, Petits Carreaux,*
> *Where we spent so many happy times.*
> *Now we're bound for the islands,*
> *For the cities want us no more.*[9]

The local authorities did not exactly welcome these fallen women
with open arms, particularly since "their reproductive capacities have
been somewhat destroyed by abuse," as a petition from Saint-
Domingue authorities to the ministry of the navy phrased it. Their
cohabiting with the former convent schoolgirls made for a somewhat
bizarre mixture, given that each group regularly crossed paths in the
narrow streets of Basse-Terre or at church. Between the narrow-
minded provincials and the whores, Guillaume-Pierre's romantic

prospects might have seemed a conundrum. Should he follow the example of his cousin Bologne and marry a pious lady, and at night slip into bed with a beautiful slave, waiting for him at the tavern? His acquaintance with Elisabeth Mérican, wife of Bologne de Saint-Georges, quickly dissuaded him from that course.

There remained the slave women. Colonists were not averse to taking their pick from among what they considered their harem. Some were perfectly capable of raping a slave woman in a sugarcane field and killing anyone daring to intervene. This was even sanctioned behavior. The *code noir* authorized them to consider slaves personal property, similar to cattle. Sexual conquest by seduction was more and more often the strategy of choice, however. In Guadeloupe, it was also a matter of necessity. The difficulty of buying slaves, a difficulty that persisted for decades, encouraged the colonists there to behave in a less brutal manner than those on other islands, such as Saint-Domingue. Indeed, in certain Guadeloupe plantations, treatment of slave women could be more paternalistic than outwardly oppressive. Slave girls might even be made to feel flattered when the master eyed their figures approvingly.

Nonetheless, this sort of behavior shocked the island's authorities. On November 28, 1730, for example, a high-level administrator sent a memorandum to Versailles, requesting authorization to put an end to relations between white men and black women. "Apart from the public scandal caused by such outrageous debauchery, which is the subject of continual complaints on the part of the clergy, consider, Monsieur, the condition of the women on this island, who not only find themselves scorned by their husbands for the sake of vile slaves but for good measure are constantly insulted by these creatures without hope of obtaining justice."[10]

One day, while crossing cousin Bologne's plantation, Guillaume-Pierre was literally stopped in his tracks by the sight of a young Senegalese woman. Her features were unusually delicate, her ebony eyes enormous, and she "was dressed in bright red and soft green, the two ends of her fichu being fastened at her waist."[11] Pretending not to notice she was being noticed, Nanon nonchalantly walked on, swaying her hips, apparently amused at the emotion she had aroused. Her manner of walking was exceedingly disturbing to this newcomer from Europe, where no woman would so innocently dare adopt such a gait. Furthermore, no corset or bustle was interposed between the master's gaze and the young woman's figure. Boullongne would take whatever time necessary, but he wanted her—and wanted her acquiescence as well. Fortunately, he had a knowledgeable tutor in the person of Plato, who initiated him into a form of broken Creole, the patois that had developed in the streets where the slaves lived from exchanges between them and the poor whites. Nanon herself had quickly learned this new language, as she mixed with those slaves who had lived for some time in the *ajoupas,* wattle-and-daub huts with pointed roofs. Little by little, she found herself being won over by the gentleness and energy of this European, who displayed none of the arrogance or brutishness of so many of the other colonists, this man who seemed amazed by everything he saw and who had become passionate about employing technology that might ease human misery. But before he could win Nanon, Guillaume-Pierre had first to buy her. The transaction would cost him over 2,000 livres (roughly the equivalent of over a year's salary for a ship's captain), which was the generous price he paid his "cousin."

Nanon had arrived on the island eight years before. She had been barely six years old when, with her parents, she was carried off by the soldiers of one of the African kings who exchanged their people for cheap goods—the cloth, trinkets, hatchets, knives, alcohol, and especially munitions and old guns used in the European wars that made up the currency of trade. Brought to the island of Gorée, off Dakar in Senegal, she was held in the fort that at that time stood some distance from the present "slaves' house" to wait for the next boat and then for the endless negotiations that would ensue between captain and vendor. The vessel would be the *Union*, the first ship built by a Bordeaux shipbuilder called Fénelon for the slave-ship owner Jean Marchais.[12] The latter had learned the rudiments of the business as a trader at Saint-Pierre de la Martinique between December 1721 and July 1723. After next spending four years in Nantes, then the capital of the triangular France-Africa-Caribbean trade, and where he was initiated into slave trafficking, he set up a business on his own in Bordeaux. Shipowners often preferred to send boats nearing the end of their useful lives to the tropics; the southern seas were found to be highly corrosive of wood. Marchais was among the first to supervise the building of his own slave vessel, which he did in partnership with two financiers.

"Union" was of course a curious and deeply ironic name for a ship engaged in the purchase and sale of human beings. Yet in this so-called Age of Enlightenment, those who amassed huge fortunes from the commerce in slaves were not regarded as social outcasts. Indeed, they made it a point of honor to swim with the tide of progressive ideas. In Nantes, for example, it was not uncommon for a slave trader to belong to a reading club, where members might discuss the latest works by the celebrated *philosophes*. Some traders formed a Masonic lodge, which proudly gave a ceremonial welcome to Benjamin Franklin.[13] And one of Jean-Jacques Rousseau's patrons, a practitioner of the *infâme trafic*, would call his slave vessel *The Social Contract*.[14]

The *Union* set sail from Bordeaux on September 11, 1729, her captain a man named François Brousse. A little more than two months later the ship reached Gorée, where she made a protracted stay. First, the cargo had to be evaluated. The ship's surgeon, who played a leading role in any slave-ship expedition, examined each piece of merchandise minutely, eliminating anyone with even the smallest wound (it might become infected during the voyage), and looking into mouths to verify age from the wear on the teeth, the way a farmer might a beast of burden. Nanon would also have watched while he weighed her mother's breasts in his hands and inserted his finger into her vagina. With the preliminary examination finished, it was time to make ready the cargo. The orders were often quite specific: "Deal only in Negroes of 15 to 20 years of age, two-thirds of them male, one-third female." The traders also purchased a few young girls and boys, who would be used for domestic tasks or to carry light loads.

Meanwhile the ship's carpenter got to work. Having been packed with goods on the outbound trip, the boat now had to be fitted out with mid-ship decks whose floors consisted of a thick wood lattice. Thus the captives crowded into the hold would not wallow in their feces, which could instead fall through and rot away. This improvement was not due to humanitarianism. The important thing was to prevent the slaves from becoming sick and therefore valueless. The voyage took months; malaria often ravaged the crew. The mortality rate for sailors during a voyage was as high as 10 percent; that of slaves, far higher. Captain Brousse's own health quickly deteriorated. Replaced by his adjunct, François Laragon, Brousse would not live to see the islands.

Marchais had instructed his crew to load up on Gorée. This was because the Senegambians were more highly prized by the traders than were the inhabitants of Benin, farther to the south. In this first half-century of the Age of Enlightenment the mercantile bourgeoisie, priding itself on its study of the animal kingdom, dutifully applied the naturalist René-Antoine de Réaumur's "differentiation" theories to their work. The Senegambian, it was averred, was more docile than the Negro of the south, certainly more robust and equipped with a finer physique, though also more apt to revolt and more prone to die during the voyage. Thus the Senegal Company, which in the preceding decades had practically acquired a monopoly over the slave traffic in the region, had exhausted all the local resources. Despite paying high prices for each piece of goods—up to 550 livres for a man and 500 for a woman, which was double the price of a few years before—Brousse and, later, Laragon could not fill their holds.

After three months of endless and exhausting delays on Gorée, the *Union* crew was forced to set sail for Anamabou, one of the jewels of the Gold Coast. There, they knew, they would find the merchandise they lacked. Indeed, the king of the nearby port of Ouidah, an excellent source for slaves, had taken to calling the French traders his "cousins and good friends." Such familiarity did not prevent the African ruler from striking a hard bargain. For weeks on end, Nanon and her mother, huddled with all the female slaves in the bows of the vessel while the men were placed aft, would have to wait for a new group of shackled slaves to join them. It was early February by the time the *Union* again weighed anchor. Her load was not excessive: 125 slaves for this small vessel of sixty-five tons, or 2 per ton. Some traders crammed in as many as 5 slaves per ton. From his stay in the Antilles, Marchais remembered the traffickers' tales of the losses they had suffered because of overcrowding. He would do his best to stay within safer guidelines.

The *Union* had to venture farther south—indeed, all the way to the equator—to pick up the favorable winds. In the holds the heat became asphyxiating, the smell unbearable. The ship therefore dropped anchor at Prince Island, off the Ghanaian coast. The slaves were disembarked and for several days would be looked after and treated relatively well in preparation for the voyage to the Windwards. It was important that the merchandise reach port undamaged.

The crossing would last nearly two months. For the slaves this meant living amid appalling filth, heat, and stench. The captain would occasionally have small groups of captives brought on deck—to "refresh" them, as he put it. At times Nanon would hear the gasping breath and moans of the ill and dying above on deck. Then, silence. After the silence would come the grim sound of leather soles and clogs as the body was picked up and tossed over the side.

The closer the boat drew to the Antilles, the worse the climate became. Moreover, the captain was under orders from the vessel's owners to step up the punishment and harassment of the crew, so as to encourage a maximum number of sailors to desert upon arrival. Once they had arrived, there would be no further need for so many hands;

the men had been recruited in large numbers to supervise the cargo and to prevent uprisings. Also, space had to be made for the return cargo—coffee and sugar—which was considerably greater in volume than the human one had been. The sailors tended to take out their revenge for the harsh treatment they suffered at the hands of the captain and officers on the slaves. The whip lacerated skin covered in filth and ravaged by lice.

The curses and blows would stop, as if by magic, as soon as land came into view. Before being put up for sale, the slaves would be held in a compound on the port, where for a few weeks they would be tended to and fed. The buyers would insist on good quality. For his first expedition, Marchais had chosen to make delivery to his old and favored clients at Saint-Pierre de la Martinique. He had a reputation to maintain.

Nanon was one of the 100 million human beings wrenched from their land over the four centuries of the slave trade—half of whom died from violence or during the crossing. Sold to one of the Bolognes, who had come to take advantage of the rare windfall of the arrival of a slave ship in Martinique, then transported to Guadeloupe on board the *Felicity*, she could have met a worse fate. In contrast to their colleagues on Saint-Domingue, Guadeloupe planters at that time rarely branded their slaves, reserving the punishment for the *marrons* after a first attempt at escape.

Nanon would grow up a beauty. Several years later her son, who by then was rich and the envy of many, made a number of trips to London, where he made friends with the head of a fencing school named Henry Angelo. Of Nanon, Angelo would write, that she "was the most beautiful gift that Africa ever offered."

That Joseph Boulogne de Saint-George was the son of Nanon has never been put in doubt by those drawn to the life of this remarkable man. The question of his paternity, on the other hand, has been a matter of some controversy, for even after he had fulfilled the midwife's prophecy and met the king of France, he left no firm indication as to his father's identity. In 1840 the writer Roger de Beauvoir, who wrote a novel about Saint-George's life, made a case for Jean de Boullongne, the wealthy and influential Parisian financier. Jean never set foot in the Antilles, however. Jean's son, Jean-Nicolas de Boullongne, has likewise been mentioned as a candidate. The name of Georges Bologne de Saint-Georges, the aforementioned planter and neighbor to Guillaume-Pierre, also figures in some biographical articles. However, Georges was an alcoholic who led a mostly dissolute life, and, as we shall see, was indicted for murder at one point. He could not have presented any child of his—particularly one of mixed race—to the French court, nor had him appointed a member of the king's personal guard, a post reserved for members of the very highest nobility. Moreover, the dossier on "Bologne de Saint-Georges" preserved in a file at the National Archives in Paris reveals that Georges was drowning in debt. For this reason alone it would have been impossible for him to entrust his son's education to the most expensive tutors in the French capital or provide him with protectors. His son Nicolas, who had bought the office of counselor to the Parliament of Metz, has also been suggested, but for similar reasons his candidacy cannot be taken seriously. Still others have posited that Joseph's father was Philippe-Guillaume, Guillaume-Pierre's brother, but he never visited the Antilles; it seems likely he was being confused with his brother. After many years of research, the "paternity suit" the present writer has drawn up makes it most plausible that the father of the man who went down in history as Monsieur de Saint-George was Guillaume-Pierre Tavernier de Boullongne. As we've seen, his property was adjacent to Georges Bologne's plantation—this can be verified on a map in the Bibliothèque nationale in Paris—and next to that plantation was the area called "Saint-Georges." Forbidden by law to take his father's name, this child of mixed race assumed the name of his birthplace, went on, just as the midwife had predicted, to achieve great fame, and then nearly disappeared from history altogether.

II

The Child and the Slaves

"Monsieur le chevalier, stop jiggling like a young goat when you play your fiddle. And follow the score. If you persist in letting your instrument be guided by your instincts, you'll never do anything but play like a *nègre*." According to Roger de Beauvoir—whose novelized life of Saint-George, published in 1840, I also evoked in the previous chapter—such is how Monsieur Plato, who every day took an hour off his duties as overseer of the plantation to give Joseph a violin lesson (as well as an introduction to the rudiments of French literature), might have addressed his young charge. Plato, it was said, was a born teacher, and took pleasure offering instruction to the slave children on the plantation.

Like most of the other planters, Guillaume-Pierre would have insisted that his servants learn to play the very latest music and perform it at formal dinners and receptions. *Les Affiches américaines*, the major newspaper of the Windward and Leeward Islands of the day, regularly ran advertisements placed by planters seeking black musicians. In this domain, merit got its due reward. Playing at planters' receptions or balls offered a sure means of building up a small savings. The colonists regarded it as their duty to keep up with the world of arts and letters; these were, it was felt, the only subjects appropriate for the release of emotion. Even in the islands, the echoes of the so-called Quarrel of the Buffoons—involving a debate over the relative merits of French versus Italian opera—launched against the composer Jean-Philippe Rameau by Jean-Jacques Rousseau would reach the planters' salons (Rousseau felt that French opera was, as he put it, an "impossibility"). In fact, these plantation owners lived in a way typical of backwater cosmopolites, taking great pains to re-create their homelands in their places of exile. This was important preparation for their return to Parisian society, once the fortune they had amassed from sugarcane and coffee was of a size guaranteed to confer respectability. When that time came, a smattering of culture would help them avoid being perceived as hicks.

Again according to de Beauvoir, Monsieur Plato had therefore been promoted to the rank of music director. It would never have been his or anyone's aim to make virtuosos of even the most gifted slaves and their children; the idea was to teach them enough that they might play a few simple melodies on the violin. Plato was delighted to find an audience he sensed was more appreciative than that of the *petits Blancs* of the port, with whom he dealt regularly. The former customs agent from Bercy who, goose quill in hand, drew up the plantation account books with unswerving meticulousness, and who made it a point of honor to see that the ledgers were kept in perfect order, had a surprising and ill-disguised talent as a ham actor. Once he set aside his pen, he loved nothing better than to turn storyteller, bringing to life before his audience his days of glory when he played the fiddle in the cafés of Bercy.

The violin had long been an instrument of the people, its chief use—along with the bagpipe-like musettes, recorders, and tambourines—being to set the crowds dancing in the Paris suburbs. With a population of only 1,400 souls, Bercy was a mere village, yet it became one of Paris's most popular watering holes. This was because of its ideal location on the Seine. Bercy was where the barges moored before saturating the capital with wines from the Marne Valley and Burgundy. Served and consumed on the spot, the wine was decidedly cheaper than it was after it had passed through customs. Moreover, people found it far more potent than the prim little wines from the slopes of Suresnes and Argenteuil. Monsieur Plato evoked it all for his audience: the open-air cafés, the dancing, the disreputable taverns, the dandies, and the gorgeous ladies. Some detail in one of his stories would often give a *petit Blanc* from the port a twinge of homesickness. At times Plato would even touch his audience of black children, most of whom would never set foot in France. For example, Plato swore he had met the notorious bandit Cartouche, who frequented the cabaret La Grande Pinte. He never tired of telling how the infamous outlaw escaped the police who came to arrest him by diving into a well in a tavern courtyard. "The idiots never caught on to the fact that it led to an underground passageway," he said, laughing. The full story of Cartouche, however, offered the strict plantation overseer a chance to turn the colorful bandit's tale into an object lesson for his rapt audience of slave children. In 1721 the police caught Cartouche before he had time to reach his well. He was thrown into a dark, freezing cell in the prison at the Grand Châtelet and publicly hanged on the place de Grève. Monsieur Plato didn't leave out one grisly detail. As recounted on the rue Case-nègre, the legend of Cartouche was a deterrent for any slave considering rebelling against authority.

Should anyone doubt his word—or his exploits as a fiddler— Plato would scowl and tell these skeptics to peer into the sound holes of his instrument. If they looked carefully they might discern a most prestigious signature. "This violin comes from Paris. I bought it for hard cash from Monsieur Exaudet, second violin at the Opéra. In those days he lived on the rue Croix-des-Petits-Champs, at the pastry-chef's, opposite the Saint-Honoré monastery. What a fine man he was, that Exaudet! He played the whole of the opera *Jephté* on this violin!" (The opera in question was written by Michel Pignolet de

Montéclair, with a libretto by the abbé Pellegrin, and enjoyed a resounding success at its performance at the Académie Royale de Musique on February 28, 1732. It was the first operatic work inspired by the Bible, and was soon banned at the urging of the Cardinal de Noailles, who found the mixture of religion and secular amusements intolerable.)[1]

Plantation life followed a routine disrupted only by religious holidays and hurricanes. At five in the morning, when the first glow of day formed a faint halo around the volcanic peak of La Soufrière, the slaves were wakened by the sound of conch shells being blown, and lined up in formation in front of the great house. Flanked by Plato and the plantation surgeon, the master proceeded to take roll call. The surgeon, in this case a sailor who had deserted from the *Union,* was not there to dispense medical care. His knowledge of medicine was limited to making obvious diagnoses and applying a few balms and unguents made from herbs. In actual fact his sole expertise was in outing any malingering slaves who feigned sickness, and then sending them off into the fields to work. For more serious cases of illness or feigned illness, Plato might defer matters to the witch doctor—the *kaimboiseur*—who was unequaled in administering medicines derived from sacred plants, or else to good Doctor Lafitte, an elderly physician from Le Baillif.

From the earliest days, Nanon had accustomed baby Joseph to get up at the same time as the workers, so that he might have breakfast with his father immediately following roll call, and after the white staff was given its orders. The boy loved watching the early-morning ceremony, when in his imagination the rows of silhouettes lined up in the semidarkness looked like soldiers standing at attention before battle in the fogs of Flanders, just as his father was fond of describing them. In those hours of dawn, General Tavernier de Boullongne's troops were there, awaiting orders to fight the imaginary enemy, each man assigned his place. Soon the sun emerged from behind La Soufrière and, without the endless preliminaries of urban dawns, abruptly shed bright rays on the regiment of slaves. Joseph could then make out the many ranks differentiating the troops.

As in Maurice de Saxe's militia, rank was designated by uniform color. The higher the rank, the gaudier the colors. First to answer the roll call were the domestic slaves: the majordomo, foot servants, cooks, coachmen, and small boys whose job it was to wave fans at mealtimes at the whites and their guests. They broke ranks as soon as their names were called in order to get everything ready for breakfast. These were slaves who enjoyed their master's absolute trust, and especially Nanon's absolute trust, for she had selected them personally. Horrific tales of poisoning went the rounds of the plantations. With his Christian name, Joseph was amused to hear names that sounded to his ears like so many mysterious evocations. Some consisted of a few syllables, exported from the African homeland, such as Zao, Zouc, Bibianne, or Arada. Others were taken from antiquity, like Aesop or Aristotle. Most of the slaves born and baptized on the island received the name of a saint: Agatha, Maria-Theresa, or Naomi. Then there were the names suggestive of workaday objects, such as Bugle, Cart, or Mill. Joseph was too young to see the extent to which in those days humans were perceived as mere tools.

The women wore brightly colored, long cotton dresses, tied at the waist with a Madras fichu; men wore vests of scarlet and white with gold buttons; coachmen were given meticulously waxed boots. Like all the other planters, Guillaume-Pierre did not skimp when it came to his servants' attire. In the little colonial world, where life was essentially spent outdoors, one could if need be stint on furnishings or interior decoration. But when it came to clothes, the staff had to rival those waiting upon the great aristocratic families of France.

The second group to answer the roll call consisted of specialized workers, the aforementioned "skilled Negroes." Unlike the valets, these did not sport multicolored attire, though their trousers and shirts made from unbleached Combourg cloth were usually in good condition. The master watched them closely, rewarding the most deserving in person every religious holiday with a new suit of clothes. In time Joseph learned to recognize each man according to his specialty. The haulers who drove the teams of oxen and mules laden with canes wore vests; so did the water-cart men and the sugarhouse workers; the *machoquets*—named after a cricket with large, enveloping wings—who poured the sugar into molds wore aprons, and so on. Some trades were particularly prized. A skilled cooper, a carpenter who could maintain the mills, a woodworker who rebuilt roofs after a hurricane, or above all, anyone with knowledge about making rum and other spirits was beyond price. And they knew it, often responding to barked commands from the drivers with a nonchalance that bordered on insolence. They were less motivated by fear of the whip than by the prospect of the master rewarding them with a few coins or offering them a few encouraging words.

Other slaves, also carefully selected, were responsible for transporting goods—delivering the sugar, coffee, and cocoa beans to port, or distributing food. They would visit warehouses and depots and bring back foodstuffs, in particular smoked meat from livestock raised by the *petits Blancs* or free Negroes or, even more prized, dried cod imported directly from Canada. Mixed with wheat flour or manioc root, this was the slaves' basic form of nourishment. Those who accompanied the agents for this exchange were usually elegantly dressed. It would simply not do to send ragged slaves into the streets of the port; the reputation of the Boullongne plantation was at stake.

Last to be reviewed were the *nègres de jardin*, who worked the sugarcane fields. No fancy clothes for them. A pair of trousers and a long hemp shirt, usually stiff from sweat and dirt, that hung down below the belt served to give protection from the sun, mosquitoes, and the whip. Some workers, particularly the youngest, preferred to work shirtless, their chests slathered with tallow to ward off insects. They would put on the clothes the master had provided them with only for a mass or a wake. When roll call was completed, the garden Negroes made their way to the fields under the watchful eye of the drivers. For the most part blacks themselves, these drivers, often freed slaves, kept one hand on the pommel of the whip attached to their belt while they roughly called any laggards to order.

By seven A.M., with roll call ended, Guillaume-Pierre gave the staff final instructions. In the meantime, Nanon had arranged for breakfast to be prepared and the table set. Joseph would take his place next to his father, who always questioned him about his progress with the violin, fencing, shooting, and his studies. This last of the line of Tavernier-Boullongnes had waited thirty-three years to have a child; there was no question of failing in the slightest respect in his fatherly duties. Each day he marveled at Joseph's agility and liveliness. "I've produced not a son but a sparrow," he would often joke.[2]

The laws regarding the children of mixed race were harsh. Since 1729 it had become increasingly difficult to free them, and the *code noir* prohibited them from inheriting a noble title from their father. Guillaume-Pierre found a way to get around the problem. Joseph would be neither a count nor a marquis; instead, his father would make him a chevalier, or knight, dubbing him as in medieval times. He never ceased to remind his son of the duties becoming his title. A noble title, especially one that had been borrowed, had to be linked to a "seignorial" property, even if fictitious. As I've noted, the land worked by cousin Georges served the purpose, being close by. Joseph would therefore be anointed the "chevalier de Saint-George." The only difference between the spelling of the land and the name was that the final "s" was dropped from the latter, an English affectation the chevalier retained his whole life.[3]

Breakfast offered one of the rare moments of familial intimacy during the day. Early on, Guillaume-Pierre had given Plato charge of this son, who was already showing great promise in many different areas. As master, he had to rush off to say the catechism to the children on the plantation before going to visit the sick in the "hospital," the name given to the rather grim dispensary where slaves with mild illnesses were thrown together with those suffering from venereal diseases, the severely ill, and the elderly. When he acquired his property, Guillaume-Pierre had had no choice but to take in the feeble and the aged. The Black Code obliged slave-owners to provide food and shelter to those slaves who were no longer productive.

This was not because of piety. In the opinion of the governor, who insisted this law be scrupulously adhered to, it prevented slaves from becoming beggars and vagabonds on the roads; it also alleviated the cost of building hospices. Moreover, by guaranteeing each slave a peaceful end to his days, the more enlightened planters were convinced they would prevent rebellion from spreading. Though they had passed the age when they were of much use in the fields or mills, the older slaves still performed small jobs: wicker- and cane-work for the men, mending and patching for the women. During the day, they could also take care of the young children, thus playing an essential role in the perpetuation of the social order.

Guillaume-Pierre took seriously this system, which combined humanity with sound business sense on an island where slave ships only rarely delivered fresh manpower. These duties done, he spent the rest of the morning in the workshops. The wagons carrying the cane to the mills—wagons powered by both water and beasts of burden—began their trek early in the morning. Sugar production could not be allowed to suffer the slightest delay. After three days of storage in the *bagasse* cabin, the canes produced an acidic sugar disdained by traders. They saw it as a mark of an inferior product and offered prices well below market value for it. Stewards, agents, and drivers all had to synchronize perfectly the work of the field laborers with that of the shopworkers. The moment the wagons stopped in front of the mills, the men unloaded the bundles of sugarcane, taking them to the middle of the one large room. There, women in long white dresses tied round with a red sash proceeded to guide the canes between the rollers—formidable grindstones made of grooved wood used for crushing the stalks. The master was sure that his daily presence there, however fleeting, helped maintain the attention essential to smooth operation. The women might feed in the cane too quickly; cramming too much between the rollers soon exhausted the animals. On the other hand, if they did not maintain a certain pace, the cane would begin to pile up. And then there was the constant risk of accidents, which usually happened in the evening, when fatigue was beginning to take hold: A fingertip might get caught between two rollers, then the whole finger, the arm, and finally the body. Since the time of Father Labat, who forty years earlier had instituted many improvements to sugar exploitation, a large bush hook was always kept near the grinding wheels, used to slice off a hand or an arm, and thus prevent a slave from being crushed.

As they fed the cane into the machine's vast maw, the slaves had to keep a watchful eye on the gutter into which the cane juice flowed, thence to be poured into earthenware pipes. These led directly to the boiling house, built on a slightly lower level.

After a brief inspection of the aqueduct and water-mill machinery, the master's morning tour normally ended with a lengthy visit to the boiling house. In temperatures that during the hot season never went below 122 degrees Fahrenheit, and in suffocating humidity, a dozen men worked around five metal vats set in the masonry of the furnace. The cane juice flowed into the first vat, where it was boiled for a few minutes, clarifying into a thin syrup. Next it was gradually transferred to the second vat, somewhat farther from the flames, by means of enormous long-handled ladles. And so it went. From vat to vat the temperature dipped and the liquid took on consistency until it became a thick syrup. Poured into earthenware molds, it gradually crystallized into the loaves so prized in the French marketplace.

Bodies dried out in this inferno, where the men labored for hours on end without the slightest respite. And yet they would not willingly have given up the job for a less fatiguing task. To reach the boiling house was to be recognized as a "worker." Twenty years earlier, when all that was needed to free a slave was to appear with him before a notary, it was not exceptional for a master to grant freedom to the one he had honored with his trust by appointing him to work in the boiler. Expertise was indeed indispensable in order to produce sugar adapted to European tastes. A few thousand miles from these tropical infernos, in the salons and literary cafés of Paris, judging the island products like a connoisseur was considered all the rage. Sugars were evaluated according to the latest criteria: too "earthy" (or not earthy enough), too acidic, too "hard," and so on. It was up to the workers to adapt. Duly reprimanded by his Parisian protector Jean de Boullongne, Guillaume-Pierre knew too well the snobbish ways of the nouveaux riches of Versailles and the Palais-Royal not to pay close attention to their tastes.

A quick midday meal and *seigneur* Boullongne was off again, this time on horseback, heading for the fields. The slaves, too, had taken a lunch break. Those who worked near the rue Case-nègre could even go home to their huts. Afterward, the drivers led them to another part of the plantation. Unless a new work detail was being organized, tradition prohibited the planters from forcing slaves to do the same work for an entire day. Whip in hand, the drivers set a beat for the labor, though it was singing that set the pace. Wherever there was work, there was song and rhythm. William Beckford, the eighteenth-century writer and traveler, wrote that "when the mill is at work at night, there is something affecting in the songs of the women who feed it; and it appears somewhat singular that all their tunes, if tunes they can be called, are of a plaintive cast. Sometimes you may hear one soft, complaining voice; and now a second or third chimes in; and now presently, as if inspired by the solemn impressions of night, and by the gloomy objects that are supposed to dwell around, a full chorus is heard to swell upon the ear, and then to die away again to the first original tone."

In this same period, another aristocrat, the Parisian Thibault de Chanvalon, toured the Windwards, carefully noting what he observed. Back in France he would set down everything he had seen in *Voyage to Martinique*, published in 1763. He, too, had been struck by the slaves' deep feeling for music: "They do no work demanding exertion save in rhythm, and almost always while singing. This is an advantage in most of their labors. Singing encourages them, and rhythm becomes the general rule. It forces the indolent to follow the others. The lack of clothing baring every muscle, one can see that there is no part of their bodies that is unaffected by this rhythm, and expresses it. . . . What appeared singular to us was that the same melody, although merely a continual repetition of the same notes, absorbs them utterly, allowing them to work or dance for hours on end." De Chanvalon concludes with the astonishingly prescient judgment that this melody, repeated so endlessly, "does not, either for them or even for the whites, produce the monotonous uniformity that such repetitions might be supposed to cause." The art of repeating the same melodies in slightly altered registers would later enrapture critics and musicians like André-Ernest-Modeste Grétry, who would applaud Saint-George's compositions. Moreover, a half-century before that, Father Labat had also written about these work songs: "One of the slaves, or else the driver, would sing an African air which all finally learned and which enlivened their work by breaking the monotony."[4]

Thus the crack of the whip served more often to accompany orders than to beat men. In Guadeloupe—Guillaume-Pierre was particularly scrupulous in this regard—the driver could not strike a slave unless previously authorized to do so. Monsieur Plato himself wouldn't have dared, except for the occasional spanking of a child when his patience was exhausted.

In earliest colonial days, children of mixed race were born, in theory, free, the Black Code recognizing this in 1685. But faced with the proliferation of illegitimate children, who represented so many unproductive mouths to feed (besides being living proof of the misfortunes of white wives), legal experts were soon able to make Roman law prevail, which stipulated that the child share the lot of his mother. In 1687, it was decreed that slaves' sons remain slaves—which meant working in the fields. Visiting a sugar plantation in Martinique, James Tobin was flabbergasted when one day his host pointed out "several mulattos who were working in the fields like beasts of burden, remarking that they were all of his blood."[5]

French philanthropists noted considerable progress. More and more births in the islands, whatever the reason, meant a proportionate reduction in the abominable trade in Negroes torn from their African homeland. Indeed, as a certain writer named Nabuco put it, "the most productive part of the slave property is the womb that provides children."

Some distance away from the Tavernier plantation, on the island of Saint-Domingue, lived a Norman gentleman, like Guillaume-Pierre the scion of an old family that had come down in the world. This was Alexandre Davy de La Pailleterie. He had four children by Césette Dumas, a beautiful slave he had purchased for an exorbitant sum. In order to pay for his return voyage to France, he sold three of them, along with their mother, to neighboring planters. But he decided to keep the fourth. Unable to hand down his name—linked to the rank of marquis—to the child, Davy de La Pailleterie gave Thomas his neighbor's name, Rétoré. As we have seen, Joseph's father also used the customary procedure. As soon as he had a little money, Thomas Rétoré "Dumas," as the fourth child was known, would buy back his mother in 1786. Then, having made a fortune in soldiering, General Dumas would acquire his sisters and their children, whom he immediately freed. He would later have a son, the writer Alexandre Dumas. (In years to come, the paths of Saint-George and Dumas de La Pailleterie would cross. At certain times they would even be inseparable.)

Joseph, for his part, only rarely accompanied his father on his daily rounds, though each time he did so he soaked up like a sponge the songs and sounds that gave rhythm to the slaves' labors. Nanon hated above all to see him identify even to the slightest extent with the white—or, worse, the black—foremen who mistreated her African brethren. However, on Sundays Joseph was allowed to follow his father around the property. That was the day Guillaume-Pierre went in person from hut to hut, giving out food for the week. The little boy trotted behind him to carry out a mission worthy of a gallant knight. He offered his black friends cakes specially prepared by his mother.[6]

Encouraging any further work at his father's side proved useless. From his earliest years Joseph knew he would never be a planter. He preferred to savor the luxuriant nature that one day he would have to abandon. Accompanied by a few domestic slaves, he spent hours wandering the paths and riverbanks. "The body of this mulatto child," Roger de Beauvoir wrote of him in the mid-nineteenth century, "seemed to have been poured into a separate mold; what struck one first of all was his physical strength, his feet being at once firm and slim, his torso as strong as that of a young tiger. As for his neck, it was vigorously set and with a real air of nobility." A few rather revolting comparisons also color de Beauvoir's portrait of Saint-George, drawn nearly a hundred years later: "His leg seemed to be akin to that of the Basque in the swiftness of its address; his arms were long and well attached. Despite his frizzy hair and his color, which was darker than that ordinarily found with mulattos, he triumphed over the Negro with all the superiority of the master over the slave." All his life, the "chevalier" would be subject to the voyeurism of the entomologists of the human species.

The little mixed-race child with the aristocratic build loved most of all to climb up the left bank of the narrow Pères—"Fathers"— River separating the Boullongne plantation from that of Bologne de Saint-Georges. On the bluffs overlooking the sugar plantation, Joseph and the servants accompanying him walked across his father's coffee and cocoa fields. They now brought in little revenue, but Tavernier de Boullongne was determined to preserve them, so symbolic of Paris with its refined salons—the very salons he vowed to conquer. As he went along, the boy tried to juggle the beans with their rough shells, as rough as the skin of the iguanas the *petits Blancs* raised for the making of a delicate dish.

The foothills of the Soufrière were the realm of the immense silk-cotton tree—"the king of trees," as the older slaves called it—as well as mango trees, with their spreading shade, papaw trees, revered by witch doctors because of their medicinal properties, and guavas. Then what bliss it was to swing on the lianas, or to escape the servants' watchful eyes and wade through the profusion of giant ferns, or to drink from the natural springs bubbling up everywhere, or to crawl behind the waterfall, or to plunge into the hot, sulfurous waters of the yellow pools. Those hot springs, so prized for their health-giving powers, were the climax of young Joseph's escapades. They were perched high above all the lands, and from them Joseph could look down on the property next to his father's, that of the Bologne de Saint-Georges cousins and the good-humored Samuel Bologne. Farther off, he could see the house of Saint-Robert, unmatched in his ability to keep the planters amused with his antics. After he came back from his long walk, Joseph would head out again with one of the few blacks allowed to carry a weapon. He would then learn how to shoot a rifle, and might bag a few partridges or a black, petrel-like *diablotin* that would later be turned over to the cook.

One of Joseph's favorite places was the town of Basse-Terre, with its profusion of fountains, its splendid houses that glowed red in the sun, craftsmen working in front of their shops in copper, wood, and leather, and stalls fragrant with a thousand spices. Nanon regularly went down there in the plantation barouche. She was without question the handsomest woman in the region, but not the only elegant woman of color: Many splendid dark-skinned women wore ruffs of lace and jewels, which always attracted outraged glances from the white wives, for it was clear where their rivals' jewelry came from. Several attempts had been made in the form of decrees signed by the governor, or even royal commands, to prohibit slave-women from attiring themselves in ways too closely similar to those of the whites. This was pointless, however. After a few weeks, a discreet article of gold jewelry would appear beneath the Madras bodice, followed shortly afterward by a lace fichu and bracelets.

Basse-Terre already boasted a cathedral and four churches and resounded with the music of small orchestras. In June 1740, when Joseph was barely six months old, the king's commissioner, Petit Maubert, deplored the liberties the blacks were taking: "The gatherings of slaves are so numerous that the streets are full of Negroes dancing day and night to the music of their instruments."[7]

Business could also be done in this teeming little city. The slaves had gained the right to sell at the Sunday market produce they had grown on the allotment given them by their owner. They sold vegetables, poultry, and fruit, doubtless hoping one day to save enough to buy their freedom. In addition, anyone gaining the confidence of a tavern-keeper might earn access to his "reserve," where he kept stolen goods that the servants stored for eventual sale. Here again, dozens of decrees were issued in an attempt to stop these fencing operations, but justice turned a blind eye. For one thing, extortion on the part of the magistrates and king's representatives had become legendary. For instance, in 1759 the governor of Martinique arrived at the scene too late to fight the English, who were besieging Basse-Terre. He had been too busy negotiating the loading of goods he had acquired on the black market on one of the only ships sailing for France.

After that, planters and magistrates realized that they had to allow their slaves a few *soupapes*, or "safety valves," to guard against rebellion, which was the nightmare of every colonist, second only to being poisoned. The last revolt, which had taken place on Christmas 1737, was still etched in everyone's memory. Had a young slave girl in love with her master not warned him in time—just before the *marrons* who had taken refuge in the forest carried off all the slaves—the French colony would have been wiped out in a bloodbath. Led by one of the king's justices, the repression that followed was so violent that the planters themselves allowed their slaves to escape before they could be burned at the stake. The priests tried to ensure that those slaves least culpable were strangled before being thrown into the flames.

In theory, *marronage* was punished as severely on Guadeloupe as on the other French islands: branding a fleur-de-lis after the first attempt, amputation of the leg below the knee for the second, execution for the third. In actual fact, the landowners made an effort to avoid extreme violence. Some settlers allowed *marrons* who had fled from the plantations during the day to come back and sleep in their huts in the evening. Moreover, mistreating one's slaves too openly was not regarded with approval. A heavy-drinking planter named Langlois was banished by the governor for having tortured four of his slaves.

Tolerance also applied to all social life. In Basse-Terre the gaming rooms stayed open all the time, even during mass. And in the rue Case-nègre, every family had the right to carouse with friends on Sundays. Several decades before Joseph was born, Father Jean-Baptiste du Tertre had written, "there is hardly a feast-day or a Sunday but that several Negroes from the same plantation or from neighboring ones meet for recreation, and at these times they dance in the fashion of their country. . . . Not only do they spend the whole of Sunday afternoon at these recreations, but at times they continue their amusements all night long, only separating one from another to return to their huts and then reuniting once more when the time comes for them to be taken to work. While the men and women dance and leap with all their might, the little children invent another dance some distance away, where it is amusing to see how they imitate the postures of their parents and copy their gestures."[8]

Escaping the condition of servitude and perpetuating the traditions and memories of the African homeland: These were the raisons d'être of those parties that sprang up all over, whether on the little squares of Basse-Terre or on the plantations. Joseph adored taking part in these gatherings and always laughed hilariously at the *calendas* and *yukas,* two dances the priests strove to ban, so offended were they to see their parishioners mimic the sexual act by rubbing their bellies together to a frantic beat.

Music and the dance were acts of resistance, and yet also symbols of integration and a certain segregation, too. Moreau de Saint-Méry stated in 1796 that "there would be balls at which the freed Negro women only danced together because the others never let them join in. . . . There are balls where the freed women dance only with the whites, not wanting to invite men of the same color as themselves."

The fine-looking lad with the handsome figure that Joseph had become soon developed a gift for these dances, in which the whole body moved to the rhythm of the music. At the time, Basse-Terre and its surrounding area were a melting pot in which sounds, harmonies, and melodies mingled to form an astonishing and improbable musical stew: classical airs from scores brought over in the royal vessels, popular tunes played by the *petits Blancs* who lived around the port, and African rhythms. This was the music Joseph's sharp ears picked up.

III

Race and the Enlightenment

The marvels of those first years on the slopes of Soufrière soon gave way to painful disappointment for the ambitious Tavernier de Boullongne. Natural disasters contrived to destroy, with crippling regularity, what he had rebuilt and restored on his property. In 1740, two years after his arrival, another hurricane laid waste to part of his plantation and destroyed a number of slave dwellings. Although Guadeloupe was without question less damaged than neighboring islands, according to the report of the governor general, it "had suffered even worse than in 1738. . . . The majority of the buildings have been razed, the others severely damaged, and three quarters of the sugar production lost." The following year, the island was hit by a disastrous drought. The king's lieutenant lamented that "the drought that has persisted here since the unfortunate hurricane has brought this poor colony to the utmost destitution." In August 1742, yet another hurricane made the governor general declare: "I have named Guadeloupe the 'ill-fated isle.'"[1]

Furthermore, Guillaume-Pierre had become extremely displeased by what he saw as the "indolence" of his slaves. He claimed that in many cases the Jesuits who preached in the slaves' huts and workshops encouraged their recalcitrance. Moreover, the company of men like Samuel Bologne, a nice enough fellow whose topics of conversation were virtually limited to the shapes of his bottles and his slave mistresses, or Vanier de Saint-Robert, who was a choleric braggart, was rather limiting. Even the kindness of the ambitious "cousin" Georges Bologne de Saint-Georges finally could not satisfy a growing thirst for new social contacts. His thoughts often turned to ways of seeking a fortune elsewhere.

The benevolent spirit that had watched over Guillaume-Pierre's prospects in Paris came once again to his aid. "His Majesty the King," as his *intendant* Boullongne duly informed Guillaume-Pierre, saw fit to offer him one of the last "free" concessions on Saint-Domingue.[2] At that time Saint-Domingue was the pearl of the Antilles, an El Dorado for adventurers the world over. Provided he was not overly scrupulous, a man could make his fortune there, decidedly more quickly than anywhere else, in the trade (whether legal or not) and exploitation of sugarcane. Moreover, the "Big Island," as they also called it at Versailles, provided, on its own, two-thirds of the exports to France. Declared off-limits to the Jesuits and their subversive influence, protected from English blockades by its size and by a large Spanish colony, the island was continually being replenished by the vessels of the slave trade. The relative precautions regarding slaves on Guadeloupe, necessary because of the shortage of manpower, no longer applied. At Basse-Terre, it took ten years to pay off the purchase of a slave. On Saint-Domingue, planters made good their original investment in a year and a half. This helps explain the savagery with which the foremen employed by the 30,000 white colonists treated the 700,000 slaves on the island.[3]

Joseph's father certainly was aware of these conditions, but he had not, after all, come to the Antilles driven by a philanthropist's zeal. Soon he and his family set sail for Cap François (now Cap-Haïtien).

They then settled in the parish of Artibonite, in La Rose, a sumptuous mansion built in the shadow of Mount Gros-Morne and bordered by the Ester river. Here the family acquired another member, an old soldier who had fought with Maréchal de Saxe and who went by the name of "Mr. Springtime." With his lofty bearing and impeccable attire, the old warrior was soon promoted to majordomo of the new property. Ever the protégé of the *intendant* Boullongne, Guillaume-Pierre was determined to hang on to his rank. He most likely thought that he could make conditions more congenial for Nanon and her son by surrounding them with an abundance of well-trained servants.[4]

The effort was in vain. One morning when he was taking a walk on the property, Joseph came across a driver whipping a slave till he drew blood. The boy tried to intervene. But, for all that he was a planter's son and dressed like a little aristocrat, he too received a violent lash of the whip. In tears, he rushed to La Rose and threw himself into Nanon's arms. After consoling Joseph for some time, his mother gently told him: "From now on, my child, you'll know that even though you are the son of a white—and not just the son of a *petit Blanc* from one of the ports, but the son of a *grand Blanc*—you're still the son of a black woman. Before this I didn't want to make you sad, but it is right that you should know where I come from, and where you yourself come from."[5]

A voluptuous sea washed Saint-Domingue, and a caressing breeze tempered the strong sun. Here one had only to stretch out one's hand to gorge on delicious fruits; lemon and nut trees and thousands of other plants perfumed the air. Could this Eden be a hell for those whose skin was not white? It did not take Joseph long to be convinced such was the case. Soon he was forbidden to have anything to do with the affairs of the plantation and above all to go around handing out Nanon's cakes to the slaves. Then, too, the tales the planters told at the evening meal were all about horrors visited upon the slaves. Malenfant, the plantation steward, would reminisce about the punishments meted out by his colleagues. "Men like the elder Caradeux or

Latoison-Laboule thought nothing of ordering Negroes to be thrown into furnaces or boiling cauldrons, or had them buried alive, standing up with only their heads sticking out, and let them perish that way. They were lucky when out of pity their friends and comrades would end their torments by stoning them!"[6] A traveler passing through the Big Island at that time relates: "I saw a colonist named Chaperon who had one of his blacks hurled into a hot oven, where the wretch expired. . . . Since then, this colonist has become the slaves' bogeyman, so that when their masters find them missing they threaten them with 'I'll sell you to Chaperon.' " Then there was the story of the elegant lady hosting a banquet who had her black cook thrown into the oven to punish him for having spoiled the pastry. And woe betide the young virgin who dared resist her master's advances. Often, the punishment was to shove a glowing firebrand into her vagina. As for the *marrons*, any slave caught running away was not given a second chance, as on Guadeloupe. He was killed on the spot, or one of his limbs was cut off. Tavernier de Boullongne had hardly settled in when another story went the rounds at the dinner table. One of his neighbors in the same parish, a certain Saint-Martin, had amputated all four limbs of five of his slaves. As was frequently the case, the crime went unpunished.

But at La Rose life was sweet. Money was pouring in, and there were lavish parties. In a few years the king's land grant had been cleared; sugarcane and cotton fields stretched from the great house to the horizon. It was time to sell. The Treaty of Aix-la-Chapelle had ended the Austrian Wars of Succession, offering what promised to be a very brief lull in France's endless conflict with England. This was an opportunity not to be missed. In two years only eight ships had crossed the seas between France and her Caribbean colonies, two of them being captured by the English. Throughout this period, cargoes had had to be rerouted around the Spanish part of the island, at a considerable increase in both costs and danger.

Eighteen years after her voyage in the hold of a slave ship, Nanon was once again to cross the Atlantic. But her son's father had taken particular care that this return voyage should avoid, as much as possible, stirring any memories of the first. Sumptuously clad, adorned with jewels and exaggeratedly perfumed with vetiver, Nanon was greeted like a princess by a crew that normally did not bother itself with civilities toward anyone with dark skin. The very crew members who, a few weeks before, on the outward-bound voyage, had shackled slaves like beasts down in the hold now vied with one another in gallantry before the Boullongne concubine.

Joseph did not conceal his pride at seeing how these whites swarmed around his mother. He quickly tried to size up this new territory on which he was to spend a few weeks—far longer than the crossing between Guadeloupe and Saint-Dominigue had taken. During the first days he would lean over the rails and admire the vastness of the jade-colored sea. The crew took a liking to this lad not yet nine years old; he was tall for his age and could already play the violin very well. From time to time a sailor pointed out to him the fins of a shark or, far off, a narwhal, that "unicorn of the seas" whose swordlike horn was imagined rather than actually seen. But no matter. Just like the whistles of the topmen echoing in the rigging aloft, the meaning of which he tried to make out, the words excited his curiosity: "mizzens," "mainsails," "studdingsails."

What he liked best were the meals at Captain Franck's table and the endless bickering between the captain and owner's representative, a certain Vitoux. His face made ruddy by spray and spirits, the captain heartily detested Vitoux, who, besides keeping a baleful eye on the cargo, prided himself on his writing talent. More pedantic than cultured, he was a conceited man who took an especially perverse delight in employing words of which only he knew the meaning. But his real genius lay in goading the ship's master. The latter did not miss an opportunity to tell Vitoux what he thought of him once he had a few drinks. Vitoux would invariably retort that the captain would do best to look straight ahead of him when he had been drinking. "This afternoon I saw you hug the mainmast again," he might snap at him in a supercilious tone of voice.

Their mutual disdain added spice to a shipboard life that quickly fell into monotony. During those first weeks of 1748, the temperature dipped a little lower the farther the ship drew away from the islands. Soon they would be swathed in icy mists; Nanon would almost never leave her cabin. From the rails Joseph could barely make out the water, which was frighteningly opaque compared with its luminous transparency back home. Moreover, it was pointless to scrutinize the horizon in search of land: The field of vision was no more than a few dozen yards. After several weeks, Joseph noted that the crew started becoming strangely agitated. Those sailors not working on the rigging hoisted great buckets of icy water up on deck and, despite the cold, began to soap themselves thoroughly and even to shave. Some went so far as to drench themselves in the cheap scents they had bought from traders in Cape François. The long voyage was nearing its end.

The next morning, Joseph was awakened by a general clamor on deck. Rushing out, he saw gigantic sailing ships passing within a few yards of their vessel, so close that the masts seemed about to collide at any moment. The shores narrowed until he could see both sides. "La Gironde," his father announced. Bordeaux was close at hand.

Having seen its prosperity threatened by the years of English blockade, the city was once again brimming with activity and intoxicated with the joy of war's end. At the quays, traders and shipowners busied themselves with chartering vessels or buying up whole cargoes. Warehouses were starting to fill up. Joseph and Nanon stood wide-eyed, watching the teeming crowds and the endless processions of carts, some of them drawn by six or eight horses. They were amazed to see that all the porters were white.

But there was no time to linger at the docks. Guillaume-Pierre was impatient to reach the city center, where a house had been put at his disposal. Wealth from the slave trade and commerce with the islands had caused luxurious properties to sprout up everywhere you looked. Finally this scion of a noble line could inhabit a dwelling worthy of his rank. As for Nanon, never before had she been treated with such respect. Though mistress of the house at Basse-Terre or in L'Artibonite, she had remained, in the eyes of the *petits Blancs*, a black woman. In Bordeaux, the *grands Blancs* complimented her on her beauty. For some years, the city had, in fact, been one of the beacons in the struggle for the improvement of the blacks' status and living conditions. As early as 1571, by decree of the parliament of Bordeaux, slaves were emancipated upon disembarkation, for "France cannot allow servitude on her soil."[7] More than a hundred years would pass before an edict dated October 4, 1691, would extend this ruling to the whole of the French kingdom. A royal declaration of 1738 had been designed to reinforce this "custom." Thus it was not unusual to see blacks moving about in the city streets. Most were paid domestics or coachmen.

Then the foremost colonial power in the world, the France that Joseph first set foot in had a peculiar attitude regarding the races. Rare indeed were the voices pleading for the universality of the human race, though the abbé Bergier, in his *Encyclopédie méthodique* (1765), ventured the opinion that "Europeans are born as guilty of original sin as Negroes," the difference in skin color deriving purely from the fact that people "are more or less distant from or close to the torrid zones."[8] The marquis de Condorcet was of the same opinion: "My friends," he said, addressing the blacks, "although I am not of the same color as you, yet I have always regarded you as brothers. Nature has formed us to have the same spirit, the same reason, the same virtues."[9] However, these opinions were isolated indeed among the other *Lumières*, most of whom obfuscated the issue of race. The *philosophes* of the day were generally content to secularize the Church's doctrine, which was founded on the pope's acceptance of slavery. This they did by stressing the differences between the races. By their lights, the black was fundamentally different from the white.

At practically the very moment that Joseph disembarked at Bordeaux, Denis Diderot was writing, under the heading "Negro" in his *Encyclopédie*: "These black men, born vigorous and accustomed to a coarse diet, find in the Americas many pleasant things which make physical life much better than in their own country. This change enables them to persist in work and to multiply abundantly." The historian Louis Sébastien Mercier recalled in his *Tableau de Paris* (Panorama of Paris) how when he was once walking along the quays with Jean-Jacques Rousseau, the latter "saw a Negro who was carrying a sack of coal." The great philosopher burst out laughing and exclaimed, "That man has the right job, he won't have to wash his face. Oh! If only the others were as well off as he."

Like Montesquieu before him, Voltaire was said to have profited to some extent from the trade in ebony; he went much further in his affirmation of the white race's superiority. "Their round eyes, flat noses, their lips, always so full, their differently shaped ears, their woolly hair, even the measure of their intelligence, all present enormous differences between them and the rest of the human species. And the proof that these differences are not due to their climate is shown by the fact that when male and female Negroes are transported to colder countries, they always produce creatures of their own kind and the mulattos are merely a bastard race."[10] As Pierre Pluchon has asserted, "[Voltaire] is a racist, like most of the enlightened minds of his day. But he is the only one to have the courage to voice his feelings openly, after which, like his peers, he can condemn slavery."

And indeed these same philosophers who regarded the blacks so contemptuously often denounced their exploitation in the colonies. The *Encyclopédie* stated that "the buying of Negroes in order to reduce them to slavery is a commerce that violates religion, morality, natural laws, and all the dictates of nature. . . . May the European colonies be destroyed rather than create so many unfortunates!" Rather cleverly, Georges-Louis de Buffon, one of the patriarchs of the natural sciences, set up the dialectic between science and conscience. "Although the Negroes have little intelligence, they never-theless have much feeling. . . . Humanity revolts against these odious treatments which covetousness has put into practice."

Thus we have the "good Negro" reduced by his very defenders to the level of an overgrown child requiring protection, or even below that. Black boys and girls were highly sought after as companions to fashionable ladies, who treated them like small pets. Hence in 1682 Pierre Mignard, one of Louis XIV's favorite painters, introduced into his portrait of the duchess of Portsmouth a young black girl, pictured offering pearls to her mistress. The custom gathered steam during the eighteenth century. A portrait of the marquise de Pompadour shows her accompanied by a young black boy.[11] A few years later, Jacques-Vincent Delacroix would rhapsodize: "Charming women, you whose whims are so fleeting, your caprices shed happiness over all; they make more people happy than does our cold constancy. The parakeet, the greyhound, the spaniel, the angora rabbit, have each in turn received your tender caresses and made you shed tears. . . . The most beautiful flame was about to be extinguished. A cold insensibility was about to take the place of rapture, of the keenest transports of delight, the most uproarious joy, when suddenly these little black creatures born in the bosom of slavery attracted your benevolent gaze. At that very moment, their bonds were broken."[12]

Mercier, that keen observer of eighteenth-century French society, summed up the matter (again in *Tableau de Paris*) in an eloquent passage: "Whereas the black child spends his life on the laps of women entranced by his exotic face, his flat nose; while a gentle, caressing hand punishes his disobedience with a slight chastisement soon effaced by the most affectionate caresses, his father groans under the whip of a pitiless master; the father breaks his back to produce that sugar which the Negro child drinks from the same cup as his laughing mistress."[13]

Little wonder, therefore, that a new trade developed, one specializing in the commerce of children. In a letter dated February 8, 1786—

one of the daily missives he showered upon his beloved during his protracted visit to Africa—the chevalier de Boufflers would declare, without the slightest hint of shame: "I'm in the process of buying a little Negro girl 2 to 3 years of age in order to send her to Mme the Duchesse d'Orléans. . . . She is as pretty not as the day but as the night."[14]

So long as he was still a child, Joseph could be sure of attracting looks that were more often curious and kindly than hostile. Thereafter he would have to use all his ingenuity to turn to his advantage the prejudices facing blacks living in France. Colonists regularly came over to spend a few years in the homeland accompanied by servants. Fantasies of all sorts rose up around the newly arriving blacks, who were often assumed to be gamblers, immature, and, above all, prone to licentiousness. One government minister named Sartine wrote to the prosecutor of the city of Aix that he was perturbed by the "harm" caused by the "multiplication" of blacks in Provence. In actual fact, seventy-one blacks and people of mixed race were recorded living there. These immigrants were rumored to have sexual prowess, as evidenced, said people, by the growing success of "black bordellos" then causing such commotion.

Thus a gradually more repressive reaction was growing to counter what was hardly an invasion. In 1738, shortly before Joseph was born, a royal ordinance was enacted that prohibited blacks from marrying on French soil; the notion was to prevent interracial marriage. The colonial lobby was chiefly responsible for the repressive measures. The slave who accompanied his master to France was, in theory, emancipated the moment he stepped on French soil. Becoming a domestic servant, he therefore returned a free man when his employer decided to go back to the islands one or two years later. And in the meantime it was feared he might have acquired a few disquieting ways. In 1753, Martinique officials wrote anxiously: "In France, the whites have no difficulty forming relationships with [blacks] and do not have the contempt for them that people here do. . . . These relationships can only have dangerous and unpleasant consequences for the colony. The Negroes who return from France are insolent, because of the familiarity they have grown accustomed to with the whites, and they have acquired habits that they can put to very bad use." One of the first countermeasures was to place a limit on emancipation. In that same year, 1753, a royal ordinance—these were often contradicted by the regional parliaments—marked a formidable step backward. It stipulated that a slave could not be considered free until he had spent three years on French soil. Planters rarely stayed in France longer than that. The only limit imposed upon the settlers' right of ownership was that they were forbidden to sell their slaves in the mother country.

Nevertheless, the colonial lobby had to acknowledge that though still classified as slaves, blacks were developing increasingly more intimate contacts with whites and continuing to adopt those habits decried by the rulers of Martinique. On June 20, 1763, a whole regulatory arsenal was set up when the duc de Choiseul, one of Louis XV's ministers, ordered colonial administrators to forbid "passage" of blacks, whether free or slave, to France. For his part, the king ordered the expulsion of all blacks before October 15 in order "to return them to the colonial plantations." This arrangement, which from the king's viewpoint had as its chief object to prevent miscegenation, was never actually put into effect. However, it illustrates quite clearly that racism was on the rise in French society.

Some professional groups were growing anxious at the prospect of competition from the new arrivals. Parisian valets and coachmen were able to win an interdiction against blacks entering their profession. This did not prevent the duc d'Orléans's wife from being driven around Paris with two black servants perched behind her carriage. In Bordeaux, the fencing masters succeeded in having access barred to fencers of color. Under these circumstances, it showed a certain panache on the part of Maurice de Saxe to recruit blacks into the regiment he planned to set up around the royal hunting Château de

Chambord, which Louis XV had presented to him as a gift following the great military victory at the Battle of Fontenoy. Thus on November 3, 1747, only a few months before his former supply officer, Guillaume-Pierre Tavernier de Boullongne, returned to France, the marshal received a petition from the minister of war, alarmed by the use these Negroes might make of their soldiering experience once they were back in their colony. But the charismatic de Saxe, for whom the king had intended to restore the title of *connétable*, or "constable" of France, couldn't have cared less. He raised a company of sixty unusually tall black men, making them his guard and personal escort. On their white horses, wearing green uniforms, Hungarian boots, and imitation-gold helmets adorned with a ribbon of Russian leather and a horsehair plume, the marshal's black *uhlans* were an impressive sight. Guillaume-Pierre was never able to admire these soldiers, whom he would have loved to outfit. Just a few months before he reached Bordeaux, his former employer, Maurice de Saxe, was killed by a jealous husband in a dry moat around the château of Chambord. In any case, other matters preoccupied the man of wealth that Tavernier de Boullongne had become in his dozen or so years in the Antilles. Chief among them were to build up his fortune and to gain his son entrée into Parisian society.

IV

An American in Paris

A festive atmosphere reigned in Poitiers in the early spring of 1748. Monsieur de Préninville, the head of the regional treasury, was about to honor the city with his presence. This individual, rumored to be a protégé of Madame de Pompadour, the king's mistress, only rarely deigned to set foot on the soil placed under his jurisdiction. He normally carried out his duties from his Paris residence on the place des Victoires, where he pored over every report and account book sent him by his provincial employees. No money could be spent unless sanctioned with his seal. The sedentary post was said to bring him a sizable income, giving him means to entertain on a lavish scale.

The very best china and silver were brought out to receive the man whose every decision was of the utmost importance to the prosperity of the province of Poitou. Yet Monsieur de Préninville had not come to Poitiers to listen to compliments and solicitations; he had come to meet the man whom he had not seen for a decade, but who now at long last had returned to France from the colonies: his older brother, Guillaume-Pierre.

At first Guillaume-Pierre had some difficulty recognizing this younger brother, who had been known as Tavernier de Boullongne when he had left and now was Monsieur de Préninville. The change was entirely symbolic, the name Tavernier having seemed too common for such an ambitious member of the nobility. He had also become very rich. In Poitiers, courtiers and spongers swarmed around him. In short, he had become a man of influence. His fortune had risen, as he told his brother with no little pride, to 514,050 livres, only slightly less an amount than Guillaume-Pierre had amassed in the Antilles. His post ensured him hefty revenues each year.

Soon the complicity forged in their "adventurous youth," as the chroniclers put it, took over.[1] Philippe-Guillaume pronounced himself moved by Nanon's beauty and noble bearing, and charmed by the irrepressible young Joseph. But they had, he insisted, to think of the future. He had made some changes to a little property on the rue de la Grange-Batelière, in Paris, where the new arrivals might stay until alterations to his home on the place des Victoires were completed. He himself had just acquired a house at the corner of the rue Saint-Honoré and rue de la Sourdière, and he suggested making his current dwelling available to his brother—and whomever he married. Indeed, Philippe-Guillaume made every effort to convince his elder brother of the urgent necessity, both for himself and for the family's name, to take a French wife. A former slave might prove an exotic housekeeper or mistress, such as one could see by the example of the comte de Mirabeau, who, after a brief stay as governor of Martinique, had brought back his Octavie. (Octavie would raise her lover's nephew, the future comte de Mirabeau, born in 1749, a year after Joseph's arrival. Before taking a leading role in the Revolution, Mirabeau would be an ardent defender of blacks.) But as a wife or even an official concubine, she would be an encumbrance for a family knocking at the doors of the French court. Préninville was not the only one to think so, he was careful to point out. Jean de Boullongne, who was now in charge of the royal treasury, shared his opinion. Jean managed the funds supporting the fabulous lifestyle of the king and his court; of the seven *intendants* of the kingdom, he was the most powerful.[2] In the government's administrative hierarchy only two figures were higher up than he: the prime minister and the minister of finance. Most important, however, Jean was a friend of the Marquise de Pompadour.

Born Jeanne Poisson, the daughter of a meat trader jailed for swindling, the magnificent, scheming Madame de Pompadour had found her way to the king's bed in 1745. Within three years she had become the most influential figure in the kingdom, which, every day, she drove ever closer to ruin to satisfy her extravagant whims. Any minister daring to stand up to her or even to suggest she moderate her expenses was immediately dismissed. She had an effective ally in the person of cousin Jean. Whenever an accountant raised objections to some expense, pleading the exhausted state of the treasury, Jean ingeniously found a way to pay for it. Having Jean de Boullongne as a godfather meant one's fortune was ensured. Nonetheless, one had to tread carefully.

Nanon quickly understood the situation and resolved to stand aside, assured that the father of her child would always have the greatest affection for her. Guillaume-Pierre pledged to keep his son close by his side in his upward climb. For her part, Nanon would receive an income of nearly 8,000 livres, enabling her to lead a very comfortable life. As luck would have it, the residence Philippe-Guillaume chose for his brother on the rue de la Grange-Batelière was situated a few steps from that of Catherine de Ravenel, the daughter of a tax commissioner. Having what was known as a "small name, but a great fortune," Catherine was the ward of a certain Jean-Marie Richard, the tax commissioner of the city of Tours—which he visited rarely—and who in turn happened to be the brother-in-law of none other than Jean de Boullongne. Things were falling into place quite nicely.

The young woman was very likely charmed by the ex-planter's commanding presence, as well as by the stories he told in such artful detail about life in the Antilles. On the other hand, she might well have been yielding to the calculations of her family. Whatever the case, she seemed prepared to forgive the transgressions of the man, twenty years her senior, being proposed as her husband. On June 18, 1748, Guillaume-Pierre de Boullongne-Tavernier, as he now styled himself, married Catherine de Ravenel. Since prudence was all, a marriage contract was drawn up before Maître François Prévost, notary of the parish of Saint-Eustache. Were the contract breached for whatever reason, each spouse could recover the assets he or she previously possessed.[3] The entire Boullongne family was present to seal the union. Marguerite, widow of Louis, "the King's first painter," appended her signature to the marriage contract next to that of Jean de Boullongne.

At that time, the royal coffers were as empty as ever. Yet ways had to be found to feed the court, which, under La Pompadour, had grown to 18,000 persons, including a military presence amounting to 9,000. Something like 2,000 courtiers with no defined function lived there in expectation of an office, a pension, gift, or sinecure. Some great families, like the Polignacs, took advantage of the weaknesses of the king and his mistress to loot the country systematically. As he was withdrawing from the government, the marquis d'Argenson remarked that "the court was the nation's tomb." To come up with the means necessary to satisfy Pompadour's whims, Louis XV accelerated the sale of offices, which resulted in an increase in the number of positions that then had to be remunerated. If the income from the sale of offices often landed in the royal treasury, the pensions remunerating them came straight out of the national budget. For Guillaume-Pierre, this afforded the opportunity to leave his plantation days well and truly behind him. Duly instructed, he quickly snapped up the mostly honorific posts of Secretary to the King and Hussar, or Usher, to the Parliament of Metz. It was but a first step into Parisian society.

Joseph and his new family thereupon moved to the handsome quarters on the place des Victoires (subsequently destroyed, later completely rebuilt), designed a half-century before by Jules

Hardouin-Mansart as a fit setting for the majestic statue of Louis XIV, commissioned by the duc de La Feuillade. Here the Boullongnes' neighbor was the widow of Samuel Bernard, who had saved the kingdom from bankruptcy under Louis XIV. Poorly compensated, Bernard, who had once been one of the most powerful figures in France, and one of the few intimates of the Sun King, had died, ruined, nine years previously. Since then, his widow, a living witness to fortune's fickleness, had been trying to withstand nearly constant harassment from creditors.

Guillaume-Pierre had made it plain that he wanted Joseph raised according to the style decreed by the academies. The *moineau*— "sparrow"—he had sired should excel in every discipline prescribed by the aristocracy: swimming, riding, dance, fencing, swordsmanship, the pistol, and even combat with the stick. He would be taught the horn, the clavichord, and the violin. Good manners were essential. "One did not need to be a poet or philosopher but one had to be an accomplished gentleman," Roger de Beauvoir noted about a century later. "Merely from the way a person took snuff from a box at Ravechel's, one could at once recognize the brilliant nobleman, the hero of the latest races or the habitué of social gatherings and supper parties. . . . These men, whom you parted from of an evening in a salon," he went on, "you would find the next day at the shoot, the stables, the dancing school, the tennis court."[4] That was precisely the sort of man the wealthy ex-planter wanted to make of his son.

The boy did indeed show promise. François-Joseph Fétis, a Belgian musician born late in the eighteenth century, declared that from the age of ten Joseph "was already surprising his teachers with his facility for learning."[5] Thus the precocious child became an object of both curiosity and affection. Relatives and servants were amused by the interest he took in everything around him: the enormous buildings going up on all sides, the elegant women, the horses with their magnificent trappings, and so forth. His new world, while not as vast as his father's old property but certainly livelier, took him each day past the cardinal's palace—soon to be the Palais-Royal—occupied by the duc d'Orléans, and then past the Louvre. One glance at the rue d'Argenteuil with its taverns in which wine was sold at all hours and he was nearly at his uncle Philippe-Guillaume's residence on the rue Saint-Honoré. If he was in the mood, he could go on to the place Vendôme, where Jean de Boullongne lived in a vast mansion at the corner of the rue Neuve-des-Petits-Champs (the present-day rue Danielle-Casanova). This street always delighted Joseph, as did the booths and hawkers that cluttered every approach to the Louvre (some enterprising souls had even set up shop in its main courtyard). But he was strictly forbidden to go inside what would have been the king's official residence had Louis XIV not moved his court to Versailles. Following the royal departure, the Louvre had been overtaken by a swarm of undesirables who were encamped there. Strange things—unspeakable things—went on, at least according to rumor. (Happily, the latest news was that La Pompadour had heard about all this from her brother, Monsieur de Marigny, and planned to do some housekeeping.) Some distance off, Joseph could make out the Grand Châtelet, which reminded him of good old Monsieur Plato and the tragic story of poor Cartouche. After this, he might have continued on to the apothecary's shop on the rue Saint-Honoré and bought a few bottles of *eau de Passy*, which, at seven *sous* a bottle, had become the latest fad among wealthy Parisians. (This pharmacy, where it is said that the invisible ink for Marie Antoinette's letters was purchased, is still there.)[6] Strange that no one from the islands ever thought of buying drinking water.

Crossing the rue de l'Arbre-Sec, Joseph might well have cast an envious glance at Monsieur de La Boëssière's fencing school, from which echoed the sound of clashing steel. But above all he must avoid getting into a squabble with Sophie Arnould, the sharp-tongued daughter of the innkeeper who lodged the painter Van Loo. Sophie had dreams of becoming an actress or even an opera singer, and envied Joseph his early success with the violin. She was forever taunting him about the color of his skin. No doubt this was partly out of spite, since her father could not afford to buy her clothes as splendid as Joseph's. Easily the most comic sight on Joseph's neighborhood rounds would have been the crowd of people snatching up royal lottery tickets at the corner of the rue Vivienne and the rue des Petits-Champs. The shouting could sometimes get so loud that he could hear it from his window on the place des Victoires. Certainly the first prize—an annual income of 20,000 livres—was enough to arouse the envy of many. To hear the colonists who used to come dine with them on the plantation tell it, gambling was a preoccupation confined to blacks.

On October 18, Joseph attended his second big wedding of that year, after his father's. At thirty-four, his uncle Philippe-Guillaume was about to marry a young woman barely sixteen years of age. "Beautiful, fun-loving, charming," according to the count of Cheverny, Marguerite de Martinville, the daughter of an extremely wealthy Farmer General, was "much talked about in Paris."[7] The count also painted a rather flattering portrait of the bridegroom: "M. de Boullongne de Préninville combined wit with the finest of educations; he would have been the handsomest of men had he not in his schooldays been struck in the left eye by a knife, in such a way that the eye could not be saved. Very rich, honorable, particular as to his friends, cheerful but shy because of his disfigurement, he had the brains to govern a kingdom; his heart was open to friendship, but one had to work in order to earn it." The Tavernier brothers had lost their father some years before. His role at the ceremony would be taken by Jean de Boullongne—whose solicitude, some felt, was somewhat surprising in so distant a relative. Almost at once, the charming Marguerite took a liking to the young Joseph. A few years later they were constantly to be seen together, which set Parisian tongues wagging, particularly those never slow to pick up an amorous trail. Friends of the Boullongne clan would do all they could to stem the flow of gossip before it destroyed family harmony. They let it be known that these shows of affection were entirely normal, Joseph being the natural son of Philippe-Guillaume rather than of his brother. The story stuck. Soon, however, more excuses had to be found for the innumerable escapades of the fair Marguerite.

Between lessons with his tutors and walks around Paris with his governesses, Joseph's life in the place des Victoires fell into a comfortable routine. One spring day in 1749, upon returning from one of his walks, he was seized by two strong arms and hurled into the air: "There he is at last, my little chevalier, my Chevalier de Saint-George! But you're quite the little man now!" The individual with the thundering voice and Herculean strength was none other than cousin Georges Bologne de Saint-Georges from Guadeloupe. When asked what he was doing in Paris, he replied, solemnly, that he was under "sentence of death." Later, at supper, Georges recounted his incredible misadventure. One Sunday in December 1747 he had been dining at the home of Uncle Samuel, along with his cousin Jean-Hugues and Vanier de Saint-Robert. The wives, all of whom except for the strict Elisabeth Mérican, Georges's wife, had partaken of the dinner and then gone home. As was his custom, Samuel had then summoned a few musicians together with his most beautiful slave women and a joyous afternoon ensued, the men dancing with the women and gulping down vast quantities of sugarcane liquor.

After supper, Georges had wanted to return home, but Jean-Hugues, who "was deep in his cups," had started taunting him about his elegant clothes, knocking him about, "throwing his hat and wig to the floor as was his wont."[8] Georges had ordered him to pick them up; instead, his cousin had trampled on them. "When you're drunk you have the damnedest manners. You're nothing but a blackguard," said Georges. At these words, Vanier de Saint-Robert, who had been inside the house, had seized his sword: "You should be ashamed of yourself, insulting my brother-in-law," he yelled from the window. He then jumped out the window, which sent him sprawling on the ground, making Georges roar with laughter. Georges then promptly took his leave, after, with some difficulty, climbing up on the horse brought to him by a young slave. Vanier had rushed down the slope, sword in hand, falling several times as he did so, trying to catch up with Georges at the sugar mill. He had therefore been obliged to dismount and start fighting. Barely had they begun when his breeches fell down to his ankles and the duel was briefly interrupted.[9]

At that point Georges had to pause in his story while the guests whom Guillaume-Pierre had hastily invited to meet this colorful character nearly collapsed from helpless laughter. But the "cousin" from the Antilles continued his tale, and at this point the story took a tragic twist: "The duel having resumed," in the words of the report written about the case, "he grazed his adversary's nose with his sword, then wounded him, though again lightly, on the arm." The fight then ended and Vanier de Saint-Robert went home to sleep it off, without even allowing anyone to dab water on his cuts, as Samuel had suggested. Three days later he was dead. Although his widow had not lodged a complaint, the public prosecutor ordered the judge to perform an inquest. The body was duly exhumed. Doctor Lafitte, although theoretically retired, was summoned and pronounced the verdict of death "due to tetanus." For the law, there was no doubt that death was due to an infected sword wound.

The "guilty party" had not even had the decency to indemnify the widow. Solicited by the dead man's family to the tune of 100,000 livres, Georges had haughtily replied that there was no question of his paying so much as a sou: "I'll be a free man for a thousand crowns and a voyage to France." Plainly put, he was convinced that in Paris he would find the support necessary to have his name cleared.[10]

On May 31, 1748, Georges Bologne, who in the meantime had fled the island, was condemned in absentia "to be hanged and strangled until death occurs on the gallows at the corner of the public square of this city of Basse-Terre." His assets were confiscated. On October 27, the sentence was carried out "in effigy," the executioner tying the rope around a figure representing the condemned man.

Bologne regaled his audience with news of the colony. In particular, he had a bone to pick with a certain Father Archange, the new priest of Basse-Terre, who seemed more interested in seducing young slaves than in carrying out his duties. After a cursory inquiry, the parishioners found out that the priest, whose actual name was Jean-Baptiste Siry, had previously swindled the congregations of Grenada, obliging them to fork out money to rebuild a presbytery. But the building never saw the light of day, the money remaining in the pocket of the priest's cassock.[11]

Now the priest was asking Uncle Samuel for 2,4000 livres to agree to bury him, when the time came, inside St. Francis Church. This was rather a hard pill to swallow. The church had, in part, been built thanks to a gift from Pierre de Bologne, Samuel's brother. In exchange, the previous parish priest had promised that Bologne's nearest descendants would be interred in one of the church chapels. But apparently Father Archange felt in no way felt bound to respect the word of his predecessor.

With his tales of drunks and a swindling, pedophile priest, cousin Georges could have gone on for months entertaining the Boullongnes and their friends, who flocked every evening to the place des Victoires. However, he felt he had to leave as soon as possible, before all of his possessions were seized and auctioned off. Jean de Boullongne's discretion worked wonders. On November 5, 1749, the governor general of the Windward Islands and the *intendant* received a royal ordinance informing them that Bologne had been pardoned by His Majesty: "The said Bologne of Guadeloupe has obtained letters of remission and is leaving for the Islands to pursue their ratification. The King's intention is that you should ensure that the judges proceed to this ratification according to this ruling."

Cousin Georges could leave for his plantation with his head held high. Having savored the pleasures of the capital, he had, moreover, announced that it was his intention to return before long. He wasn't going home empty-handed. In his pouch was a certificate appointing his brother Pierre "Councilor to the Parliament of Metz," an office Pierre had been pleading for for years. In his letters of application, Pierre had even claimed kinship with the great house of Bologna in Italy.

This intervention in favor of his "cousin" allowed Jean de Boullongne to point out an astonishing gap in the kingdom's administrative system—to wit, all the provinces had a treasurer based in Paris, who saw to it that they functioned smoothly, in addition to overseeing their expenses. Curiously, however, no one had thought of appointing one to the colonies, which were still administered directly by the Department of the Sea. Some means had to be found to rectify this situation forthwith. Boullongne whispered the idea to La Pompadour, who found the idea all the more remarkable in that the post would be sold for the impressive sum of 600,000 livres, which would immediately fall into the royal purse.

By great good fortune, the *intendant* in charge of the royal treasury had a cousin who had recently arrived from the Antilles, and who would be prepared to invest this sum—for the good of the colonies, naturally. The king's favorite was not slow to agree that the man was highly suitable. Though for Guillaume-Pierre the outlay was on the heavy side, he nonetheless pledged to pay it. On December 23, 1749, two days before Joseph's tenth birthday, he borrowed 90,000 livres from a financier named Jacques Challard. Guillaume-Pierre's new wife, Catherine, being still a minor, it was her tutor, one Richard, who signed the acknowledgment of debts in his name—a situation that was beginning to be a trifle humiliating for a man who had held in his hands the fate of several hundred slaves. Still, his appointment, eleven days later, as Second General Treasurer of the Colonies provided him with lucrative consolation.

The tutor's watchful eye over his ward could not, however, extend to the conjugal bed. It was not long before she gave birth to a little girl, Catherine-Jeanne. Guillaume-Pierre began the custom of changing homes whenever he climbed a step up the social ladder. The family took over a townhouse on the rue Saint-Honoré, opposite the convent of the Jacobins and two steps from Philippe-Guillaume's home and the church of Saint-Roch. (Guillaume-Pierre's townhouse must have faced what is today the rue du Marché-Saint-Honoré.) The question arose what to do with Joseph, who was getting too big to stay at home. It was time to think about his education.

Having so often passed by La Boëssière's fencing school, the elegantly dressed young boy had finally caught the attention of the owner and his son, who was five years Joseph's junior. The new Second General Treasurer of the Colonies was eager that his son be given as impeccable an education as the one he had received from his tutors. On this point he was immediately reassured. Monsieur de La Boëssière, a native of Bas-Poitou, had come to Paris some twelve years earlier to escape the priesthood to which his family was dooming him. In addition to his gift for wielding the foil, he liked, as he was fond of putting it, to "offer sacrifice to the muses." He would write a comedy, *Crispin*, an opera, *The Coquette in the Country*, and, much later, publish an elegiac poem on the death of the Prince of Brunswick. In 1752, when he took in Joseph as a boarder, La Boëssière was reputed to be one of the best fencing masters in Paris, even though he had not yet won the braid of a master at arms, and therefore could not yet keep a *salle ouverte*, or "open hall," meaning he could not take in fencers whom he had not himself taught. That would happen in 1759. Nonetheless, this somewhat shy, seemingly withdrawn man had two trumps that were immediately appreciated in this neighborhood, perhaps the smartest in Paris. On the one hand, he attached at least as much importance to his pupils' intellectual and moral education as to their performance at sports. For him—and he would communicate this ethos to Saint-George—the result did not count so much as the manner in which it was achieved. On the other hand, he was a tireless worker; his protégés quickly learned that if they wanted to stay under his roof, they had to spend hours practicing, over and over, a tedious series of moves facing a wall before even being allowed to cross foils.

La Boëssière also invented the protective mask, worn by fencers to this day. And he had an eight-year-old son who immediately conceived an immense admiration for Joseph, now thirteen. The father also quickly took a lively and affectionate interest in the young man of mixed race, often taking him hunting. Indeed, an enduring bond developed among the three of them.

In 1818, the younger La Boëssière took up his pen to commend to posterity the talent and character of the two men who had meant the most to him. In the preface to his *Treatise on the Art of Weapons* he wrote: "From the age of eight, when my father put a foil in my hand, and having always practiced under his guidance, I had the inestimable advantage of learning from his lessons and being raised with M. de Saint-George, who was until he died my friend and companion in arms. Out of respect for the memory of these two famous men I thought it my duty to preserve for posterity the principles which made each one shine." These preliminaries are followed by a second preface, a seven-page biography of Saint-George, as if the teacher in the younger La Boëssière had wanted to preach by example before embarking on the first of the fifty-eight lessons that are contained in the treatise. Cutting short his introductory remarks, he declares: "Perhaps the most extraordinary man ever known in fencing, and even in all physical exercise, was the famous Saint-George; one might well say of him what Ariosto said of Zerbino: 'Nature made him and then broke the mold.' "[12]

Joseph's childhood friend goes on to describe how the older boy's days were organized: "At the age of thirteen he began to board with M. de la Boëssière, staying there for six years. Mornings were taken up with his education, the rest of the day being spent in the fencing hall." The classics made up a large part of this "education," but it also was firmly based on the moral teachings imparted by his fencing master. "However favorably one has been endowed with talents, these talents only shine forth in all their brilliance when they are guided by sound principles. M. de la Boëssière could take pride in having developed the talents of M. de Saint-George." And then—most important in his father's eyes—Joseph also had regularly to attend the royal riding school at the Tuileries gardens. In theory, to be admitted one had to have an introduction, since only gentlemen could take lessons from its director, a man named Dugast. But, as ever, the best guarantee remained the goodwill Madame de Pompadour felt toward the Boullongne clan (she had agreed to be godmother to Jean-Nicolas, the son of Philippe-Guillaume and Marguerite, and therefore Joseph's cousin). And thus did the young "chevalier" find himself face-to-face with viscounts and marquises at Dugast's riding school. Once again his father had shown exceptional farsightedness. Joseph delighted everyone with whom he came in contact. "The Chevalier Dugast who headed the Tuileries riding school liked to consider him one of his best pupils," the younger La Boëssière wrote. According to his admiring friend, Joseph's dancing master also pronounced himself very well satisfied with his unusual pupil: "Saint-George's natural grace had made him a good dancer; everyone agreed that if he had devoted himself to the ballet, he would have done amazing things."

Music was absolutely expected to have a preeminent place in these "academies." Guillaume-Pierre would reveal the importance he attached to it when he obtained for his son the services of Jean-Marie Leclair, the most brilliant violinist of the kingdom.[13] Leclair was the founder of the Violin School of France and a former musical favorite of Louis XV. As for composition, it would be taught by the most renowned musician of the time, François-Joseph Gossec, the man who would, as we will see, set the French Revolution to music.

In the fencing hall on the rue Saint-Honoré Joseph simply dazzled those around him: "At fifteen," his friend and biographer continues, "his progress was so rapid that he beat the best swordsmen. At seventeen he had acquired the greatest speed. In time, he combined with his prompt execution an expertise that finally made him without peer." Perhaps the younger La Boëssière realized he was taxing credulity, for he adds: "In the other arts, we have monuments of the skill of those who distinguished themselves: Paintings survive the artist, marbles the sculptor, works of music and poetry survive the composer and poet. It is otherwise with exercises of the body: dancing, fencing, and riding leave no trace of the perfect execution of those who distinguished themselves in those arts. Only contemporaries, who witnessed these prodigies, can remember them."

Happily, "many people who saw Saint-George are still alive and can attest that everything one can cite about this marvelous man would be inferior to what amazed them. I who saw him close at hand, who never left his side, confess that I am still filled with admiration for his attacks, each one more astonishing than the one before." There most certainly was innate talent. But it was also the result of ceaseless work over those fifty-eight lessons, in which Joseph was often held up as the exemplar. He never balked at taking up his stance at the practice or "touching" wall, an exercise that dueling machos very often despised. And there he "touched" with increasing speed the same point, always with surgical precision but using different approaches. André Grétry, the great composer and musicologist, would in his turn hear Joseph "touch" his violin, that is, establish themes in different tonalities, to the ceaseless delight of his listeners.

In those six years he spent as a boarder at La Boëssière's academy, Joseph became an adolescent, then a young man. "Saint-George had grown to a height of five feet ten inches [exceptional for the time]. He was very well built, with a prodigious strength of body and extraordinary vigor. Lively, supple, and slender, he astonished everyone with his agility. No one in the class showed more grace, more consistency." Joseph always remembered that his father had not made him a chevalier for nothing. "He made it a duty never to trick his opponent, that is, not to make false movements before beginning. If he happened to do so even to the slightest degree, the thrust did not count. . . . If he saw his opponent make a feint, the foil was knocked out of the other's hand by parries and beatings so powerful and elastic that arms were broken. . . . When fencing with his friends he was accommodating, but you would be wise not to take advantage of that, for if he noticed he would take his revenge. To judge his talent, it was not enough to see him fence; you had to be sufficiently well advanced in the art of swordsmanship to fence with him—then you could recognize his superiority."

And what superiority. "Imagine what a swordsman can do with such speed! One who could make whatever attack was called for, who had an exceptional length of lunge, who always thrust out of tempo and yet with the most impressive *garde*. If you engaged his blade, you would find the point so light you could not feel it. . . . In a word, you dared not try anything: Straight thrusts and disengagements would rain down on you one after the other and overwhelm you." The writer of this glowing homage was himself one of the best fencers in Paris.

Interestingly, the younger La Boëssière never mentions the other student of mixed race whom his father would take in some years later, Thomas "Dumas" Davy de La Pailleterie, father of Alexandre Dumas, author of the *The Three Musketeers* and *The Count of Monte-Cristo*. He was simply among the masses of other pupils who regarded his elder colleague with a mixture of envy and admiration, another islander like himself who drew all eyes. But no matter. "Not once did M. de Saint-George yield to the insinuations of jealous mediocrity," insists his early biographer.

While the son was inspiring all this admiration, the father continued, perhaps less brilliantly but just as surely, his ascent in society. In 1751 the ever-helpful cousin Jean finally put his cards on the table. He had sent a group of genealogists to Picardy and French Flanders to establish if in fact he was linked to the old noble family known as the "Tavernier de Boullongne." The court painters' heir had an obsession. He had long dreamed of being appointed Controller General of Finances (the equivalent of a minister for finances) but, as we've seen, given that he was the son of an artist admitted to the nobility only in 1721, he was constantly being edged out by members of the old families. Were he officially related to an ancient lineage, the outlook would be decidedly more positive. Thus on December 8, 1751, the representatives of the three branches of the Boullongne clan were all brought together in Jean's vast residence on the place Vendôme (site of the present-day Boucheron jewelers). Jean presented the result of the genealogists' research in Arras. He was without question the last-born of a minor branch of the Boullongnes, but they all shared the same ancestor, a certain Claude de Boullongne, a native of Tournai. Agreement was therefore reached: The Taverniers de Boullongne would bear the principal family arms, but Jean would also be entitled to a coat of arms, very slightly modified. The Marquis d'Argenson, one of Louis XV's ministers and a personal enemy of Jean's, was furious: "Le sieur de Boullongne has a fine genealogy drawn up to show the king that although he is a painter's son, he comes from a noble line in Picardy." And, he added, the *intendant* "is taking steps to increase the king's credit (that is, his debt) so as to be able to provide for the court's expenses and drain the people even more."

Where there's a will there's a way. On August 25, 1757, Louis XV finally signed the appointment of Jean de Boullongne to the post of Controller General of Finances, the promotion that he had just missed getting on several occasions. At once Jean arranged for the transfer to his son, Jean-Nicolas, of his post of *intendant* of finances, which had hitherto guaranteed him a way of life fit for a nabob. This was but the first stage of a period of frenzied nepotism. A few months later, Guillaume-Pierre was promoted Treasurer General in the Event of War, one of the most expensive, and therefore the most lucrative, posts in the kingdom. And Philippe-Guillaume rose to the post of Farmer General, the most reviled because it was the most remunerative in the *ancien régime*. The people hailed the financier's promotion. A song was even composed to sing his praises:

> *Who's the one who by his labors*
> *Can make order out of chaos?*
> *Boullongne, Boullongne, Boullongne.*

Who, without filling the hospital,
Can stuff the royal treasury?
Boullongne, Boullongne, Boullongne.

Who can provide the money
Lacking up to now?
Boullongne, Boullongne, Boullongne.

Who'll give everything back to his king
And keep nothing for himself?
Boullongne, Boullongne, Boullongne!

Alas, just as the new hero was busy building up his career by blindly subsidizing La Pompadour's costliest caprices, the English were busy building forty ships. Without declaring war, they attacked the French colonies and ravaged the islands of Ré and Aix off the west coast of France. The kingdom had no funds with which to mount a counteroffensive. Expedients were sought, and a certain Etienne de Silhouette came up with the brilliant idea to "issue confidence bills which individuals would purchase with gold." This paper-money policy, unfortunately reminiscent of the national bankruptcy under the Scotsman John Law, shocked Jean de Boullongne, who, when all was said and done, was still a financier at heart. He saw no merit to the idea, and the danger of increasing public distrust of the king. Louis XV, however, had an ear only for good news.

On March 4, 1759, the count of Saint-Florentin presented himself at dawn at the door of the house on the place Vendôme. "The king is pleased with your services," he announced to the master of the house. No further explanation was necessary. The controller general understood that he had been dismissed. The insignificant Monsieur de Silhouette, who would not even dare blink at the royal demands, and would be remembered in history as a shadowy common noun, would take his place. Obeying custom, which decreed that dismissal be followed by a period of "exile" from the capital, the ex-minister retired for several months to his château near Alençon, some 120 miles west of Paris and a few leagues from that of Fresnay-le-Vicomte, the fief of the third branch of the Boullongnes.

At least those men whose success Jean had been so instrumental in creating kept their posts. For Guillaume-Pierre, being appointed Treasurer General in the Event of War meant being a sort of secretary of the armies. On the one hand, he oversaw the purchase of equipment, provisions, arms, and munitions, about which he had learned while in the service of Maurice de Saxe. On the other hand, he was responsible for paying the soldiers' wages as well as the salaries of general officers, provincial governors, and fort captains. In addition, he exercised the power of oversight over all the elite regiments: musketeers, light horse, king's guards, and mounted grenadiers. He was the only person of distinction in the kingdom authorized to raise levies, when necessary, on the king's treasury. But he derived most of the resources of his post by taxing the district tax collectors as need arose. In so doing, he was assisted by the provincial treasurers of war, who, like him, drained resources as they pleased but only paid him back when necessary. He was also skilled at securing loans across the country in the name of the public authorities.[14] In short, this descendant of a small landowner who had fled northern France and had had to style himself "de Tavernier" to escape his creditors now sat atop a colossal goldmine. No one controlled him, nor was he accountable to anyone. All he was asked to do was to come up with the funds necessary for the outfitting and functioning of the armies. No one would have thought of reproaching him for slipping into his purse a considerable part of the gold levied on the country.

In the meantime, Saint-George fenced every day with La Boëssière. Little by little the pupil rose to the level of, and at times surpassed, the master. La Boëssière, sixteen years older than Joseph and not as tall (five feet six inches versus five feet ten inches), had maintained his reputation by spending endless hours experimenting with positions, searching out the best methods of attack, and devising the most effective parries. Authorized in 1759 to try to enter his school into the highly exclusive club of the Royal Academy, of which there were twenty members, he was finally ready to do so—thanks in part to his prize pupil. He himself would have to beat one of three fencing masters opposing his bid. For his first match, La Boëssière chose the strongest and beat him in two touches. At long last he had won the coveted title of "Master of Arms of the Royal Academies," and the braid to go with it.

Now that it was a royal academy, his establishment could take in fencers from outside and open its doors to spectators. The public immediately flocked to the school, curious to discover this "Negro" whom Monsieur de La Boëssière had taken under his wing. So, too, did the best swordsmen show up, one after another, to cross foils with the amazing chevalier de Saint-George. More than one dueling hotshot found himself pinned down thanks to Joseph's speed and agility and the precision of his thrusts, each of which would be accompanied by a resounding "Ha!" The young man knew he had to be accepted and, like his teacher, usually displayed a playful disposition. But woe betide anyone who dared make fun of his complexion. One such unlucky man was the chevalier de La Morlière, who just before a match had seen fit to make some glib remark about taking on an opponent who was a half-caste. Before anyone could intervene, Saint-George had hurled himself, howling with rage, on the young man, tossed him the length of a balustrade, and systematically broken a bundle of foils on his back. It was a humiliation that would never be forgiven. Similarly an obscure swordsman named Chardon turned up to duel Saint-George, whom he knew only by reputation. Eyeing Joseph's stature, he apparently realized too late that he didn't measure up to his impressive opponent and therefore contented himself with parrying and retreating, without making a single attack. Joseph threw down his sword in a rage, strode up to his opponent—who was paralyzed with fear—and carried him upside down all around the hall. The audience got their money's worth.[15]

Over the following months, the chevalier de Saint-George was judged unbeatable. The question was, was he the best in all France? In Rouen a famous fencing master named Picard disputed any such claim and announced that he would triumph easily over "La Boëssière's mulatto." Joseph had to take up the gauntlet—or so his friends advised him. However, he was not combative by nature and disliked that the pending match was being described as a "duel." His father came up with a convincing argument, according to Henry Angelo, the English fencing master in whose house Joseph would later stay. If his "sparrow" won, he would be given a one-horse chaise in the English style with trappings fit for a prince. And his father would send specially for an English horse. The dandy that Joseph had become could not refuse. In 1760 he went to Rouen, and "like Caesar, he came, he saw, he conquered."[16] Picard was forced to acknowledge that, at twenty-one years of age, the chevalier de Saint-George was indeed the best fencer in the kingdom. In the most fashionable quarters he was already being compared to Giuseppe Tartini, the Italian violinist virtuoso, then sixty-four years old, who in his youth had been a formidable fencer. However, Saint-George had yet to prove that he could wield the bow as well as he did the sword.

V

The Foil and the Bow

Y ke voi roi de France un jou, the midwife had predicted. "One day he meet the king of France!" The midwife's prophecy seemed destined to become true. Versailles was still some distance off, of course, but at La Boëssière's fencing establishment or at the Royal Academy riding school Joseph was now routinely testing his prowess against young nobles who were habitués of the court. A number of them had already accompanied him through the teeming quarters of the Palais-Royal, where he stood head and shoulders above the crowd. Others could not bear to think of recognizing as their equal a "piece of merchandise," as the *code noir* described the children of slaves.

Paris society was rife with debates over semantics. To the older nobility, while Saint-George might call himself a chevalier and earn praise for his gifts from the gossip press, he would never be anything other than a "Negro." The qualifier "mulatto" was used most frequently in census reports and official memoranda. Enlightened souls as well as the younger aristocrats had begun calling him "the American," in part because he was a breath of fresh air in stuffy high society. Joseph himself debated what term to use to define his racial identity.

He finally decided upon "Creole." The term was sometimes used to designate whites from the Antilles and Guiana. However, administrative and police reports often referred to "Creole Negroes," to distinguish them from Africans or Indians. "Creole" it was.

Like La Boëssière the younger, the great British fencer Henry Angelo describes Joseph in his memoirs as the consummate athlete. "No man ever united so much suppleness with so much strength. He excelled in all the bodily exercises in which he engaged—an excellent swimmer and skater," Angelo declared. He also relates how Saint-George impressed the young nobles by swimming one-armed across the Seine. Challenged to repeat the exploit in winter, Joseph made himself the talk of the town by diving into the icy water in January before an astonished crowd.[1] Another observer noted that "no one could match him in running; in the dance he was the model of perfection; an excellent horseman, he rode the most difficult mounts bareback and made them docile."[2]

Restless for pleasure and constantly on the lookout for novelty, Parisians went wild for "the American." At nineteen, Joseph stopped boarding at La Boëssière's school and went to live with his father, who had again moved house and was now installed on the rue de Richelieu, in a townhouse directly overlooking the Palais-Royal gardens. This section of the city was a favorite meeting place for wealthy young people, who thronged there on summer evenings. They vied with one another in elegance, compared the richness and showiness of their carriages, and sent kisses to the young ladies, who returned them by blowing delicately on their fans, a coquettish gleam in their eyes. Then they would trot to the Champs-Elysées, newly planted with trees, where riders and carriage drivers competed in audaciousness. On crowded evenings, as many as 2,000 carriages might be there, watched by crowds of spectators: coaches of two, four, or even six horses for princes of the blood, broughams, phaetons, and two-wheeled chaises in the English style. Saint-George always created a sensation when he turned up in his own buggy amid this new aristocracy so in thrall to anything English. Some went to stir up trouble. One of the stars of those evenings was Rosalie Duthé, whom the duc d'Orléans had presented to his fifteen-year-old son Philippe that she might teach him the facts of life. One night she emerged on the Champs-Elysées in a coach-and-six. In theory, only princes were entitled to own such a carriage. The joke did not sit at all well with certain young aristocrats, who sang, to the tune of a popular air, "La Duthé a dû téter" (more or less, "La Duthé must have suckled royally").

At times these boisterous corteges made it as far as the Passy hills, where the nouveaux riches had built themselves sumptuous second homes. While members of the old aristocracy divided their time between the court and their provincial châteaux, the new elite worked in Paris, the center of business. Soon some from this group felt the need for their own escapes from the din of clogs on cobblestone and the raucous shouts of street vendors. By far the most desirable site was on the western outskirts of the capital, where one was close to Versailles, the unmistakable seat of power, but could also maintain a prudent distance. The professionals among the newly rich feared like the plague being contaminated by that idle crowd that clung to its past and closed its eyes to its future.

Gilded youth—the scions of those highly placed at court, the sons of speculators and merchants—often attended the fêtes held by the so-called *noblesse de robe* and newly wealthy bourgeois in their "Trianons." In summer, one masked ball would follow another. And the music being played, more and more, was breaking free from religious influence and appealing directly to pleasure. The Château de la Tuilerie, which Jean de Boullongne had built in 1734 on the hills between Auteuil and Passy, was one of the most frequented at the time. On many occasions the controller general welcomed Saint-George, who might show up with a band of friends in his wake. As he grew older, Joseph's most appealing character traits became more pronounced. "Despising wealth for himself, what he possessed belonged to his friends," La Boëssière the younger observed, adding, "He made his gifts the more precious by the delicacy with which he pressed them upon others. He particularly liked children. Gentleness, goodness, and confidence were innate in him, and despite the spontaneity of his character he watched his manners so well that no one could ever complain of any fit of temper on his part."

However, there was one area in which the young Saint-George would lose composure: commentary on the color of his skin. "It was dangerous to push him to the limit," says La Boëssière in this regard. His father had been the witness to one of Saint-George's rare explosions of anger. One day, when master and student were walking together and chatting, an unknown individual took it into his head to accost Joseph, calling him "badly bleached." Joseph threw himself on the man, grabbed him, and plunged his head in the gutter. "Now you're as badly bleached as me," he yelled at him.[3] Still, these outbursts were short-lived. "Once himself again, he did everything possible to make one forget anything offensive in his speech," according to his biographer.

Although his abiding concern was to be accepted by Parisian society, he spared neither time nor money for his friends. "Kind to the point of weakness, he allowed himself to follow along, often forgetting that his own interests called him elsewhere," writes La Boëssière. Above all, he was determined to prevent rancor from becoming tinged with racism. "He did not want to have a single enemy." Such had been the aim of his education all along. The Boullongnes had quickly learned that in a society that judged a man's worth by the antiquity of his name, it was crucial not to arouse enmity. Thus the duc de Luynes would say of Jean de Boullongne that he had only friends. Philippe-Guillaume Boullongne "de Préninville" and his brother Guillaume-Pierre always made a point of being agreeable. The least sign of commonness and they might be reminded that they were the descendants of an obscure "Tavernier." This lesson served Joseph's career very well.

The Château de la Tuilerie stood close by the country home of another rich financier, Le Riche de La Popelinière (sometimes referred to as La Pouplinière), a patron of the arts and letters whose principal residence was on the rue de Richelieu, a mere stone's throw from Joseph's father's house. Joseph became a friend of the family. In the early 1760s the young man would regularly ride through the iron gates of the vast park in his chaise. The financier, who was then sixty years old, had just become infatuated with a very young girl named Félicité, later known as Madame de Genlis. In her *Memoirs* she would recall the courtly way the rich landowner wooed her: "He would often say as he gazed at me, sighing deeply, 'What a pity that she is but thirteen years old.'" Yet the girl—who was in fact fourteen—was very aware of the older man's charm: "I was angry with myself that I was not three or four years older, for I admired him so much that I would have been delighted to marry him. He is the only old man who inspired that idea in me."[4] For some time, this future mistress of Philippe, duc de Chartres (later "Philippe Egalité") took up residence along with her family in the "old man's" house. Shortly afterward, her father, a bankrupt Burgundian nobleman, would set sail for Saint-Domingue, no doubt intending to bring home the fortune he needed to regild his coat of arms. Meanwhile, the future colonist could benefit from advice from Guillaume-Pierre, now of course Treasurer General of the Colonies, who was a constant caller on Le Riche de La Popelinière, as were all the members of the Boullongne clan.

La Popelinière was fond of giving parties on his vast estate. There were rustic balls at which, to the music of violins and musettes, the guests danced the *farandole*, winding their way through the hedges and topiaries; games of blind man's bluff, which often ended in "general mischief," as young Félicité had already found out; ballets and theatricals held in the host's elegant private theater, in which he had his guests act in plays he wrote himself. "I played the part of an ingénue and then a *soubrette* in two plays entitled *The Indolent Young Woman* and *The Players.* . . . At these performances I danced a solo dance, which received great applause," remembered Madame de

Genlis. In fact, the "old rake," as Louis Petit de Bachaumont dubbed him, relied chiefly on the services of a talented black named Crébillon, who wrote several—often racy—plays for him. Saint-George had only just celebrated his twentieth birthday. In *tableaux vivants* straight out of a painting by Watteau or Fragonard, he aroused admiration for his talents as a dancer and the skill with which he played his violin. The instrument had been made for him by Andrea Amati, Stradivarius's teacher, and bought for a small fortune by his father. No one was as gifted as he at giving those *fêtes champêtres* their intoxicated cadences.

Le Riche de La Popelinière, who had lately been following the teachings of Rameau, his former concertmaster, was especially sensitive to the creative genius of Gossec, whom he had appointed to succeed the older composer. "Every Sunday we had a musical Mass in the private chapel," reported Madame de Genlis. "Madame de Saint-Aubin played a little organ. Gossec and the other musicians performed beautiful symphonies." This composer, who was of Belgian origin, wrote no fewer than thirty of his forty-five symphonies during his stay at La Popelinière's estate, and was constantly on the search for new ideas. It was he who introduced the clarinet on a large scale to symphonic works, paving the way for Mozart. Similarly, his impressive Mass for the Dead, written in 1760 for his patron, is startlingly audacious. The *Tuba mirum* is scored for two orchestras, one that would play outside the church and the other inside. It would be a priceless lesson in orchestration for Saint-George, whom Gossec had introduced to composition.

At La Popelinière's country house, the days were always meticulously planned. "Supper was at nine o'clock. After supper, we played a little music on our own," noted Madame de Genlis. "At half past eleven we went to bed." Tuesday was devoted "to the sparkling wits and the wise." A frequent guest was the painter Quentin de La Tour, who once impressed his listeners by declaring that rather than face the pitted roads from Paris he had thrown himself in the Seine. As he couldn't swim, he explained, he had clung to a boat and let himself be dragged all the way out to Passy. Among the other guests were the poet known simply as Bertin, born on Réunion island and an expert in erotic literature, and Madame Riccoboni, the darling of literary Paris, whose books were disappearing from bookstore shelves. She had just published *The Letters of Milady Gatesby* and was already planning *Ernestine*, the novel that would make her famous—and that Saint-George would later turn into his first opera.

The center of attraction at these bucolic soirées was undeniably the flutist Jacques de Vaucanson, admired above all for his talents as an engineer and maker of musical automata. To the delight of all, Vaucanson had devised a mechanical flute player as well as an artificial duck "which both ate and digested." La Popelinière simply could not do enough for this inventing genius, particularly since the day the latter had told him the following story. Related at his patron's expense, it still aroused hilarity among dinner guests many years afterward. In 1744, Thérèse, La Popelinière's young wife, who held a popular salon, seemed not indifferent to being fervently pursued by the duc de Richelieu. Suspecting a liaison, her husband gave his presumably unfaithful wife a memorable thrashing and then locked her up in their home on the rue de Richelieu. For years the poor woman could not leave the house unaccompanied. Seeing this, the duke proceeded to acquire the property next door, which struck the jealous husband as highly suspicious. Richelieu then summoned Vaucanson, who promptly discovered that a wall in one of the fireplaces could be made to swing open, permitting the duke to enter whenever he pleased the husband's residence. The latter took the affair very badly, even retiring from society for several years. But time proved healing, and he was graciously tolerant when the episode gave rise to numerous jokes, even inspiring some licentious scenes in his plays.

The wooded slopes of Passy and Chaillot were still home to animals that could be hunted. In those days it was the fashion for the hunter to be accompanied by a young Diana, particularly one whose charms were not lost on the hunter. Saint-George was paired with a girl named Marie, who was "pleasingly plump, more a Diana than a Venus. Her bosom, round and firm, stimulated the senses, but her gestures and bearing were modest." Such is the portrait of Marie sketched by the writer Odet Denys. The rule was that the actors in the hunt should leave their position when they heard the summons of the grounds steward. But when the horn blew, the young woman and her handsome huntsman were nowhere to be seen. They would soon meet in a house owned by one of Marie's friends on the heights of Chaillot.

Eventually the young woman's family learned of the liaison. Nothing was considered more natural than for a white nobleman to bed a beautiful black woman. But for a black man, even the son of the Treasurer General of the Colonies, to be linked with a noble girl was intolerable. Exiled from Paris for the whole summer, Marie would write passionate letters to her American, using the house in Chaillot where they had their assignations as an address. The ruse was soon discovered, and Marie's compliant friend ordered to refuse all mail. Joseph would not see his beloved again until months later. Hidden behind a pillar in St. Paul's Church, he watched her mount the steps to the altar on her father's arm and marry another man—white, of course.

This blow to his love and pride was no doubt the inspiration, some years later, for one of the romances that made Saint-George famous in the salons and concert halls, *The Other Day Beneath the Trees*:

> *Oh the joy of being loved tenderly,*
> *And yet what disappointment follows in its wake!*
> *Why do you approach so slowly*
> *And then so quickly turn away?*

Never again would he think of marrying.

Soon after that he was able to console himself by making a triumphant entrance into the famous corps of musketeers that formed the king's Horse Guards. Few attained membership in this elite unit, the envy of the whole aristocracy. In theory one had to provide "proof of nobility." The chevalier had other assets to show, however. Attending the Tuileries riding school, one of the few royal academies of the equestrian art, had in fact introduced him to the sons of old noble families. And he had proved himself one of the best horsemen. After his victory over Picard, no one disputed his title as best fencer in the realm. Yet more than simply being a fine horseman or an exceptional duelist, Saint-George was the son of the man who controlled the purse strings of both companies of musketeers (known by their colors, gray and black).

In those days one could not ignore the power of Guillaume-Pierre de Boullongne-Tavernier. In 1761, out of his own pocket, he offered the king a ship of thirty guns that was christened *The Citizen*. With this gift the former colonist became one of the kingdom's benefactors, following the disaster of the Battle of Krefeld, where the French fleet had been partly destroyed by enemy fire. Nobody, surely, would object to Joseph's joining one of the companies of musketeers.[5] The younger sons of the great families, who prided themselves haughtily on serving in these two elite companies, did just that, however, and the law was on their side. Even if Monsieur de Boullongne dared recognize Joseph as his son, a law signed in 1729 refused noble title to any man of color. Lampooned and ostracized by these so-called gentlemen (among them was La Morlière, whom he had beaten and humiliated at La Boëssière's), Joseph resolved to quit the musketeers on his own initiative. He was immediately named a gendarme in the King's Guard, another prestigious corps. This title meant that he was still a member of Louis XV's military household, although the gendarmes traveled on foot and the musketeers on horseback—somewhat vexing for Saint-George, who was after all the finest student at the most prestigious royal riding academy.

In private, Saint-George would confess how humiliated he felt by these sons of old families who stamped their little feet in rage on ground that was shaky, as France's indisputably was at the dawn of the Revolution. He would not, however, display his wounds in public.

In any event, rejected though he might be by these well-born men, he would soon be welcomed with open arms by their wives. His compelling presence, his physical grace, and his talents as dancer and musician made him an irresistible figure in a period when women were seizing upon previously male prerogatives with refined voracity. Many of them disputed openly their husband's supposed monopoly on independent thinking. Others paraded their official "favorite." Still others went so far as to set up so-called *caravanes*, love nests in which couples formed, dissolved, and exchanged partners.

This was the moment when Louis Petit de Bachaumont began writing his voluminous *Secret Memoirs in Service to the History of the Republic of Letters in France,* which was published in London beginning in 1777.[6] Bachaumont made no attempt to conceal his admiration for the "manifold gifts of nature" with which the American had been endowed. Joseph not only played the violin "in superior fashion," he wrote, but was "a very valorous champion in love." Saint-George was also noticed by another exceptional chronicler of his time, François Métra. At noon each day, Métra would settle himself on the terrace of the Feuillants, at the Tuileries, wearing an incredible hat edged with gold, and read an excerpt from his *Nouvelles à la main* (News at Hand) to an always sizable and appreciative audience. He, too, remarked that Saint-George was "born with the most marked gifts for physical talents and exercises," an expression that he intended to be understood in its broadest sense. Indeed, this well-informed gossip, after insisting on "the surprising degree of perfection" that the Creole had attained, concludes with a dubious pun: "One of his mistresses has been reproached for her appetite for *le vit nègre*," a licentious pun on "life" and "limb." Métra seemed a little insecure about his bon mot, since he felt the need to justify its use: "The word is acceptable, is it not, given the fashion for puns?"

Frequently attired in vests of white satin, breeches of pearl-gray velvet, silk stockings with gold clocks, and shod with scarlet-heeled shoes, Saint-George knew how to show off his uncommonly fine physique. And even the color of his skin, though dark for a man of mixed race, inspired praise. Madame de Genlis adopts a nearly enamored tone when she describes Joseph's teeth as "two rows of pearls set upon black velvet."

Love letters piled up in the elegant apartment in the mansion on the rue du Bac where the family had settled in 1763. (Two years before, his father had added to his collection of posts that of Treasurer General of the Order of Saint-Louis, the highest decoration in the kingdom, just at the time he presented his warship to Louis XV. Once again he marked this new step up in his career by moving house.) Here Joseph could lead the life of a prince.

This was an age when society worshiped stone. While Louis XIV's descendants continued to expand Versailles, the rising affluent displayed their wealth by building châteaux in the provinces or townhouses in Paris. This taste for ostentation gave rise to a staggering number of bankruptcies. The owner of the house on the rue du Bac on which Guillaume-Pierre had set his heart had himself been a victim of the frenzy that led families to ruinous displays of their wealth. The former owner, elder son of Samuel Bernard, Louis XIV's financier, had bought the house on the death of his father, in 1739, convinced that the proceeds from his post as a counsel of state and superintendent of the queen's household would bring him sufficient income to maintain the luxurious property. Fourteen years later he died, riddled with debts. Two notable creditors thereupon showed up: Chancellor Guillaume Chrétien de Lamoignon, whose actions against the parliament of Paris and the provinces would be one of the harbingers of the Revolution, and Voltaire. The latter was not one to forgive a debt, even when it meant harassing a dead man's heirs. He regularly appeared before the Geneva authorities to collect the so-called *signes de vie,* or "signs of life," which he shipped by mail coach to Maître Louis Bronod, the Bernards' notary. Here, for instance, is one dated

August 7, 1761: "We, Etienne-Jean, baron of Montperoux, residing on behalf of the King in Geneva, do hereby certify that François Marie Arouet de Voltaire, gentleman ordinary of the King's chamber, residing near this city in the château of Ferney in the district of Gex, is at the present time living as I have myself seen him on this day."[7]

The 438,000 livres Guillaume-Pierre de Boullongne-Tavernier paid to become owner of the Hôtel du Bac were most welcome. They allowed the debt owed the seigneur of Ferny to be repaid. The new proprietor was requested to pay "in coin of the realm," without "any notes or royal securities no matter what their denomination and what currency they might have."[8] In fact, the paper money issued by the crown only inspired mistrust—even if it was disbursed by a dignitary of the crown.

Situated at the heart of the now fashionable quarter of Faubourg Saint-Germain, the property extended across more than two acres between 46 rue du Bac (part of it is still visible today in the form of a door over which there is a bas-relief depicting "Prudence" and "Law," and a cartouche carrying the monogram "SB") and the rue Saint-Dominique (today part of boulevard Saint-Germain). In addition to the main mansion, the property included a large house facing the rue Saint-Dominique. This was the Hôtel des Vertus, bought from Princess Marie-Claire of Brittany. Under the terms of the contract, Guillaume-Pierre was obliged to honor the three-year lease granted by the former owner to the Portuguese ambassador, who had taken up residence there. There were stables capable of housing forty-one horses, a dozen "water lines," and a large crawfish pond. Everything bespoke magnificence. The layout of the property prevented annoying congestion beneath the porch: Carriages entered the courtyard from the rue du Bac and exited on what is today boulevard Saint-Germain.

As they approached the entrance, visitors and their coachmen could admire the pond, shaped into a figure eight, into which water flowed from a great basin decorated with an oversized cluster of reeds made of lead. Above this was a group of marble statues representing

Diana with a stag and a hind. A statue of Apollo completed the decorations, which were devoted to the hunt and the arts. In the center of the courtyard was an enormous sundial. In summertime, blossoming orange trees and oleanders lent an exotic touch to the open area.[9]

Two more fountains decorated with masks of gilded lead spewing water had been installed in the *salle des buffets*. From there one entered one of the most richly ornamented dining rooms in all Paris. But the luxurious impression it made was nothing compared with the elegance of the salon on the second floor. The walls of this vast room, approximately forty feet long and twenty-five feet wide, were entirely covered in wainscoting decorated with gold leaf. Over each doorway hung paintings by Van Loo, Pierre Restout, and Dumont, dubbed "the Roman." (The main elements of this decor were later reinstalled in the Hôtel Rothschild, 41 Faubourg Saint-Honoré, then donated by Baron Edmond de Rothschild to the Israel Museum in Jerusalem, where they can be admired today.) Amid this decor, which two centuries later was considered "one of the outstanding works of French decorative art," Saint-George performed wonders as master of ceremonies.[10] In the summer, his father organized fêtes and balls in the garden. For cards and other games the guests withdrew to the salon, where tables were set up for piquet, quadrille, brelan, and trictrac.

Also richly decorated, Joseph's apartment was nonetheless one vast mess. In his romanticized history of Saint-George, Roger de Beauvoir would describe it thus a few decades later: "Near the mirror, on a panel patterned with goddesses in the Van Loo style, hung a pair of foils; over here was a pair of skates, over there a violin wrapped in cotton serge, farther on a worn-out shoe fetchingly crossed with a master fencer's stick [used for instruction in the art of dueling]. Here and there one glimpsed horns attached to the wall hanging, then next to the cerise-draped daybed, a large whip—a royal whip, as could be seen from the fact that the handle was encrusted with precious stones. . . . On the mantelpiece, with its marble nymphs and cabriole legs standing out in curved silhouette in the bright sunlight, lay a bundle of music scores." As for the bedroom, it was "hung in damask of three colors, giving it the look of the most graceful of rainbows. The pier glasses and friezes offered to the gaze garlands of pompom roses, held aloft by genies with inverted torches. Beneath trellised bowers of green, shepherdesses with pouting lips held up in their left hand the corner of their skirt with its flounces and gussets, as though the opera violins were awaiting their orders beneath the foliage of some neighboring grove."

Every corner was littered with flasks and bottles of perfume—from Jollifret's, naturally. Scattered across the sofa were paste buttons, jabots, Brussels lace. With so many servants at his disposal, why would the chevalier take the trouble to arrange all these objects meticulously? Between the parties and the assignations and the training at La Boëssière's academy, Saint-George spent little time in his apartment. He mainly went there to sleep and to practice his violin.

In an age when Greek civilization was glorified and pagan gods had replaced Christian inspiration as subjects of art, the accepted term to denote the very best in every domain was "god." Hence the gazettes called Gaetan Vestris the "god of the dance"; Mademoiselle Guimard the "goddess of the dance"; François-Joseph Talma the "god of the theater"; and Pierre-Jean Garat the "god of song." As for Saint-George, he was soon consecrated the "god of arms." No one had succeeded in beating him. Soon the Arms Patent conferred by the royal academies would bear his effigy, as well as those of the other great swordsmen of the age. His reputation rapidly crossed borders, with the result that the Italian "god of arms," Giuseppe Faldoni, came to Paris in the summer of 1766 so it could be decided who was the better fencer. The chemist Lewis Delavoiner introduced the Italian to Joseph. As he had done with Picard, Joseph refused to agree to a match. He found the high stakes and the passions aroused by the prospective encounter vulgar.

Faldoni hit upon a clever way of forcing the chevalier to fight. He combed all the fencing schools in Paris and fought and defeated the leading teachers and most famous assistants. Eventually, there was no way for Saint-George to avoid him. Egged on by his friends, he finally relented. The match was arranged for September 8. The great names of the nobility and the most skilled fencers of the court and the city of Paris reserved seats for the event. After an interminable match, one full of unexpected turns, the Italian, who was somewhat younger than Saint-George (by now twenty-seven), finally won the day, four touches to six. The day after his victory, Faldoni wrote his father to describe what had happened. Saint-George, he said, was a swordsman of unbelievable speed and strength. His parries were "almost impenetrable," and without any doubt he deserved to be called "the first fencer of Europe."[11] After Faldoni, that is, the newly crowned "champion" of the world.

VI

"Quarreling Buffoons"

Civility finally returned to French salons in the early 1760s. Polite society began to recover from the conflict that had rent France less than a decade before. Joseph, then an adolescent, was having his first violin lessons under Leclair when the crisis broke. Though not mentioned in the history books, it tore families apart, pitted old friends against one another, and caused open combat between clans. The reason for all this destructive rage? The mass resignation of parliamentary magistrates in protest against the king's absolute power? The peasants' revolt against the crushing burden of taxes? The war with the English and the total annihilation of the French fleet? The persecutions against the Jesuits?

None of the above. This great schism was provoked by the aforementioned Quarrel of the Buffoons, which erupted in 1753, following the appearance of Jean-Jacques Rousseau's *Letter on French Music*. In his *Confessions*, Rousseau later summed up, with his customary lack of modesty, the causes for the flare-up: "This was the time of the dispute between the parliament and the clergy. The parliament had just been exiled, unrest was at its height, and revolt seemed imminent. The pamphlet appeared; in an instant all the other disputes were forgotten; people thought of nothing but of the peril to French music and the only revolt was against me."

The philosopher, happily, emerged from the "revolt" relatively unscathed, the mob content merely to burn his effigy on the plaza in front of the Opéra. In actual fact, Rousseau's appropriating to himself paternity for this quarrel was fairly shameless. In 1749 a young German philosopher, the baron de Grimm, had barely set foot in Paris when he began to vilify French opera, which had, he said, a tendency to bore audiences to death. Everything was wrong: Rameau's harmonies, sounds too pedantic to charm the ear, stilted characters, contrived plots based on an endlessly rehashed mythology, inflated language with its "flames" and "chains," abuse of deus ex machina, and ballets that invariably disrupted the action. All this conspired to drive away the public. Musically, what was intolerable was the total lack of connection between the dramatic thread and the melodic line. Music and libretto were divided; each element lived its life almost without ever meeting the other. Indeed, the "poet" and the composer were rivals for stardom, and it was not unusual for a singer to be forced to sing a tenderly amorous ode to some grotesquely pompous air. For example, the work of Philippe Quinault, Jean-Baptiste Lully's librettist, was often declaimed in the salons without music. And operas at that time were usually signed in the first instance by the writer of the libretto, not that of the music. This custom was long in dying out: Up to the mid-nineteenth century, music publishers still occasionally placed Mozart's name after that of the librettist Lorenzo da Ponte's.

The press was awash with criticism of the music of official opera. "Bawling," "roars," "continuous barking," "yelps": The epithets were legion. Grimm echoed these in his *Letter on Omphale*: "Singing, a shamefully profane term in France . . . it is what we call shouting."[1] In short, as the encyclopedist Jean Le Rond d'Alembert declared, French opera consisted of "three hours of noise and boredom."[2]

Happily, the Italian "buffoons" came back to the capital, their return having graciously been granted by the Regent. These were the musicians and players of the Neapolitan school, so often painted by Watteau, who had earlier staged their *opere buffe* for Parisian audiences. At first their pantomimes might have disconcerted the most tradition-bound spectators, but they quickly charmed the public with their straightforward plots, their heroes drawn to human scale, and their touching melodies, which one could hum on leaving the performance. It was all a far cry from Rameau. In 1752, Giovanni Pergolesi had scored a phenomenal success with his *opera buffa La Serva padrona* (The Servant as Mistress), which premiered on Tuesday, August 1. Soon afterward, the Quarrel of the Buffoons—also known as the "Quarrel of the Corners"—broke out. In the theater, supporters of the Italians would gather beneath the queen's box: This was the Queen's Corner. Supporters of the French assembled below the box occupied by the king and Madame de Pompadour: This was the King's Corner. Rousseau and most of the philosophers quickly took up their positions in the Queen's Corner. "Soon, I became so infatuated with Italian opera that, bored with gossiping, eating, and gambling in the boxes, I would often escape my fellow spectators and go over to the other side. There, all alone, shut up in my box, despite the length of the opera I gave myself up to the pleasure of enjoying it until the end," he would write in *Confessions*.

The philosophers eagerly championed the Neapolitan singers Anna Tonelli and Pietro Manelli, praising them for having introduced grace and delicacy to the stage. Having spent several weeks in France in 1752, the Italians still drew enthusiastic audiences two years later. Rousseau, never afraid of seeming treasonous, thought French music "a fat, waddling goose" compared to the liveliness of the Neapolitan school. Amid the uproar, he wrote his own opera, *Le Devin du village* (The Village Soothsayer), based on simple arias. It was a huge success and even performed at the Paris Opera in 1753, with the queen's support.

The King's Corner had no choice but to react. A strenuous appeal was made to stir up national sentiment against the foreigners, to no avail. Voltaire made a mockery of this pursuit of chauvinism: "I go to the temple of song in search of peace. I am greeted by shouts: Are you for France or for Italy? I am for my own pleasure, gentlemen." La Pompadour's reaction was to commission a composer by the name of Mondonville to write an unmistakably French opera for her. The work, a turgid absurdity, could be performed through to the end only thanks to the intervention of the soldiers loyal to the comte d'Argenson, the minister of war. The king's favorite could not let such an insult go unanswered. In 1754, Louis XV dismissed the Italians from France, leaving the field clear for Rameau's music. Sixty years before that they had been expelled by Louis XIV, to give Lully a monopoly over musical aesthetics.

Officially, dispatching the foreigners ended the war and proclaimed the victory of French opera. Italian opera had been defeated by a deadly dull work. For thirty years, from 1744 to 1774, the year Saint-George would begin to commit to paper the first measures of his operas, only thirteen new works—total—would be performed on the stage of the official opera house. That meant less than one every two years. In fact, the war had ended with the annihilation of French opera. Having won an arbitrary victory, it was vanquished by taste.

Nevertheless, the Quarrel of the Buffoons had another unexpected result. According to Grimm, it helped ensure the survival, at least for a period of time, of the absolute monarchy in matters of royal prerogative. All representatives of the Enlightenment who grumbled against absolutism and the scandalous expenses of the court and Madame de Pompadour had hurled themselves into the fray. What better way to show one's hostility to Louis XV, and get away with it, than to join the Queen's Corner and yell at the top of one's voice against that of the king? "The quarrels between the Paris parliament and the court, its exile and the transfer of the upper chamber to Pontoise: All these events were topics of conversation for a mere twenty-four hours. Whatever that august body had done over the past year to gain the public's eye, it never was able to seize the thirtieth part of the attention paid to the revolution in music," wrote Grimm in his *Literary Correspondence*. On a more serious note, he adds: "The Italian actors who have been performing for ten months on the stage of the Paris Opera, and who are known here as 'Buffoons,' have so absorbed the attention of the people of Paris that the Parliament, despite all the measures and procedures intended to bring it renown, could not but fall into complete oblivion. One wit has said that [the singer Francesco] Manelli's arrival prevented a civil war, because without that event people with nothing to do would no doubt have been preoccupied with the quarrels between the Parliament and the clergy, and the fanaticism that so easily inflames people's minds might have had fatal consequences." In 1757, three years after the expulsion of the Italians, Louis XV escaped assassination at the hand of Robert Damiens.

Forced out of France, the "Buffoons" would leave an indelible trace in the French musical heritage. Rousseau and the philosophers were not alone in rebelling against the stilted academic harmonies of Rameau and his followers. Some of the most established French musicians were also charmed by the Italians' lightness of touch. For example, Jean-Marie Leclair, the former court violinist and favorite of Louis XV who was imparting his expertise to Joseph, had unhesitatingly supported this new school, whose emphasis on melody constituted an enduring homage to the role of the soloist. Day after day he initiated his young pupil in what was to be the new musical art, one less straitlaced and more creative. As Louis Striffling would write 150 years later, Leclair was "the most distinguished representative of this French school, not only an excellent composer but combining those virtuosic feats of execution in which the Italians excelled with qualities of clarity and precision to which the French audience was extremely sensitive."[3]

From then on, music became more spontaneous, more playful. Spectacular progress in manufacturing would permit violinists to take hitherto forbidden risks. The "sparrow," as his father called him, could amuse himself by imitating the bird songs he used to listen to for hours in the tropics, weaving garlands of trills in the high notes like no one else in Paris.

This love of the descriptive was reflected in the tastes of the day. No more gardens in the French style: Le Nôtre, like Rameau, was now held up to public ridicule. No more affected pictorial art. Make way for gardens in the English style, for the nymphs of first Watteau, then Boucher, and then Fragonard's swings. Racine was old hat. Hail to Pierre de Marivaux. Liberated from its harmonic sclerosis, music, too, became descriptive. Rousseau himself had decreed that music must be "imitative." The organist Claude Balbastre excelled in imitating thunder; François Couperin's nightingale was dusted off; Rameau's hen brought him popularity with the general public that he had never found through his operas; Louis-Claude Daquin was acclaimed for his swallow and his cuckoo. And, a few decades later, Joseph Haydn would be won over by these rustic fashions and celebrate in his music the lark and the rising sun.

Now first violinist in La Popelinière's orchestra, under Gossec's direction, Saint-George ruled over this aviary. He would become something of a prisoner in this gilded cage with *The Loves and Death of the Poor Bird*. All his life he would be asked to play the piece—in Paris, Versailles, Lille, Rennes, even London. The actress and singer Louise Fusil, who became devoted to Joseph, later wrote in her memoirs:

> Saint-George had a feeling for music to the highest degree, and the expressiveness of his execution was his principal merit. One piece that brought him great applause on the violin was *The Loves and Death of the Poor Bird*. A brilliant song, full of delicacy and ornament, announced the first part of this little pastoral piece; the bird's warbling expressed his happiness at the return of spring, which he celebrated with his joyous singing. But soon afterward came the second part in which he cooed his love. This song was soulful and full of seductiveness. One could almost see him hop-

ping from branch to branch, pursuing the cruel beauty who had already chosen another and was flying swiftly away. The third motif was the poor bird's death, his plaintive singing, his regrets, his memories, mingled at times with reminiscences of his joyous notes. Then his voice grew weaker and weaker and finally was heard no more. He fell down from his solitary branch; his life expired with a few throbbing notes. This was the bird's last song, his last sigh.

In fact, this "imitative" music would soon open up a generous place to sentiment, foreshadowing Schumann's piano piece *First Loss*. The warbler is "plaintive," the linnet "startled." Pieces of music devoted to women describe them as "insinuating," "indifferent," or "seductive."

The taste for ornament—even Marie-Antoinette's lambs could not escape it—had repercussions in music as well. Trills, mordents, tremolos, plucking, and hammering were so many illuminations added to the melodic line. In his *Art, or the Philosophical Principles of Singing,* which he published in 1756, Jean Blanchet stressed that "grace-notes are a melodic salt which seasons singing, giving it the taste without which it would be dull and insipid. Grace-notes are in singing what facial expressions are in eloquence, and to remove those kinds of ornaments from music would be to take away the most beautiful part of its being."

In this domain, too, the Guadeloupe-born fencer who had carved out for himself a reputation as the best "buttoner" in France was a peerless virtuoso in the way he linked together dotted and sixteenth notes. He would take a mischievous pleasure in the art in a little piece, less than eight minutes long, called *Les Caquets* (The Chatterboxes), in which his violin imitated the chattering of gossips. (Marius Casadesus recorded an amusing version of this piece for Polydor in 1936). His music is a call to joy and to dance, to those voluptuous bucolic soirées in the gardens. This is no doubt one of the reasons several writers, including Lionel de La Laurencie, an undisputed expert on the history of the violin, would compare his style to Watteau's.[4] Louis Striffling, too, writes apropos of the music of that era: "Graceful images will come before our minds, and on hearing a clavichord pick out those delicate trills, those lively mordents, we will imagine those artificial beauty spots, shaped like hearts or half-moons, those coquettish, roguish, or bewitching patches with which ladies of quality . . . ornamented their faces to enhance their complexions or accentuate their expression." He adds: "It is an art perhaps wanting in depth and force, but full of intelligence, very refined, highly nuanced, reminiscent of Marivaux and Voltaire. . . . A few measures of this music suffice to call to mind with all its charms the intelligent, amiable society for which they were composed."

It was in the salons that this new fashion took flight. At the time, France had only a few real orchestras or large concert halls where the Rousseauists and the "Ramistes" might confront each other. The King's Concert, the Queen's, and that of Madame de Pompadour competed as alternatives to church performances, as did the few large groups owned by rich patrons such as La Popelinière or the Prince de Conti, and the newly founded music academies. The salons, on the other hand, resounded with performances by singers and instrumentalists between lectures and poetry readings.

In the historical imagination, appreciation of the salons tends to be excessive. They are lumped together in one enormous homage to the Age of Enlightenment, as though they were all characterized by the same degrees of excellence and brilliance. It is true that dazzling gatherings, such as those organized by Madame de Lespinasse, who received Mozart; or by Madame de Montalembert, whose house on the rue de la Roquette was a magnet for the greatest wits; or those hosted by Madame de Rambouillet and Madame du Deffand were abuzz with the intellectual ferment that was making the *ancien régime* wobble on its pedestal. But in a multitude of other salons the tone tended toward the gallant and the mundane.

In his *Observations on Music,* written in 1757, F. N. Ancelet describes the atmosphere of these "little society musicales" as noisy and distracting. "By far the majority of the people only go there to amuse themselves, to chat and to be seen. A great many unthinking people attend salons whose only aim is the gathering itself. They come to show themselves off and blame what they should applaud by thinking only of external appearances. Fathers and mothers bring their children to teach them a certain boldness and confidence, essential to be able to play or sing in public; they also want to get some return on the money they have spent on their education. One is stupefied by the nascent talents that one is forced to applaud in order to please the parents." And he describes this scene, probably repeated a thousand times: "A shy young lady has to be begged over and over to sing; she is persuaded to go to the harpsichord. After a great many curtsies she announces that she has a cold, and finally sings her teacher's lesson by heart. By dint of speeding up the tempo, the cantatilla ends and the curtsies resume. Those with real talent have barely had time to be heard."[5] It is as if, besides the right to pursue happiness, exercise freedom of expression, and proclaim the primacy of law, the salons of the Enlightenment also invented the piano lounge.

For an artist to show off his talent in these circumstances was difficult in the extreme. Yet artists had to make a living. Although chaperoned by Grimm on his second journey to Paris in 1778, Mozart himself would have to stoop to play for a few livres before an uninterested audience. In a letter to his father, he tells of how, when he was invited to play at the duchesse de Chabot's, he had to wait for a half-hour in an ice-cold room. When the mistress of the house finally deigned to come and ask him to sit at a harpsichord, he felt obliged to answer: "I said that I would be delighted to play something, but that it was impossible at the moment, as my fingers were numb with cold." And he added: "I asked her to have me taken at least to a room where there was a fire." Whereupon he was asked to play on an execrable pianoforte before the duchess and her guests, who in the meantime had produced pencils and paper. "What vexed me most," Mozart continues, "was that Madame and all her gentlemen never interrupted their drawing for a moment, but went on intently, so that I had to play to the chairs, tables, and walls. Under these detestable conditions I lost my patience. I therefore began to play the Fischer variations and after playing half of them I stood up."[6]

Mozart also knew that he could not stop doing these appearances. His father repeatedly reminded him that he had a pressing need for money, which, if he was a good son, Wolfgang would send him from Paris. On February 5, moreover, he had mailed him a list of individuals—which he added to later—most likely to appreciate his talent. Essentially, these were patrons who had crowned the young prodigy with laurels on his first trip to Paris fourteen years earlier. In some cases the addresses were out of date. For example, that of Madame de Boulogne, "Ruë [sic] St. Honor., opposite the Jacobins." She was none other than Catherine de Ravenel, the wife of Saint-George's father. By then, however, the Boullongnes had moved to the rue du Bac. Among Leopold Mozart's recommendations were also some intimates of Joseph's: the duc de Chartres, the marquis de Dufort, with whom Joseph often hunted at Villers-Cotterêts, and the Robecqs, to whom in 1773 Saint-George dedicated his first six quartets and who had since become his "cousins" by marriage. Shortly afterward, on April 20, Leopold advised Wolfgang to "give warm greetings" to the leading French musicians of the day, notably to Gossec, then on April 29 to Le Duc, that other great friend of the black composer.

There remained one way to attract notice: virtuosity. The audience of the salons wanted more of this, and on the scale introduced by the Italians. Only the most adept or audacious performer managed, occasionally, to impose silence on these noisy gatherings. Competitions came to be organized. Duels were staged between violinists: Jean Baptiste Anet against Jean Pierre Guignon, Guignon against Jean Joseph Mondonville, and so forth, all of whom engaged in a curious sort of combat, bow in hand. A composer's score became the pretext for improvisations before an audience, which looked more for

technical feats than for aesthetic interpretation. Dexterity of finger-
ing, speed in scales and arpeggios, precision in double-stopping
became, according to Louis Striffling, the most reliable criteria by
which to judge a musician's abilities.

Saint-George in no way scorned these instrumental jousts, though
they were not to his taste. As Leclair's pupil and Gossec's protégé, he
much preferred to make his Amati sing, weep, or throb rather than
indulge in vulgar demonstrations of dexterity. But the showman in
him could not resist the desire to arouse the admiration of the ladies,
who, barred from fencing matches, crowded around the great soloists.
Following a slightly perverse custom, in fact, the prettiest women
were placed in the first row to "inspire the player."[7] But what a contrast between Saint-George, who had to be coaxed into taking out his
violin before an audience at his father's house or that gathered at one
of Madame de Montalembert's salons, and Mozart, begging for intro-
ductions from his friend Grimm. The one steps down from his chaise
or is deposited by coach on the arm of a pretty woman. The other, to
save money, often walks the interminable distances between the man-
sions where he is invited to play and the modest apartment he rents
with his mother in the suburb of Montmartre. "You say," he tells his
father, "that I ought to pay a good many *visiten* in order to make new
acquaintances and revive old ones. That, however, is out of the question. The distances are too great for walking—or the roads too
muddy—for really the mud in Paris is beyond all description. To take
a carriage means that you have the honor of spending four to five
livres a day, and all for nothing. People pay plenty of compliments, it
is true, but there it ends. At first, I spent a lot of money driving
about—often to no purpose, for the people were not at home."[8]

Singers competed similarly. The epic battles between two sopra-
nos, La Todi and La Mara, took place a little later, and unleashed
fierce passions. On this subject, too, the salon audiences were becoming expert. Sophie Arnould, the young girl who had made fun of
Joseph's color when, newly arrived in Paris, he crossed the rue de

l'Arbre-Sec, was one of the first victims of these ruthless critics. "The finest asthma that I ever heard sing," was the comment offered by the abbé Galiani, notorious for his caustic remarks. Even cruder was this from the Concourt brothers: "a paltry organ and a wretched throat." By contrast, Antoinette Saint-Huberty and Louise Dugazon, the singer with whom Saint-George would, for a short time, find love, knew how to kindle both emotion and enthusiasm.

The appetite for these jousts faded, as did all musical fashions in this fast-moving century. Ten years after the Italians were expelled, those same music lovers who had previously praised the virtuosi to the skies suddenly criticized them as "musical acrobats," demanding that a little more feeling be shown in the interpretation. When he was passing through Paris, the German flutist Johann Quantz, once the teacher of that excellent flutist and composer Frederick II (who wrote no fewer than 120 concertos for the instrument), described the wide disparity he found between music composed in the Italian style and the new French music, now free of the ponderous hand of Lully and Rameau. "The interpretation of the Italian artists is exuberant, artificial, complicated, often insolent and bizarre. . . . That of the French is strict and modest, clear and precise, neither profound nor complex."[9] This precise yet expressive manner of playing, always respectful of the composers' scores, lent itself perfectly to collective performance, to a dialogue among instruments. Trios and quartets began performing in the salons, though some considered them a poor man's orchestra. "The quartet," writes André Tubeuf, "repudiates the pomp of the baroque churches, their trumpets and gold. It flees the warbling and the plumage of opera. With the quartet, music learns how to say: neither God nor master."[10]

One essential characteristic of chamber music is that players complement one another. Each musician must be able to listen to the others and play as part of an ensemble. This suited Saint-George perfectly. Always in search of friendship and participation, he found in this music a way to satisfy his need for them. It was therefore natural for him voluntarily to rein in his virtuosity to follow the rhythm of colleagues less gifted than himself. The amateur composer Jean Benjamin de la Borde wrote of him: "Of all men, Saint-George may be the one who was born with the most, and the most varied, talents." To these should be added, de la Borde believed, "the rare merit of great modesty."[11]

Two months before Joseph's twenty-fifth birthday, his teacher, the violinist Jean-Marie Leclair, was murdered in front of his house. Combining a deep feeling for music with virtuosity, Leclair is still considered the founder of the French school of music.[12] His death left a gaping hole in the musical world, a hole that to some degree Saint-George filled. At once the Italian composer Antonio Lolli, who was then living in France, turned to Saint-George, whom he deemed the best of Leclair's students. In 1764, Lolli dedicated two concertos to him: "To M. de Saint-George, Gendarme of the Guard of His Most Christian Majesty." Two years later Gossec, acclaimed for the glorious *Dies Irae* that he would later include in his sumptuous *Requiem*, paid Saint-George an enormous compliment by dedicating to him his six trios (opus 9).

> To M. de Saint-George, equerry, Gendarme of the King's Guard.
> Sir,
>
> The fame which you have acquired by your talents and the favorable welcome that you have extended to artists, have encouraged me to take the liberty of dedicating to you this work, as an homage due to the merit of such an enlightened lover of the arts. If you give it your vote, it will have certain success. I am, Sir, respectfully, your very humble servant.

Conductor of two great orchestras and an admired composer, Gossec was showing Saint-George a deference normally shown only to rich patrons, and combining it with an unfeigned admiration for his talent. Joseph is hailed as an undisputed master of the violin. In

1768—that is, two years after this dedication—Saint-George received yet another when an Italian maestro named Avoglio dedicated six sonatas for violin (opus 4) to him.

Adored by audiences, hailed by composers, celebrated by critics, writers, and poets, Saint-George had succeeded in bringing about a startling reversal: the black man as Enlightenment hero.

VII

The "Famous" Saint-George

His defeat at the hands of Faldoni in 1766 traumatized Saint-George far more than he let it appear. Behind the consoling remarks that were offered he often sensed insincerity, even malicious pleasure on the part of people only too happy to see him stumble for the first time. So long as he was unbeatable, people seemed able to ignore his color. He was the "American." After he had proven human, he was the "Negro" or, worse, the "half-breed."

Fortunately Gossec, who was only five years older than Saint-George, was perceptive enough to see what he was going through and kind enough to help. The Belgian musician had been among the first to recognize Joseph's talent. Even while forcing him to study tedious composition techniques, Gossec had behaved more like a big brother than a taskmaster. Moreover, Gossec, already well known as a master of the art of understatement in his compositions, admired the way the younger man produced with his violin what he, Gossec, had wanted to express in his scores. One composed the music and the other gave it life, and between them grew a feeling of friendship that got stronger each day.

Now twenty-seven, Joseph saw that the time was drawing near when he would be forced to make choices. Most probably he had not thought about this possibility before the match with Faldoni, caught up as he was in the whirlwind of a charmed life. Now he knew that though it might be some time before a French swordsman could beat him, his best years with the foil were behind him. In fact, unlike the others, he did not have to give private lessons at the fencing school in order to live. The tidy income his father paid him and the elegant lodgings he provided for his son on the rue du Bac kept Joseph from having to depend on his sword for a living. Nor did he even have to pay for a housekeeper. If we are to believe Roger de Beauvoir, the person who tended to Saint-George's every need as soon as he got home, and who put together his clothes with such taste, was none other than Nanon.[1]

In this period of transition and doubt, the trios that Gossec dedicated to him seemed to Joseph like a summons to take command of his future. He would always remember Gossec's generosity, just as he would himself extend a hand to a friend in need. The Belgian could be persuasive: Should Joseph choose the violin, he could also be the first in the field. Leclair's death had left a huge void in the French music world. Now it was up to his most brilliant pupil to take up the torch. Joseph began to turn up less frequently at La Boëssière's fencing school, even though its master remained his friend and confidant. On the other hand, he was much more likely to be seen in the cavernous Hôtel de Soubise, the greatest non-royal edifice in Paris, home of the Concert des Amateurs. (Today, the Hôtel de Soubise, probably the finest building in the Marais district, houses the Archives nationales.)

Founded by Gossec in 1769, the Concert des Amateurs soon became a formidable rival to the other great "private" music organization, the Concert Spirituel, founded in 1725. Both represented the first attempt to take music out of the palaces and the churches and make it available to the public. It was thanks to the Concerts that, for the first time, musicians were able to live on their art, without depending on royal whim or the clergy, and free of the machinations of court rivalries. But it had been a tough fight.

The utmost diplomacy had been necessary to loosen Lully's dead-handed legacy, which is what these concerts essentially did—threatening the institutional dictatorship the court musician had handed down to his successors. Upon his appointment in 1672, Lully's first concern had been to give the Royal Academy of Music—the Opéra—which he directed, absolute control over all musical activity in France. No one was permitted "to allow any entire piece of music to be sung, whether it be in French verse or in other languages," before an audience without the authorization of Louis XIV's appointed representative and those who would succeed him.[2] In his lifetime Lully never granted any authorization, however small.

In those days, every minimally cultivated man was expected to listen to and appreciate music, even to play an instrument. We might recall the advice the music master gives Monsieur Jourdain in Molière's *Le Bourgeois Gentilhomme*: "A person as magnificent and who has an affinity for the finer things of life such as yourself must give a concert in your home every Wednesday or Thursday." Yet Lully's censors couldn't be everywhere, and semi-clandestine private concerts organized in the homes of wealthy music lovers could be overlooked. But for Lully's successors to permit permanent public performances was quite another matter. For the more forward-thinking members of Parisian society, London served as a model. Music there was starting to become more democratic. Several Masonic societies served as a screen behind which musicians could play in taverns, the most famous of these being The Goose and Gridiron, whose name was a gastronomic joke linking stringed instruments—the gridiron—with the winds, as symbolized by the goose's neck and beak, which were evocative of the first cornettes (an ancestor of the saxophone). At the beginning of the 1720s, the violinist and composer Francesco Geminiani, a student of the elder Scarlatti's, had founded in London the Philomusicae Apolloni, of which he was the self-proclaimed "director and dictator."[3] Half Masonic brotherhood—requiring its own initiation—and half musical organization, the Philomusicae boasted thirty-nine musicians and played on every other Thursday. Its creation had largely been made possible by the support of a powerful protector, the duke of Essex.

The society soon became talked about in France because of Geminiani's frequent visits there and also because of French musicians who had performed in London. These musicians realized that escaping the clutches of the Royal Academy, like their London counterparts, would mean both finding a strong protector and using diplomacy. Life was not always fun and games for those in the public eye. The chevalier de Rohan Chabot, for instance, could thrash with impunity the young Voltaire for insolence.

Beginning in 1720, the prince de Conti, heir of the junior branch of the house of Condé and the first great protector of musicians, formed a music society called *Les Mélophilètes* (The Music Lovers) in his townhouse. Concerts were usually given free of charge.[4] Since the regent himself often honored these occasions with his presence, it would have been awkward for the Royal Academy to raid the place.[5] It was more often the case that musicians and their protectors got around the problem by organizing performances that were strictly private, at least officially. In 1724, Madame de Prie had invited some Italian musicians to play at her academy. The theory was very simple: Subscribers would contribute toward the music organizations whose performances they alone were entitled to attend. Since the public was not admitted, the concerts were not subject to the Royal Academy's censorship. Organizations such as these began to spread across France, notably in Lyon in 1728, then in Dijon in 1758. They were not very successful, however, since the "academicians" could rarely agree on the type of music to promote.

Thus, gradually, the idea took hold that it was possible to break free of the Academy's iron grasp, and to survive, even thrive, without the patronage of a prince or king. But those musicians who performed for popular audiences obviously could not count on finding a powerful protector. To avoid the police, they were forced to adopt a ruse. The Italian musicians—known as "Buffoons," as we've seen—began to give the public an active role in their performances. They adapted old ballads by substituting their own words, and from these songs patched together an opera scenario. The "arias" based on these ballads were repeated in the form of vaudeville-type refrains in which the audience would join in as chorus. The results were spectacular. When the constabulary bore down on the stage to arrest the musicians, the spectators' voices drowned out those of the performers as well as the sound of the instruments, making it all but impossible to enforce musical law and order.

Meanwhile, the resourceful Anne Danican-Philidor, formerly music manager to the prince de Conti, took the initiative in 1725 by exercising the right to organize occasional ticketed concerts (though he had to fork over 10,000 livres to the Academy). It had not escaped his notice that theatrical performances were by law suspended on religious holidays, such as All Saints' Day and the feasts of the Purification or the Assumption, as well as the weeks preceding Easter. He came up with a brilliant stratagem. He argued that it was not right to deprive music lovers of their beloved art during these periods and suggested that "spiritual" music be performed outside places of worship during these religious holidays. The idea (as well as a substantial payment to the Royal Academy) gave birth to the Concert Spirituel.

Initially, the new group's repertoire was confined strictly to sacred works, the so-called "music of the chapels." But eventually it would liberate itself. "A solid, ponderous machine set in motion for more than sixty years to an almost immutable rhythm," as Michel Brenet put it, the Concert Spirituel was the principal vehicle of eighteenth-century French musical life until the Concert des Amateurs joined it.

Though led and inspired by the finest professionals, the latter was also made up of enlightened amateurs (the term having not yet acquired the pejorative sense it has today). Many of the leading aristocrats devoted three or four hours a day to practicing their musical instruments so as to not be outshone by the professionals. La Pompadour, who could afford to pay professional players, nevertheless included "amateurs" in her orchestra; almost a third of her performers were nonprofessionals. The duc de Guines was judged one of the best flutists in the kingdom. When he was appointed ambassador to the king of Prussia—a move designed mainly to remove him from the side of Madame de Montesson, the future wife of the duc d'Orléans—it provoked a diplomatic incident of some magnitude. Frederick believed his cousin the king of France had intended to humiliate him by sending to Sans-Souci as his representative from Versailles an instrumentalist who was better than he was. The result was that poor de Guines was never again asked to appear at court with his flute. Among the other "amateurs": agricultural minister de La Haye, the baron d'Ogny, and the ultra-rich baron de Bagge, a passable violinist who, despite hours of practicing his instrument, despaired of ever achieving the stature of the greatest.

These concerts were regularly attended by anywhere from a few hundred to some two thousand spectators willing to pay between three and six livres. But a way had to be found to tack between various shoals: the censorship of the Royal Academy, the demands of the Church, which was trying to impose religious music as well as aesthetic canons, the greed of rapacious people of every order, and wide-ranging public tastes. Clerical vigilance was, in the end, the easiest to get around. The Church included in its ranks some cardinals who were both liberal and libertine, and for whom any evening or nightly performance afforded an excellent excuse to escape the sacristy. One example was the celebrated abbé de Pellegrin, immortalized in a popular song:

> *Catholic in the morning, pagan at the end of the day,*
> *He dined at the altar and supped at the play.*[6]

On a more aesthetic level, the Church, which itself maintained certain chapels, tried to keep a watchful eye on the changing forms of musical expression. In the abbé Galiani, who was of Neapolitan origin, it found both a scrupulous critic and (as we have seen) one whose acerbic comments could do real damage. One of his neighbors in the Salle des Gardes in the Tuileries Palace, where the Concert Spirituel was performing, whispered in his ear one night: "This hall is deaf!"—a comment on the room's acoustics. Glancing at the orchestra, Galiani replied, "It's certainly lucky."

Censors so insistent on musical quality were perforce less so where religious canons were concerned. Like the Buffoons, the director François-André Philidor and his successors finally matched profane and even decidedly racy words to music taken from the liturgy. The Royal Academy pretended to have been taken unawares, not wanting the public to reject this goose with the golden egg whose annual payment was practically equivalent to a royal subsidy. As for the governor of the Tuileries, who was supposed to enforce the law, the sizable fee exacted from the Concert Spirituel for its use of the Salle des Gardes (though lent free of charge by the king when he was not residing in Paris) dissuaded him from stepping in.

The only "spiritual" thing about the Concert was its name. Four motets—examples of sacred music—were offered as alibis, becoming a regular part of the repertoire. These were soon followed by concertos, and later by symphonies. But given the cost of seats, filling the hall was not an easy matter. Philidor and those who came after him had to use their wits to come up with "attractions," and not simply musicians, that might satisfy the public's craving for novelty. For instance, the Concert invited the Héricourt brothers, aged twelve and thirteen, each of whom played two flutes at the same time. Then there was the young prodigy, said to be seven years old, named Zygmuntowsky—Slavic names being fashionable in those days—who played the cello to perfection dressed as a sailor and perched atop a table. The audience also saw a "young Negro from the colonies" who came to "demonstrate his talent on the violin."[7] Among the other curiosities was a woman who, it was said, played the violin as expertly as a man. Sometimes the star performer was an instrument, such as an impressive dulcimer or cymbalom (played mainly in Hungary, an instrument with strings stretched over a trapezoidal resonance chamber that are hit with sticks). Daringly, Vivaldi was played on the bagpipe-like musette. Christoph Willibald Gluck was struggling to earn his living in London by playing concertos using water-filled glasses.[8]

On the musical level, a way had to be found both to attract the public with original works and at the same time to retain its loyalty with familiar melodies. Some of the Concert's directors had no scruples about pirating works that had already had a successful public premiere. Thus the late-nineteenth-century musicologist Michel Brenet would report: "When he happened to lack copy, [Jean Joseph] Mouret would borrow a sarabande from Montéclair's *Jephté*, a bergère from Lully's *Roland*, add a few odds and ends of his own, fit to the whole patchwork the words of the *Pange lingua* and, thanks to Mademoiselle Lemaure's performance, easily succeed in having this novelty heartily applauded."[9]

Nonetheless, the nouveaux riches and cultural parvenus who filled the halls did not merely crave novelty. Genuine musical creativity was brewing in Paris. Throughout the second half of the eighteenth century, the city was a crucible in which met, clashed, and fused the most diverse musical cultures. The Italians had breached the once-unassailable Lully-Rameau fortress. Gossec and Grétry brought innovations from northern Europe, Geminiani and François-André Philidor—Anne Danican's brother—a distinctly English influence. Then, too, the influence of the Mannheim school, which had nurtured Haydn, Mozart, and even Beethoven, was pervasive in Parisian musical life. It was represented by the Stamitzes—Johann, the father, and Karl, the son. Mozart, no paragon of virtue himself, hated them, calling them "drunkards and pornocrats." Yet they had demolished, as surely as the Italians had done with opera, the old canons of instrumental music.

Until then, the orchestra had been limited to a handful of stringed instruments. Now it boasted woodwinds, brass, and percussion. The newly invented clarinet was given a role of its own, and the horns, hitherto thought of as simply belonging to the ceremonial of the hunt, were used to heighten symphonic effects. Music itself became even lighter, the visual equivalent of the paintings by Watteau, Boucher, and especially Fragonard. It threw off its courtly and religious vestments to pursue reverie and pleasure, and drew its inspiration from rustic themes. What could be more natural? It was the fashion to celebrate nature, the body, harmony.

Johann Stamitz became notorious by frequenting taverns of ill repute. Fifteen years later, Karl Stamitz, then music director to the duc de Noailles, followed his father's example by getting roaring drunk and chasing after soubrettes and marquises. For all their loutish behavior, they filled the concert halls with graceful music. When they happened to be in Paris, Mozart studiously avoided them, offering as excuse their licentious ways. But whenever he left Salzburg or Vienna, he usually spent several weeks in Mannheim, which was very much under the Stamitzes' musical tutelage. It was as if he felt an irresistible need to draw from the springs of his own musical heritage before rubbing shoulders with musicians abroad. Yet Amadeus was too proud to admit to any influence at all—save, perhaps, that of his father.

In Paris, the Stamitzes were everywhere. They played at the court before the dauphine, Marie-Antoinette. No reception or salon was held without them. And, above all, they were present in the scores of their fellow musicians. Haydn and Mozart were not the only ones to be influenced by the Mannheim masters: Gossec, the undisputed master teacher of the day, Grétry, that most fertile of composers, and Saint-George all followed in their tracks.

As soon as the Concert des Amateurs came into being, in 1769, Gossec named Saint-George first violin and timekeeper. With his baton, he set the tempo during rehearsals. He also directed rehearsals when Gossec was away. The role played by timekeeper was critical; orchestra directors preferred to rely on him rather than on the recently invented metronome, which they found too impersonal. Only musicians experienced in composition could claim this post, which was considered the second most important in the orchestra. As first violin, Joseph had the privilege of playing standing up during the performance. Since the orchestra director was only occasionally present during concerts, the first violin frequently replaced him and conducted in his stead. Despite some internal jealousies—and sarcastic remarks regarding the thick layers of powder he used to hide the color of his skin—Joseph rapidly became the orchestra's guiding spirit. Financed by wealthy patrons, the Concert des Amateurs had the means to attract the very best performers. His prominent roles in it thrust Saint-George into the limelight. Another honor was soon added to his expanding collection: In 1770, Karl Stamitz dedicated his Six Quartets (opus 1) to the violinist's father. Why this rather astonishing homage to the Treasurer of Colonies and Wars? For Stamitz it was a way, he wrote, to give thanks to a man "who has presented artists with an inestimable gift in the person of Monsieur his son."[10]

Respected for his leadership of the orchestra when he filled in for Gossec, admired for the exceptional sensitivity of his playing, Saint-George now turned seriously to composing. As early as 1765, the year his half-sister, Catherine-Jeanne, married the marquis de Montmorency—vicomte de Laval, colonel of the Auvergne regiment, and first groom of the bedchamber of Monsieur (Louis XVI's younger brother)—he had sketched out some quartets. Originally, quartets were designed for the performance of symphonic pieces on a reduced scale. Gradually, however, the genre acquired its own personality, blossoming in the early 1770s, thanks notably to Haydn and Gossec. Saint-George would wait until 1773 to have the scores of his first six quartets engraved, all of them being dedicated to the prince de Robecq, otherwise known as Anne-Louis Alexandre de Montmorency, a cousin of his half-sister. Their publication was then hailed in a supplement to *Les Annonces,* one of a variety of gazettes devoted to the arts and society, and in an article in the *Mercure* in June. (The quartets were later published by the music publisher Jean Georges Sieber, who had a shop on the rue Saint-Honoré, and were also printed in Lyon by another music publisher named Castaud.) Clearly, the music was intended to be played to the restricted—and often quite noisy—audiences of the salons vying for the chevalier. They were mainly intended to charm.

Having cut his teeth on the quartets, Saint-George embarked on his first compositions for orchestra. This was a significant change in scale. The Amateurs' orchestra had no fewer than seventy-six instruments: forty violins, twelve cellos, eight double basses, in addition to the normal number of flutes, oboes, bassoons, horns, and trumpets, and that newcomer, the clarinet. Composition had to account for this new fullness. So dear to the baroque composers, the monotonous figured bass, which the public had ended up abhorring, would no longer suffice. Through practice Saint-George learned how to master his subject. Dilettante or not, he had grown up in an atmosphere of perfectionism. La Boëssière's portrait of him depicts him as a glutton for work who could repeat the same fencing move for hours on end until he was convinced he could not improve upon it. In 1772 his first concertos aired in the Hôtel de Soubise. All of Paris society assembled for the occasion. The response was enthusiastic. The mulatto was no longer merely the protégé of a few notables, if indeed he ever had been. He was recognized as one of the best musicians of the age.

The following year, Gossec left with two of his best violinists, Pierre Le Duc and Pierre Gavinies, to assume direction of the Concert Spirituel. He handed over his baton to Saint-George. The idea of a black conductor aroused more than a little resentment. Most jealous of all was one Jarnovic—an Italian whose full name was Giovanni Mane Giornovichi—who claimed at the time to be the leading violinist in Paris. For years he would heap sarcastic comments on "the black." Joseph treated these attacks with scornful silence. That is, until the day that Jarnovic slapped him and challenged him to a duel. This was very foolish, for Saint-George had continued to work at his fencing and was still in top form. Jarnovic was out of his league. But Saint-George refused the duel, merely saying, "I admire his talent too much to fight him."[11] Several days later, the jealous violinist visited the rue du Bac and stammered an apology. They became friends.

Saint-George kept his musicians busy. Twelve times a week the orchestra met in the elegant salon of the townhouse belonging to Charles de Rohan-Rohan, Prince de Soubise et d'Epinoy. As Emil Smidak recalls, "these were subscription concerts" at which much new music was played, especially great symphonies and concertos.[12] Even Gossec admired the quality of the players. The group, he wrote, had "the most skillful artists of Paris in each orchestral part." Yet, as mentioned earlier, a great number of these musicians were not professionals but noblemen who had learned music from childhood and could practice for hours on end, having no need to work for a living. This could present problems, however. To win the obedience of the heirs of great families, often very protective of their social rank, called for great tact. Even bewigged and powdered, Joseph could never forget that his mother was born a slave. Still, he possessed two advantages: uncommon talent and an ability to avoid giving offense. Then, too, the frenetic pace of work he imposed on his musicians left them little time to brood.

Above all else, the orchestra's success was such that no one could doubt the capacities of its director. Thus Saint-George would wield the scroll of paper—the ancestor of the baton—for eight years. Critics praised the precision of the direction, the energy of the execution, the consistent quality of the playing.[13] As Smidak notes: "More than Gossec, who only directed for four years, it was Saint-George who ensured the orchestra of the Amateurs its brilliant reputation." Then in 1775 came consecration: the *Musical Almanac* called the Concert des Amateurs the "best orchestra for symphonies that exists in Paris and perhaps in Europe."

Joseph found himself adorned with an adjective that in his day and beyond would become affixed to his name, as Alfred Marquiset wrote in 1919, in a biographical essay entitled *Le Don Juan noir*: "Men who have earned a place in history, for whatever reason, generally see their name endowed with a characteristic epithet: thus we have the 'renowned' Cardinal Lauzun, the 'valiant' General Lassalle, the 'witty' Labiche, and so on. The individual who concerns us here is the holder of the word 'famous.' There are few memoirs, dictionaries, and histories that, when they mention Saint-George, fail to refer to him as the 'famous' Chevalier de Saint-George. This adjective has never left him." One of Haydn's biographers, Marc Vignal, cites the "famous" Chevalier de Saint-George, and the same adjective is used by Madame Vigée-Lebrun, La Boëssière, Grimm, Bachaumont, the *Mercure français*, Félix Clément in his encyclopedic dictionary of musicians, and so on.[14] In fact, the majority of music dictionaries published in the nineteenth century describe him as "famous." There was the occasional exception. On February 28, 1777, the *Journal de Paris* reviewed a concert directed by "the celebrated M. de Saint-George."

VIII

The Salon Man

At Versailles, intelligence and talent were harder to come by than servants and courtiers. To truly savor life, one had to go to Paris. There, in the elegant townhouses of the old families or the nouveaux riches, people could meet and gossip, play cards, or remake the world far from indiscreet ears. Women were no longer ladies of the court, wives, or mothers. They discovered that they could also have a life of the mind. During the day, while the men were busily fulfilling their duties at Versailles or out hunting, their wives held salons.

Some have claimed that these *conversazioni* paved the way for the Revolution, though not all were as literary and philosophical as history has sometimes described. The salons of Madame du Deffand, Madame d'Epinay, or Madame de Montalembert attracted philosophers and writers, however, and owed their reputation to the wit and intelligence of these hostesses, who knew how to enliven an argument on some difficult subject and how to get their guests to take some kind of intellectual stand. The Bastille dominated people's thinking, for it was a constant reminder that the written word was still subject to censorship. But the spoken word was free. Other salons limited themselves to artistic endeavors or diverting pastimes: painting, debates, and the especially popular amateur dramatics, at which the guests improvised sketches based on proverbs. Evenings were given over to elegant receptions, enhanced by concerts or theatrical performances.

For the intellectually ambitious, and for musicians, admission to a salon constituted an indispensable first step up the social ladder. Once in, the aspirant needed to shine (though not too much), avoid faux pas and indiscretions, and try to attract the notice of one of the other guests in order to be invited later to his or her own receptions. In her memoirs, Madame de Genlis depicts the atmosphere of these elegant yet exacting little worlds: "Bad manners or scandal would exclude or banish an individual from this society." She continues, "But to be admitted it was not necessary to give proof of either a blameless life or superior merit. Two things only were expected: good form and noble manners, and a kind of esteem acquired in the world either by rank, birth, or influence at court, or by elegance, riches, and personal charm."[1] Writing in hindsight in 1820, she was at once dismissive of the salon—calling it a "predatory and contemptuous circle"—and aware that it did serve to raise the intellectual sights of its members, these being "all those who had a well-recognized superior merit."

Joseph's entry into this world was smoothed by his father's position. Guillaume-Pierre did not have to knock on doors; others knocked on his. Given that at the time France was in a state of permanent conflict with its neighbors, people flocked to the man who with a flourish of the quill could decide the future of a fleet, a fortification, or a regiment. And, as Treasurer of the Colonies, he was much sought after by shipowners alarmed at the risk of a blockade of the Antilles and nobles panic-stricken at the thought that they might have to do without chocolate or coffee. No colonist visiting Paris dared neglect paying his respects to him. Guillaume-Pierre de Boullongne—"Tavernier" had by now been definitively dropped from his signature—was not considered one of the brightest lights of the day, but he enjoyed mixing in society. And his sister-in-law, the dazzling

Marguerite de Martinville who, according to the comte de Cheverny, "created many a rumor in Paris," was unmatched in her ability to enliven the salons, though her escapades at masked balls set tongues wagging.[2] At the Boullongnes' there was much talk of cannons, frigates, and uniforms. But hosts and guests also enjoyed dramatics—and music, indispensable at any fête. The marriage of Joseph's half-sister Catherine-Jeanne to Paul-Louis de Montmorency drew that family, one of the most fashionable of the upper nobility, to the rue du Bac. Far from resenting what might have seemed a bad match with the petty nobility, these latter-day representatives of a line that had produced a constable *and* a marshal took keen pleasure in coming to hear Saint-George, whose first quartets, penned in the year of the union of the two families, were dedicated to the prince de Robecq, Anne-Louis Alexandre de Montmorency. The latter was also "lieutenant general" (equivalent of a general in today's terms) of the same regiment in which served his cousin Montmorency de Laval, who had married Joseph's half-sister.

Sometimes Mars and the muses, to adopt the language of the times, were bedfellows. During his stays in Paris, a certain artillery captain with radical ideas was a frequent visitor to the mansion on the rue du Bac. He argued strenuously that the fortifications constructed a century before were incapable of withstanding the firepower of modern cannon. The military establishment upheld the dogma of the invincibility of Louis XIV's fortresses, which had been built by the legendary military engineer Sébastien Le Prestre de Vauban, and in another age such insolence might have landed Captain Choderlos de Laclos in prison on the king's orders. More freethinking than authoritarian, this society could not be too angry with the officer, who was in any case as eager to make his mark in literature as in military strategy. Anyone meeting Laclos for the first time would find it hard to believe that this soldier, who was attached to a provincial garrison and apparently suffered from morbid shyness, would in 1782 create the character of Valmont in *Dangerous Liaisons*. For the time being Laclos committed to paper what he dared not express openly, achieving thereby some success, if not happiness. Every hostess who received him was thus presented with a madrigal from his own hand. For example, these four lines could not fail to delight the ravishing Marguerite de Martinville:

> *Her eyes lowered and in modesty stare,*
> *Fixed they remain upon her bosom fair,*
> *Her milk-white breasts, which no effort compels,*
> *To fall and rise, breath-driven swells.*

Guillaume-Pierre's salon door was always open to Laclos, who was also a native of Picardy and the scion of a noble house that had seen better days (his father had been the secretary of the *intendant* of Picardy). A friendship soon sprang up between this introverted military man and the talented but exceedingly modest Joseph, two years his senior—despite their differences. For example, Laclos practically never openly declared his love for women for whom he nonetheless harbored devouring passions. Saint-George couldn't help charming women, particularly with the beauty of his playing. Laclos could count his feminine conquests on the fingers of one hand. It was said that Saint-George slept on a pillow stuffed with locks of hair he had stolen from each of his lovers. (Such collections of fetishes were all the rage at the time. The prince de Conti took a ring from each of his conquests; at his death, four thousand were found in a drawer.[3])

The close friendship between these men amused Saint-George's father, though it meant he had to be especially diplomatic when he received Madame de Vauban, now the chief defender of her late husband's fortifications. Madame de Vauban was herself far from insensitive to the charms of the handsome mulatto whom the financier had brought back from the islands. Soon she would receive Saint-George in her salon, where he would first perform one of his rare trios and several dozen of the songs termed *romances*, all dedicated to his hostess.

The Mars-muse alliance on the rue du Bac also emerged during one of the frequent visits from the marquis de Montalembert. A respected intellectual, an engineer specializing in armaments and fortifications, and a general, the marquis also acted as Laclos's protector in Paris. In copious memoranda, studies, and reports, the younger man set out boldly what the older one could not manage to put into words. Montalembert's chief ambition was to find as large a readership as possible for his impressive book, *Perpendicular Fortifications*. But to publish such a tome, complete with engravings and illustrations, would cost a fortune. One reason he often turned up at the treasurer general's house was to attempt to convince him of the validity of his theories and solicit financial support. (Montalembert's book would finally be published, though not until after his death.)

His young wife, who had been barely twenty when he had married her in 1770 at the age of fifty-seven, normally accompanied the old marquis. Their townhouse on the rue de la Roquette, purchased in 1771, attracted the brightest stars of the Enlightenment: Voltaire, Rousseau, Benjamin Franklin, Jean le Rond d'Alembert, Jean-François Marmontel, and several of the musicians then in vogue. The beautiful marquise's eyes bewitched more than one of these masters. But the young woman soon had eyes only for Saint-George, whom she made the star of her soirées—in every sense. A society paper written by a retired lawyer and sold clandestinely in the Popincourt quarter of Paris stated that the charming theater Madame de Montalembert had had built in her townhouse was mainly used for amorous assignations with the handsome mulatto. Shortly thereafter, rumor would attribute to Saint-George the paternity of the child whom the *philosophes'* muse had just brought into the world.

Poor Laclos found it unbearable to be ignored by his protector's beautiful wife. In 1779, overcoming his timidity, he determined to send a verse epistle to Madame de Montalembert. In eight stiff-sounding stanzas, each full of ponderous allusions, he trumpeted his passion and threatened to seek his fortune elsewhere should she ignore him further. In his attempt to prove he could be as insolent as any grand rake, Laclos instead only managed to appear foolish, or so Roger Vailland, his biographer, would later observe.

Joseph mixed with the cream of Parisian wit and refinement on the rue de la Roquette, where he often encountered a musician from the Concert des Amateurs. This time, however, it was not the second violin or first viola with whom he spoke, but a count or a marquis. Nonetheless, his modesty and courteousness continued to sustain him in a society whose members hated nothing more than arrogance or unseemliness. Madame de Genlis, once again, described these salons as cozy places of conviviality. "There, in groups too large to permit the sharing of secrets and which, at the same time, were not so large as to preclude general conversation; there, in assemblies of fifteen or twenty persons, were to be found all of France's amenities and graces. Every means of pleasing and interesting others was here combined with surprising good sense. One felt that, in order to distinguish this group from bad company and the society of the vulgar, one must, in one's address, preserve the tone and manners that best proclaimed modesty, reserve, kindness, indulgence, decency, gentleness, and nobility of sentiment. Thus good taste alone decreed that, merely in order to shine and to charm, one must adopt all the forms of the most amiable virtues. . . . Backbiting was banned from these general conversations; its bitter taste could not be combined with the gentle charm which each person brought to them. Never did discussion degenerate into argument."

Having made his debut in society and earned his stripes, Saint-George was soon asked to appear at the home of the prince de Conti. Every Monday the prince held a "supper" at the Temple, in Paris's Marais district. These were sizable occasions—at least 150 people took part in the banquets; in order to salute the prince before going to table, guests had to muster the courage to pass between several rows of men. But the heir to the house of Condé did not design these evenings as mere frivolities. Madame de Genlis recalls that "the Prince de Conti was the only one of the Princes of the Blood who was interested in the sciences and literature, and who could speak in public. He impressed everyone by his looks, his figure and manners; no one could say kind words with more delicacy and grace." His salon was also one of the high points of Parisian intellectual life. Many well-known writers attended regularly. Among the most notable guests was the abbé Raynal. Cultivated to the point of pedantry, a free-thinking apostate and iconoclast, the abbé was above all a formidable advocate of anticolonialism who would later become famous for his exhortation: "Peoples, do you wish to be happy? Overturn every altar and every throne!" Another free-thinker who regularly attended these soirées was Prince Louis, the future Cardinal de Rohan. His somewhat dissolute ways and spicy conversation hinted, some said, at a very promising ecclesiastical career indeed. Saint-George also often met the omnipresent baron de Bézenval, commander of the Swiss Guard and one of the great personalities of the dying *ancien régime*. Soon the baron felt compelled to invite Joseph to his receptions, which were not known for wit and intellect. What the baron sought above all was pleasures. De Bézenval, recalled Madame de Genlis, "had a charming appearance and was a great success with the ladies. Extremely ignorant, and unable to write even a passable note, his mind was fit only for small talk, which he delivered lightly and with grace. He was accused of being malicious. He was wholly irresponsible and unprincipled."

Shortly after that, Saint-George found a hostess of quality in the marquise de Chambonas, "renowned for the elite company present at her soirées."[4] She announced her intention of including the violinist among her guests at each of her receptions. He was, after all, a peerless violinist, a much-admired dancer, and he willingly played in the little theater pieces organized by the more wealthy hostesses. However, success did not turn Saint-George's head. He also knew how to get attention by seemingly not trying to. In her memoirs, which she completed several weeks before being led to the guillotine, Madame Roland remembers going as a young woman with her mother to the gatherings at Madame L'Epine's. Celebrated by Stendhal (for whom she was "the divine"), Lamartine ("the soul of the Gironde"), and the great historian Jules Michelet ("the marvel of the Revolution"), Madame Roland retained a vivid memory of the evening when Saint-George and a few other musicians turned up at one of these gatherings. Madame L'Epine had twice braved her family's rage, first by marrying a sculptor, an assistant to Jean-Baptiste Pigalle, then by becoming a singer. By sheer tenacity she had managed to form a "concert of amateurs composed of skilled people and to which she admitted only what she called good company."[5] Saint-George had nothing to gain by showing up, but the young woman's persistence and her passion for music had won him over.

There was a world of difference between the elegant townhouses, some of them with lavishly decorated theaters, like that of Madame de Montansier's on the rue du Beaujolais, where Saint-George was also a frequent caller, and the modest lodgings where musicians played for an audience of aesthetes. According to Madame Roland, "Mme L'Epine's apartments were not very elegant; the concert room was a little cramped but it opened onto another room whose large doors remained open; there, seated in a circle, one had the double advantage of hearing the music and seeing the players, and being able to chat in the intermissions." One day, as he passed through this section of the city, the composer Grétry was almost literally struck by a melody coming from a nearby house. He sat down by the roadside to listen to the "finale" of one of Saint-George's concertos, which was being played "with full orchestra," he relates in his memoirs. "It gave me a pleasure that has never faded." One of these refrains, he notes, is repeated twenty times and yet is so engaging that one never tires of it; quite to the contrary— "At the end of the piece one is distressed to hear it no more."

Saint-George had a special reason for his regular appearances at Madame L'Epine's gatherings: She had a nearly perfect coloratura soprano voice. Therefore, in addition to his work as a composer of quartets and concertos, he threw himself into writing ariettas and *romances*. At this time, the genre was in its early stages; it would reach its peak in the first days of the Revolution.

Despite his gifts, Saint-George was not one to cash in on his talent. If he happened to be out walking and inspiration struck, he would simply take his violin out of its case and treat onlookers to a free concert. Without question his favorite place for such impromptu concerts was the gardens of the Palais-Royal. Elisabeth Vigée-Lebrun, who became a portraitist of Marie-Antoinette and one of the most accomplished women in Paris, describes in her memoirs those summer evenings when Saint-George and other artists would entertain the public: "The Opéra was just nearby; it was adjacent to the Palace. In the summertime the show finished at half-past eight and all the elegant people left even before the end to stroll in the garden. It was the fashion in those days for women to carry enormous bouquets of flowers which, combined with the sweet-smelling powders with which each of them scented her hair, truly perfumed the air one breathed. Later, but before the Revolution, I saw how these parties would go on until two o'clock in the morning; music was played in the open air, by the light of the moon. Some amateur artists, including Garat and Alsevédo, sang there. People played the harp and the guitar." She adds: "The famous Saint-George often played his violin there as well. The crowds flocked to hear him."

The year was 1771. Elisabeth Vigée, then seventeen years old, would soon marry a man more interested in the considerable sums paid her by the queen and dignitaries of the kingdom for his wife's portraits than in her beauty. However, Elisabeth hid part of her earnings from her husband, keeping a nest egg with which she funded a salon. As soon as she could, she invited the "famous" Saint-George. One evening when he appeared in the concert chamber of the royal family's official portrait painter, a large crowd formed. The corpulent duc de Noailles, unable to find a seat, was forced to sit on the floor, and when the concert was over, several strapping youths had to come and help him up.

Before long, Saint-George's reputation as a virtuoso and "gentleman" reached Versailles. In 1774 the young queen Marie-Antoinette, then nineteen years old, invited the chevalier to come and play music with her. The court thought that by now it was used to the liberties the young queen took with protocol. The arrival of a "colored" man into her immediate entourage, however, was a bombshell, particularly since he wasn't there to serve beverages or wave a fan. Saint-George would become Marie-Antoinette's musical adviser and even for some time her music teacher. The prediction that the midwife had made the day he was born had finally come true. Practically every day Saint-George's path crossed that of Louis XVI. And in the evenings he described the pomp of Versailles down to the slightest detail to Nanon.

This association with the queen did not last long, chiefly because Saint-George could only barely tolerate the poisonous atmosphere of the court with its eternal intrigues and conspiracies. At the worst, envious courtiers set one trap after another for this "Negro," who was not to be allowed to defy the laws of genetics with impunity. At best, "friends" tried to exploit him, eager to take advantage of his daily contact with the queen in order to gain an introduction or a sinecure. Soon a new face appeared at court: that of the "chevalier" Gluck, who had taught music to the future queen when she was a child in Vienna. After years of travel, the German composer had arrived straight from Italy, where, finally, his talent had begun to be recognized. He dreamed of seeing his career crowned at Versailles and in Paris, the cultural beacon of Europe. He also had some sound ideas about opera. Saint-George passed to Gluck his post at Marie-Antoinette's side without regret. Right up to the Revolution, Joseph would enjoy a privileged relationship with the queen, who would regularly travel to Paris to attend his concerts, even going to watch him skate on the frozen Seine in January 1789.

Meanwhile the family continued to feather its nest. On his deathbed in 1769, Jean de Boullongne, the Controller General who had set himself up as protector of the "tribe," had been able to contemplate the success of his work. Jean-Nicholas, the son whom he had arranged to be appointed Farmer General, gave elegant parties in his mansion on the rue Saint-Honoré. Philippe-Guillaume, also a Farmer General, bought up lands and châteaux in the provinces. Guillaume-Pierre was able to acquire a marquisate in the Ardennes. A few years after buying the townhouse on the rue du Bac, his eye fell on a superb château in the Ile-de-France he was determined to make his secondary residence. Purchased from bankrupt financiers named the Savalettes, and located less than thirteen leagues from Paris, Magnanville boasted no fewer than seven salons on the ground floor and fifty apartments, each luxuriously furnished and each equipped with an antechamber, a bedchamber, salon, and bathroom as well as lodging for domestics.[6] The estate was tailor-made to attract wealthy Parisians. "How would these fine financiers not be caught up in this endless succession of fêtes, to which each one brought his contingent of imperturbable gaiety, inexhaustible goodwill, and particular ingenuity in discovering a new distraction, an amusement not imagined the evening before?" writes the nineteenth-century financial historian Didier Thirion.[7] He adds, "In this society there were Boullongnes of Magnanville and Préninville, Santots, Martinvilles, ten financiers, holding either one title or several simultaneously, positions worth millions, all mixing with members of the most fashionable society, youths prodigal and elegant, gallants, as well as ten women who were coquettes, flighty, and immense spenders, with no aim in life other than to amuse themselves. Thus they banished from their minds all preoccupations and cares; all they thought about was pleasant gatherings, balls, both elegant and fancy dress, plays, games, rustic parties, and delicious feasts."

Above all, Magnanville became known in Parisian society for its sophisticated theatrical performances, which Boullongne offered free of charge. Usually the guests, backed by a few professional actors or singers, acted out the roles. People flocked to this pleasure dome. "How many comings and goings of visitors to Magnanville, what noise, what confusion in the salons, the corridors, and even the kitchens, when the château was filled from cellar to attic!" writes Thirion. Saint-George shone in his role as master of ceremonies. He regularly brought along his musicians as well as some female singers. Soon Magnanville's theatrical soirées rivaled those held at La Chevrette, the château where Madame d'Epinay (who was, we might remember, Rousseau's benefactress) received painters, actors, writers, and musicians, and which was standard-bearer of the age. Here Saint-George tried out his *romances* before presenting them to the outside world. Falling on responsive ears, his melodies, delicate and flowing but also very melancholy, made the rounds of Paris. One that he presented to Madame de Vauban (widow of the fortress-builder) might also easily have been dedicated to Nanon:

> *Sleep, my child, close your eyes,*
> *Your cries tear my heart.*
> *Sleep, my child, your poor mother*
> *Has enough sorrow.*
> *When with gentle tenderness*
> *Your father won my love,*
> *He seemed to me in his caresses*
> *Naïve, as innocent as you.*

> *You cannot yet feel*
> *What it is that wrenches these sobs from me.*
> *The sorrow that consumes me*
> *Never troubles your rest.*
> *Sighing for what one adores*
> *Is the hardest thing to bear.*

> *Let us join our sad destinies*
> *And live together forever.*
> *Two unfortunate victims*
> *Must help each other tenderly.*
> *I took care of your earliest years,*
> *You will watch over my old age.*

Saint-George's *romances* were played not only in Paris and Versailles but also in the provinces and abroad, notably in London,

Vienna, and Rome. Some of them were actually composed in Italian (in particular, the three dedicated to the comtesse de Vauban).

The Rousseau-ian notion of a natural paradise seemed an inexhaustible source of inspiration. In Saint-George's *romances,* the brook always runs clear, the grass is soft, the bushes inviting. The carefree, rustic décor of these melodies, which seem straight out of a Boucher painting, invariably suggests an Eden, a place of everlasting happiness. Love, however, is ever fleeting. There are few coquettish glances, if any, in his long *lamento*s. Without exception, these mourn a passion condemned to prove ephemeral. When the object of desire finally surrenders, it is but for a few brief moments. The dichotomy between the joy of communing with nature and enjoying the camaraderie of friends and the sadness permeating his life would surface again and again in Saint-George's concertos, whose middle movements display profound sadness. For all the unfailing good humor he showed toward his friends and to society at large, Saint-George was profoundly melancholy. He was, in fact, doomed never to find enduring love. Because of his birth and especially the society in which he moved, he tended to meet young ladies of nobility and wealth whose families would never have consented to mixed-race descendants. The scenario of his love affair and break-up with Marie would be endlessly repeated.

> *My mistress does forget me,*
> *Ah, Love, let me die!*
> *When love's caresses are no more,*
> *What cruel torment is life!*

The theme is hardly original, and is strikingly reminiscent of the *Plaisir d'amour* of his contemporary and friend Johann Paul Martini, an exile like himself. Though we might now see them as too naïve, too affected, they are hardly more so than the *romances* that would become the rage a hundred years later.

While Saint-George was pining for love, Mozart was writing a rather surprising letter in verse to his mother, the severe Maria Anna:

> *Oh, mother mine!*
> *Butter is fine.*
> *Praise and thanks to Him,*
> *We're alive and full of vim.*
> *Though we're rather short of cash.*
> *But we don't find this provoking*
> *And none of us are choking.*
> *Besides, to people I'm tied*
> *Who carry their muck inside*
> *And let it out, if they are able,*
> *Both before and after table.*
> *At night of farts there is no lack,*
> *Which are let off, forsooth, with a powerful crack.*
> *The king of farts came yesterday*
> *Whose farts smelt sweeter than May.*
> *His voice, however, was no treat*
> *And he himself was in a heat.*
> *Well, now we've been over a week away*
> *And we've been shitting every day.*[8]

(Mozart tended to indulge in vulgarity when under the pressure of meeting a deadline for one of his compositions.)

Magnanville and its cultural life opened up new horizons to its proprietor. "Tavernier de Boullongne" had become (having passed from "Boullongne-Tavernier" to simply "de Boullongne"—or "de Boulogne," so that no one could associate him with a relative who ran a cheap bistro) the marquis de Busancy, after the property he had bought in the Ardennes, which included eight villages. Then he changed his name yet again. Henceforth he would sign himself "Boul-

longne de Magnanville" or "Guillaume-Pierre de Magnanville," so
that no one in Paris could fail to know that he presided over that
enlightened place where intelligence and pleasure went hand in hand
and where the finest food and wine was plentiful. When one was at
Magnanville, one was no longer in France; one inhabited a mytholog-
ical world that was an endless source of inspiration for *fêtes galantes*
and painters. Guillaume-Pierre was its Jupiter, Saint-George its
Apollo, and Bacchus was everywhere.

The walls surrounding the vast park with its marble urns carved
by Girardon muffled the groans of a suffering populace. And yet, as
Thirion would later note, "it was nonetheless not in Magnanville's
destiny to bring good luck to its owners, despite its manifold delights.
Savalette was almost completely ruined there while Boullongne
gravely compromised his fortune." Guillaume-Pierre did not sense
the change in the wind when, in 1770, under the pressure of public
opinion, a revolt broke out against the *traitants*, or farm tax collectors,
and the money-handlers. There were bankruptcies and suicides by the
dozen throughout the provinces. Guillaume-Pierre himself suspected
nothing. He was, after all, friends with the king's own secretary and
benefactor of marshals. By 1774, however, faced with the abysmal
failure of his Treasurer in the Event of Wars for the entire northeast,
he found himself financially crippled and no longer able to fulfill
his commitments toward the royal treasury. The formidable minister
of finance, the abbé Terray, managed to balance his budget by pleading for credit from the Necker Bank. Guillaume-Pierre de Magnanville had therefore to cede his office to his brother, who bought it
for his son.

For the former Swiss banker Jacques Necker this was not punishment enough. He had kept an eye on this nouveau riche who had purchased himself a little Versailles on the backs of the people and yet
seemed incapable of fulfilling the duties of his post. Necker was probably the first to devise the ethics of responsibility according to which
anyone who goes bankrupt has to pay up. Until then, bankruptcy

might ruin ordinary people and the middle class, but those responsible for them usually emerged unscathed, especially if they enjoyed some kind of rank, since in theory the nobles' assets could not be seized. In this atmosphere of impunity, certain members of the nobility had even made bankruptcy into an art form. Having lost a fortune worth thirty million livres, the prince de Rohan-Guéménée had in the process ruined the lives of thousands of humble people, yet his cousin the Cardinal de Rohan proudly declared: "Only a sovereign or a Rohan could go bankrupt in so splendid a fashion." The colorful cardinal had also not noticed that times were changing. Implicated in the so-called "Affair of the Queen's Necklace" a few years later, he was arrested on the king's orders in Versailles while wearing his ecclesiastical habit and thrown into the Bastille. Necker, who was both government minister and banker, was planning to draw up a genuine national budget, balancing expenses and receipts over the course of a year. He believed this was the only way to get around the dictatorship of the caste of Farmers General and treasurers general, who fleeced the people but paid back only fractions of the amounts needed for the state to function. The feudal attitudes of these financiers was coming back to haunt them. Between these men, who in a single generation had managed to hoist themselves up to the level of the higher nobility, and Necker, who was intent on prosecuting them, a ruthless conflict arose. Necker wanted to set an example. He had scarcely taken his seat in the government when he responded to a request for an audience from Magnanville, now on the defensive. Receiving him late one morning, out of politeness Necker felt obliged to invite Guillaume-Pierre to lunch. The former treasurer general declined the invitation. His health, he said, condemned him to take "no food other than milk" (at that time, milk was the diet of choice for people wanting to lose weight). "Well, then," replied Necker, "why insist that your position be reinstated? You don't need a fortune to live on milk."[9]

Guillaume-Pierre was soon forced to sell Magnanville. Shortly afterward, he would have to give up his Busancy holding, which had been bringing in a comfortable income. The townhouse on the rue du Bac was the last to go. One misfortune after another rained down on the would-be aristocrat. The victim of yet another fraud perpetrated by one of his clerks, he was within a hair's-breadth of complete ruin. Happily, a few friends kept an eye out for him and his banker forgave a debt of 180,000 livres. His brother Philippe-Guillaume, who had an opulent house on the rue de la Chaussée-d'Antin, arranged for him to live there. (Préninville was lucky enough to remain Farmer General. But that later exacted a price: The post would guarantee him a place on one of the last carts bound for the guillotine.)

Guillaume-Pierre's daughter, Joseph's half-sister, was not spared the indignities attending this decline in fortunes. Her husband being first gentleman of the bedchamber of Monsieur, the king's brother, in 1780 Catherine-Jeanne claimed an equivalent title in the service of Madame. She was immediately given to understand that the daughter of a planter, a planter who was, moreover, bankrupt, could not aspire to the same position as a Montmorency. A few years later, Joseph's half-sister would become furious when she learned that her son, who bore the legitimate title of viscount of Montmorency, wasn't promoted to the rank that was his due. She complained about it to the maréchal de Ségur: "In the old days, it was easier for a Montmorency to get a constable's sword than it is today to get a colonel's epaulettes." "Messieurs de Montmorency have always been treated according to their merits," came the stinging reply. Guillaume-Pierre resented this series of insults endured by his children, and made no secret of it.

As for Saint-George, for the moment at least he was far from claiming a colonel's rank, which would undoubtedly have further enraged his vindictive half-sister. He was but a modest chevalier, a title that had been invented as we have seen, not conferred. Still, his career seemed sufficiently assured that he did not suffer in the least from the series of misfortunes striking his father. He was forced to tone down his life-style, Guillaume-Pierre having significantly reduced his allowance. The sale of the rue du Bac residence did not much affect him. He was immediately offered a large apartment in the Palais-Royal, of which he had long been a regular. Fortune smiled on him, in fact, when Madame de Montesson, who in 1773 had married the duc d'Orléans—the second most powerful man in the kingdom—decided to lure Saint-George away from the marquise de Chambonas and make him director of her theater and leader of her small orchestra in 1775. Still very beautiful, the wife of the rotund duke was then thirty-eight; Joseph was two years younger. Inevitably, tongues wagged.[10] "*On ne prête qu'aux riches*" (One lends only to the rich).

Madame Charlotte-Jeanne de Montesson was a truly remarkable woman, able to wed the duke discreetly on the express condition—imposed by the king—that she not assume the title of duchesse d'Orléans. She was just sixteen when in 1753 she married Monsieur de Montesson, who was seventy-eight years old and the possessor of 80,000 livres in income, as well as a quite sizable belly. The marquis had the ill grace to wait sixteen years before departing this world, bequeathing to his still relatively young wife his lands and his château of Villers-Cotterêts. It was here that the marquise bewitched the duc d'Orléans by fellating the first prince of the blood when, during a hunt, he was lying stretched out beneath a tree, overcome by the heat.[11] The very next day the duke dismissed his mistress, a onetime oyster salesgirl who had become a dancer at the Comédie Italienne. Shrewdly, however, the marquise refused to sleep with the duke until they were married. The duke waited patiently. For years the good fellow had been the laughingstock of the court on account of his wife, Henriette de Bourbon-Conti, who had amassed an impressive list of lovers, including Louis XV, the prince de Soubise, our old acquaintance the maréchal de Saxe, the duc de Richelieu, the abbé Bernis, and even the painter François Boucher, who had depicted her draped in a spray of flowers as "Hebe giving a drink of nectar to Jupiter's eagle." Apparently not satisfied with aristocratic conquests, she would go— so rumor had it—in disguise to the gardens of the Palais-Royal and the taverns of the surrounding area and bring some drunkard back to the princely apartments. In short, Madame d'Orléans had claimed her sexual rights. Thus her unfortunate widower could not help falling in love with a woman who so prized her virtue . . . even if the gossip columns recalled that the marquise de Montesson gave her suitor exclusive rights to that virtue.

By 1775, the marquise de Montesson presided over one of the most brilliant salons in Paris. Her two great passions were the theater and music. Her niece, Félicité de Genlis, who was not close to her, would relate what Pierre Alexandre Monsigny, her music teacher, had told her, namely that the marquise had asked him to compliment her in public (that is, before the duke) and to be sincere in private. She longed to learn how to write poetry and to play the harp; she surrounded herself with the finest minds. At times this craving brought her perilously close to resembling one of Molière's pretentious know-it-alls. She was once heard to inform someone, in learned tones, that the Baltic Sea was particularly beautiful along the Turkish coast.

Such slips were readily forgiven. Madame de Montesson was a genuine patron of the arts, especially with regard to writers and dramatists, for whom she spared no expense. (She herself had dreams of being published, and privately printed her complete *œuvre*. Sales did not exceed twelve copies, proof, incidentally, that not everything could be had for money.) At Villers-Cotterêts and in her own townhouse on the rue de la Chaussée-d'Antin, her orchestra and actors, together with friends and courtiers, made up a very creditable theatrical troupe. The architect Alexandre Brongniart—designer of the present-day Paris stock exchange—had installed a theater in the huge mansion the marquise ordered built in 1768, next door to that of the duc d'Orléans. Home from the hunt, the duke would good-humoredly give in to the whims of his wife, whom, intelligent but exuberant and capricious as she was, he adored, agreeing to play the small parts she entrusted to him. Often he appeared as the country bumpkin, the simpleton of the play. This amused the marquise de Créquy: "As she did not succeed in being the duchesse d'Orléans, she demanded that the duc d'Orléans be a Montesson." Roger de Beauvoir goes further: "Her dominant trait," he wrote, was "the overriding need for approval."[12]

Odet Denys recalls the brilliant cast of characters in her theater: "You'd find d'Aguessau, a high magistrate from the famous chancellor's family, acting alongside Lamoignon [president of the Paris Parliament] in *The Barber of Seville*. . . . The productions were of the highest quality. The marquise gave an intelligent performance as Pergolesi's 'Servant as Mistress' and as Aline, the queen of Golconda, nor was she above appearing as a shepherdess or a servant. She herself, as well as her niece Mme. de Genlis, wrote several agreeable plays for her theater."

Recruited to this theatrical troupe, Saint-George soon became its director. He decided on the programs, hired the professional artists, cast the roles, supervised rehearsals, and added music and ballets to the performances. Moreover, he brought the theater up to the standard to which he was then lifting the Concert des Amateurs. Soon the gazettes would all report, with ill-concealed irony, that the Comédie Française, which was under the king's protection, was being drained of its talent—to the advantage of Madame de Montesson's theater.

Before long, La Montesson was never seen without her chevalier. She made him her first equerry. But she had far loftier ambitions for him: Her desire was to make him the duc d'Orléans's captain of guards. First, though, he should be given some noble title. This task was entrusted to Madame de Genlis's husband. In acknowledgment of Joseph's help in smoothing relations between the duc d'Orléans and his son, Philippe, duc de Chartres, the elder duke created a post for Saint-George, that of "Master of the Hunt of Pinci." From then on, several times a week, the chevalier would accompany his protectress to Le Raincy, where the duc d'Orléans had organized a hunt. Elisabeth Vigée-Lebrun remembered these occasions. "In 1782 I spent some time at Le Raincy. The duc d'Orléans, Philippe Egalité's [the duc de Chartres's post-Revolution name] father, who lived there at that time, had invited me to paint his portrait and that of Mme. de Montesson. Except for the pleasure of watching the great hunting meets, I was somewhat bored at Le Raincy. . . . Saint-George, the mulatto who was so strong and skillful, was among the hunters."[13]

Her sudden passion for a half-caste must have seemed surprising. The daughter of a slave-trading captain from Saint-Malo—Béraud de La Haye—the marquise de Montesson never left the house without her two black lackeys riding postillion on her carriage. In her mind, Saint-George was not like the others. "One thing above all pleased her about Saint-George," Roger de Beauvoir would observe. "He never wore the same suit, the same jabot, the same boots two days running; he had amorous adventures, he was a good raconteur; he wrote minuets and danced them." Above all, he shone at the *ambigus*, or mixed-genre entertainments, that the marquise excelled in organizing, in which people played music, sang, and danced. Alfred Marquiset would describe this period of Joseph's life: "A rooster receiving the adulation of a swarm of beauties, he was the star of all theatricals, suppers, and fêtes."[14]

John Adams, who would be the second president of the United States, was living in Paris at that time. On May 17, 1779, he wrote in his diary: "[Admiral] Landais gave Us an Account of St. George in Paris, a Molatto [sic] Man, Son of a former Governor of Guadeloupe, by a Negro Woman. He has a sister married to a Farmer General. He is the most accomplished Man in Europe in Riding, Running, Shooting, Fencing, Dancing, Musick. He will hit the Button, any Button on the Coat or Waistcoat of the greatest Masters. He will hit a Crown Piece in the Air with a Pistoll Ball." From such descriptions are legends born.

IX

The Voltaire of Music

Problems arose all too quickly for poor Louis XVI. In 1776, having been on the throne for barely two years, he had to confront two very troublesome situations. First came the revolt of the nobles and financiers against his Controller General of Finances, the Baron de Turgot. As many had predicted it would, naming a reformer such as Turgot to such a post was bound to cause problems. And the "physio-crat" himself had introduced a few. For example, Turgot's lowering of interest rates, designed to encourage trade and the economy, angered both Versailles and the bankers so indispensable to the court, and his plan to abolish the guilds, a move intended to enable every worker to become his own boss, irked the bourgeoisie.

In the preamble to his formal presentation, Turgot had set forth some rather radical ideas: "God, by giving man certain needs and making him dependent on the resource of labor, made the right of labor the property of every man, and that property is the primary, the most sacred and unprescriptible of all." Ridiculous. And now here he was providing for the establishment of provincial assemblies in which no attention would be paid to the distinctions among the three orders—the Church, the nobility, and the commoners. Not long before, Louis XV had dismissed the excellent Jean Boullongne from the same post for far less. Though slightly put out by having to reverse his decision so soon, the king, to satisfy his entourage, fired the eccentric Turgot. It was a simple formality. Everyone quickly forgot the youthful error. After all, even a king needed a period of apprenticeship.

Far more aggravating was the whole business then convulsing the music world. The scars from the Quarrel of the Buffoons had scarcely had time to heal when the king was annoyed to see that factions—"corners"—were again forming, and that a new war was erupting in the very bosom of his court. The reason? The music master whom Marie-Antoinette had engaged at the beginning of Louis XVI's reign, in 1774, a certain Monsieur de Saint-George, was applying for the post of director of the Académie Royale de Musique, which meant the Opéra. It was said that the musician had all the qualities necessary to revive an institution adrift, one in which nothing new was being created. The Concert des Amateurs, which he directed, was the envy of every court in Europe. Moreover, the chevalier was drawing audiences away from the Comédie Française to fill the theater of the clever but scheming Madame de Montesson. In short, if this American put his talent exclusively at the service of one of the crown's institutions, he would once again fill the Opéra and, as important, empty the theater owned by the muse of the king's cousin, the duc d'Orléans. Such was the course the queen urged her husband to pursue.

The man's candidacy would certainly have been crowned with success were he not half-black. His father, it was true, seemed an honorable gentleman, despite the failure of his principal office two years before. But the question was, would he, the king, risk becoming the laughingstock of European courts by appointing a Negro at the head of his own opera house? How humiliating for France to reveal to the whole world that there existed no native-born French musician worthy of taking on the post! Certainly this Monsieur de Saint-George was prodigiously talented, but could that by itself justify so honoring him just when the arrival of the chevalier Gluck into Marie-Antoinette's entourage looked like a fresh snub of French musicians? Despite all of this, the good-hearted Louis was prepared to give in to the queen, who assured him that the mulatto musician's gifts really were quite extraordinary. But in Versailles and Paris, people were enraged. According to Smidak, there was even talk of the "threat of a great revolution."[1] The affair dragged on, became public, and finally, so Gérard Gefen claims, "created as big a stir as the Quarrel of the Buffoons."[2] Which was precisely what Louis wanted to avoid.

In the face of the racist hatred being unleashed against him, Saint-George's best friends' efforts were of no avail; matters had gone too far. The final blow would be dealt by none other than Saint-George's childhood nemesis Sophie Arnould, who persuaded another Opéra singer, Rosalie Levasseur, as well as the lead dancer at the Opéra, La Guimard, to oppose Saint-George's candidacy. The three divas addressed a petition to Marie-Antoinette wherein they stated that "their honor and the delicacy of their conscience would not permit them ever to be subject to the orders of a mulatto."[3]

The idea may not have been theirs. Saint-George's chief ally being Marie-Antoinette, the petition may have been intended to give the queen, then only twenty-two years old, pause just when others were trying to change her mind. Sophie Arnould's determination to oppose Saint-George may have had its roots in their childhood quarrels. There is little reason to doubt she found it vexing yet again to find him crossing her path. There was more to it than that, however. Mademoiselle Arnould's voice was nothing out of the ordinary, and her "asthmatic throat" could, as we have seen, prove debilitating. For an opera singer, this was a serious handicap. Nor could her physical appearance make up for her vocal limitations. When Madame Vigée-Lebrun studied her with her artist's eye, the analysis was fairly severe: "Mlle. Arnould was not pretty; her mouth marred her face, while only her eyes gave her an expression mirroring the remarkable wit for which she was famous. An endless number of her bons mots have been repeated and put into print."[4] These bons mots were useful for denigrating the competition, but not enough to launch a career. Arnould, who had made her debut at the Opéra in 1757 at the age of thirteen and taken part in the marvels of the Tuileries stage, now received far less adulation than in the past. Her idiosyncrasies were becoming increasingly troublesome. For example, she continued to demand that her box at the Opéra be given to no one else, even on those nights when she was not singing. As for the dancer, La Guimard, the verdict was decisive: She was far from being a top talent and, besides, even though still said to be a *grande amoureuse*, she had lost her looks. (The portrait done of her by Fragonard tends to support this judgment.) And moreover, at forty-five, it was perhaps time for her to hang up her dancing slippers.

The letter-writers proclaiming their dignity wounded at the prospect of having a black director imposed on them had everything to fear from Saint-George. At that time he was often in the company of Madame Saint-Huberty, the aunt of his young friend Louise Fusil. Remembered Vigée-Lebrun: "You had to have heard Mme Saint-Huberty to experience the full effect of tragic opera. Not only did Mme Saint-Huberty have a superb voice, she was also a great actress. By good fortune she sang the operas of Niccolò Piccinni, Antonio Sacchini, and Gluck, and that beautiful and expressive music was perfectly suited to her talent, which was full of expression, truth, and grandeur." The appearance of this eighteenth-century Callas could cause riots, as happened during one of her performances in Marseille.

But the crowning touch was Saint-George's passion for the remarkable Louise Rosalie Dugazon. The newspaper *Mercure* had long singled her out on the stage of the Concert Spirituel for her "light, flutelike voice and powerful emotion." Vigée-Lebrun believed Dugazon was "the most perfect talent that comic opera ever possessed. Never did anyone bring to the stage so much truth. One ceased to be aware of the actress: it was Babet herself, or the Countess d'Albert or Nicolette."

Hunkered down in their pride, refusing to be directed by a mulatto, the three divas in fact were betraying their fear of the future. Should Saint-George get the Opéra position, retirement for them would surely follow. Racism cloaked strong personal resentment and plain self-protection. Arnould, Levasseur, and Guimard were right to see the danger being posed as very real. Saint-George was probably in love with La Dugazon; he was reputed to have fathered the son that the great diva produced at the time. Gustave Dugazon would later have a fine career as a musician, becoming so successful that some journals would often ascribe it to his suspected ancestry.[5]

Describing the three *artistes'* rebellion, Grimm noted, with a touch of irony: "Such an important consideration made all the impression expected of it."[6] The king's reply, in essence, was that it would be Saint-George or nothing. The divas refused to back down. Eventually came another decision: The mulatto, who deserved the post based purely on his talent, would not be appointed director of the Opéra. However, neither would anyone else. The king delegated his *intendant des menus plaisirs,* or Superintendent of Royal Entertainments, to see to the institution's financial needs. Without artistic direction—without a soul, essentially—the Académie Royale was in grave danger of becoming a rudderless ship.

This episode may well constitute the first great racist scandal in modern French society. Before it happened, people had paid little heed to the talents of blacks, who were so much cattle to be bought from African traders and sold in the marketplace. At best, they were fit to be made servants or pets. Saint-George was forcing whites to respond to a basic question: When they weren't being turned into domestic drones, might blacks not develop the same skills as whites? Marie-Antoinette's reply would have been "yes." "No," declared the enlightened minds of the day. For the progressive-thinking cleric Abbé Grégoire, there was no mistaking what was at stake. He turned

Saint-George into a symbol, calling him "the black Voltaire." After all, François Marie Arouet—Voltaire's full name—also had had to suffer beatings and humiliations because of his ideas.

Grégoire's comparison was touching but not quite accurate. For one thing, Voltaire would never have stooped to defending a black man—unless, of course, he was the victim of a Jew. Nevertheless, the sobriquet was descriptive of Saint-George's musical style of composition, evoking both liveliness and delicacy as well as Voltairean gravity and indignation. The author of *Zadig* also wrote a serious poem on the Lisbon earthquake and was a passionate advocate in the so-called Calas Affair, fighting to clear a Protestant named Jean Calas of the charge of murdering his son, purportedly because the son was about to convert to Catholicism. These were qualities Saint-George shared. He could be nimble and witty yet also was prone, musically speaking, to an unshakable melancholy and deep seriousness, using trills in the treble and rapid alternations of high and low notes. His music reminds many listeners of Watteau and Boucher in its fast movements, Jean-Baptiste Greuze in its slow.

Following the painful business of the Opéra rejection, Saint-George threw himself into composition, writing no fewer than one *symphonie concertante* (a concerto with two or more soloists—violin and viola, two clarinets, two violins, and so forth) and five violin concertos in a matter of a few short months. Happily, his friends closed ranks around him. The duc d'Orléans presented him with commodious lodgings and a handsome pension. And to show that he had been the musicians' candidate for the Opéra position, the directors of the Concert Spirituel—in principle the fierce rival of the Concert des Amateurs—proposed that Saint-George write his first *symphonie concertante*. And the famous Pierre Le Duc conducted the premiere. It was a tremendous honor and magnanimous gesture, aimed at silencing the petty quarrels and wagging tongues. It was also but the first in a series. Even when Saint-George was unable to conduct them himself, the Concert Spirituel would often perform his works. His success with the orchestra did not diminish: In 1775, he directed the New Year's Eve concert, and in both 1783 and 1787 he opened the musical season.

Saint-George's name often alternated with that of Mozart on posters and announcements. For example, on March 26, 1782, the Concert Spirituel performed his clarinet concerto for the second time. The next day the program announced one of Mozart's symphonies. The day after that, March 28, Joseph's name again appeared in large print, announcing his concerto for bassoon. The best violinists of the century—such as Rodolphe Kreutzer, to whom Beethoven dedicated his famous sonata—were eager to perform his works. In the prolific correspondence Mozart maintained with his father and others during his second stay in Paris, he never once mentions Saint-George's name. Was this a case of jealousy on the part of a composer, who was often loath to acknowledge any talent in his rivals? Very possibly. And yet Wolfgang's letters refer to musicians considerably less admired at the time than was Saint-George.

Paradoxically, for a violinist and composer, one of Saint-George's most frequently played pieces at the Concert Spirituel was his clarinet concerto, which was in particular demand on religious holidays, like Christmas and Easter, and for the season openings in February. There was hardly a spring when it was not played.[7] Saint-George was deeply grateful to the Le Duc brothers, who directed the Concert Spirituel. When Simon Le Duc died, Saint-George was chosen to conduct the concert given in his friend's memory. The *Journal de Paris* gave an account of the concert, performed on February 28, 1777: "In the middle of the adagio, the celebrated M. de Saint-George, touched by the feeling in the piece and recalling that his friend was no longer among the living, dropped his bow and started to weep. The emotion soon caught on from one player to the next, until all the members of the orchestra abandoned their instruments and gave vent to the keenest grief."

Meanwhile, his first six quartets began to take on a life of their own. Printed and distributed in 1773 by music publishers in Paris and several of the larger provincial cities, they could thus be passed from salon to salon and performed.[8] As an habitué of salons, where the guests tended to be interested in frivolity, Saint-George wrote his quartets in two movements, somewhat speedy in tempo, whereas Mozart preferred quartets of three movements with a central adagio. Gérard Gefen believes that these six quartets were "contemporaries of Haydn's 'Sun' quartets and Boccherini's opus 11 . . . and in no way inferior to them." The great musicologist Lionel de La Laurencie writes, "The writing is clear, flowing, airy. The melody strikes one as more supple, more singing, and more emotional than those of Gossec and, notably in the rondos, it clearly bears the signs of mulatto melancholy." One can hear elements of the greater works to come in these rapid movements—indications that the composer sought to combine delicacy and deep emotion.

The first and perhaps most refined of these quartets was written at the time of his half-sister's marriage into the powerful Montmorency family and, as we have seen, was dedicated to one of its members. La Laurencie describes it as "charming and tender . . . delicately enfolded in the caressing, rocking sonorities of the accompanying instruments." The first movement of this quartet already gives a foretaste of a dichotomy in Saint-George's compositions. The notes tumble out. Then, suddenly, at the turn of a phrase, comes a note that gets drawn out, like a long sob in the midst of a joyous celebration.

The quartets reveal a composer caught up in and playing with current musical customs and tastes. The future lieutenant of the hunt to the duc d'Orléans includes a "hunt" in the rondo of his sixth and last quartet. The genre was then at the height of fashion. With its charm and elegance—and scattered Vivaldi-like touches—Saint-George's *chasse* takes sly delight in piling on the pastiches. A discreet one-note accompaniment mimics the drone of the hurdy-gurdy, a relative of the viol and the instrument of the masses par excellence. A shower of pizzicatos suggests the Italian style. In the end, the music returns to the harmony of rustic pleasures with a charming minuet.

His music alternates between high spirits and profound sadness. Even in the sprightliest of his melodies, darker visions are never far off. This is most obvious in the concertos, which were his preferred domain. Here the violin could develop its melody at leisure, free to follow its own inspiration and yet supported by an orchestra whose sole purpose was to heighten its effects. The orchestra doesn't try to compete with the soloist.

As La Laurencie observes, "Saint-George's concertos impress with their gracious thematic development, which has a tinge of characteristically Creole languor and melancholy sentimentality. The composer is fond of stating his themes twice over, the second time in the lower register." Most of his concertos are constructed on the same model. There is an allegro first movement, the general theme of which is announced by the orchestra. After this *tutti,* as it was called, the violin is then free to indulge itself, aligning trills in the high register, alternating high and low notes to a hair-raising rhythm. Yet despite being one of the great violinists of his century, Saint-George never indulged in virtuosity simply for its own sake, as Giuseppe Tartini or Niccolò Paganini were fond of doing. Even in the wildest passages, the brio serves a melodic line that remains supreme and is designed to express the beauty of the instrument.

After all the joyous preparation, another Saint-George emerges from beneath the melancholy of his second movements, whose dramatic intensity and emotional charge rank them among the most moving pages in the classical repertoire, such as the largo of Antonin Dvořák's *New World* symphony and the second movement of Mozart's no. 21 (K467) piano concerto or of his clarinet concerto. One cannot help wondering at the striking similarity between the second movement of his ninth concerto (opus 8) for violin and the Albinoni *Adagio*—which was in fact not written by the early eighteenth-century Venetian master of that name, but by a twentieth-century musicologist named Remo Giazotto.[9] The same attack, same rhythm, same sweep. One might almost suggest Saint-George had a hand in this famous *pasticcio*.

Two passages in particular place these concertos among the most beautiful adagios in all music, those in the Concerto no. 2 (opus 3) and the Concerto in D Major (opus 4). Here the violin does not sing, it weeps, like a Negro spiritual—or a mother's tears. You might hear in it the lament of a man who will never find a bride to take to the altar. Perhaps it is simpler than that: the sweet sadness of being left by one lover and seeking consolation in the arms of yet another. We cannot know. Yet Saint-George gave everything of himself to others, as we are told again and again by those who knew him. The same goes for his music, freely offered to whoever is there listening, caught up in the magic of his bow.

His last movements give wing to melodies that sing, dance, and shout out the sheer joy of being alive. This is the Saint-George of the fêtes. Here the music is like Fragonard's paintings, inviting us to be swept up in a mad *farandole*, threading our way around the topiaries and statues of a magnificent English-style garden. You leap, spin, brush your lips across a bare shoulder, discreetly lift your mask to share a conspiratorial glance. You stop a moment to catch your breath and swallow a little quince liqueur or Champagne—just long enough to look around for your inamorata before being caught up once again in the whirl of the dance. Saint-George's music has all of that. It is Champagne music, a music fit to celebrate a new age. It places us either in Magnanville or in the gardens of the Palais-Royal, where his violin set both the pretty ribbon-sellers and the rugged street-porters to dancing. We could be listening with the rich people at play or with those drawing up the plans for a more just society. Saint-George's music captures an age in which the idea finally took shape that it was man's primary duty to be happy. Like a Smetana or a Grieg, Saint-George makes music pictorial. La Laurencie may have been mistaken to dub him the "Watteau of music." Saint-George arrived on the scene well after that artist's death. Given the grace of his themes and the delicacy of his musical line, he is instead far closer in sensibility to Boucher, or to the Fragonard of the *Fêtes galantes*. As suggested earlier, he might also be compared to Greuze—Diderot's favorite artist, by the way—because of the emotional intensity driving the melancholy passages in his music.

Two hundred years later, Saint-George's music seems eerily modern. It speaks to the human spirit and touches the soul, yet contains melodies that engrave themselves on the mind. Musicologists explain the enduring popularity of *The Magic Flute* by the fact that, having heard its arias only once, the spectator can hum or whistle them after the curtain has come down. This is a feat Saint-George's works can match. His melodies leave a permanent impression. The depth of his engagement with his music, whether it jumps and spins, laughs or weeps, makes him one of the heralds of Romanticism.

X

Toward a More Perfect Society

"On this thirteenth day of the twelfth month of the year five thousand seven hundred eighty of the True Light [December 13, 1780]," five high-ranking knights of the Grand Orient of France welcomed a distinguished visitor on the plaza of the Respectable Lodge of St. John of Scotland of the Social Contract. Sword in hand, they led him into the temple, where a few dozen brothers stood awaiting him, and introduced him to the order. Next, preceded by the Grand Expert and Master of Ceremonies, they escorted him through the temple to the East, where he would preside over the lodge at the side of the Worshipful Master. The distinguished brother wore decorations proclaiming him a member of the philosophical degree of the Black Eagle. He did in fact belong to the thirtieth degree of an order that had thirty-three. Applauded by the assembly of some five hundred brothers, the chevalier de Saint-George, who had come as a friend (he belonged to the *Loge des Neuf Sœurs*, or Lodge of the Nine Sisters, into which Voltaire had been initiated), mounted the three steps of the East and took his place at the right of the Altar of Oaths, a huge desk behind which sat the Worshipful Master.

Until now, Saint-George's membership in the Masonic order has been a matter of conjecture rather than fact.[1] Indeed, the only evidence for it was a sale in the Netherlands of Masonic objects—some of which could have belonged to Saint-George—and the correspondence of François Jouve, a member of the Grand Orient who was a Worshipful Master of the United Hearts Lodge in Basse-Terre, Guadeloupe. A former frigate officer, Jouve defended a lodge brother accused of marrying a woman of mixed race, writing in 1784, "Did we not have as our brother, Brother Saint-George, of the respectable Lodge of the Nine Sisters?" This assertion had at the very least to be checked to make sure it did not involve a "claim" on the part of the inhabitants of Basse-Terre, proud of sharing their birthplace with the black Don Juan, as Saint-George was dubbed at the time, particularly since Freemasons tend to annex historical figures never actually initiated into the order.

In any case, the date suggests that Saint-George was the first person of mixed race to "receive the light" in the Grand Orient of France. At that time, a period of between fifteen and twenty years was in theory necessary to move from the first degree—that of "apprentice"—to the thirtieth. Moreover, it is unlikely that because of his origins Saint-George would have been accorded any favorable treatment, such as a reduction in that time period. He was therefore most probably initiated in 1773, the year of the creation of the Grand Orient, or shortly thereafter. Masonry historian Alain Le Bihan supports the claim that Saint-George represents "the only known case of a mulatto's membership in a Parisian lodge in that century."[2]

His initiation therefore took place in secret. No records of it exist in any of the Masonic archives, the so-called "pieces of architecture," nor does "Saint-George" appear on any lodge tablet, that is, any membership roster. According to an unverified rumor, he went through the initiation "trials" with a sack over his head instead of wearing the traditional blindfold. Some brothers, potentially hostile to the presence in their midst of someone of a different race, were made to believe that this was a highly exalted dignitary of the kingdom.

Segregation extended to those of mixed race as much as it did to blacks. As Pierre-Yves Beaurepaire has noted, "The mulatto is dangerous because he is the product of the crime of nondifferentiation, the monstrous mingling of differences."[3] Indeed, most of the colonial lodges mercilessly hunted down any brother who stooped to "marry" a black woman. Some even risked jeopardizing obedience to their vows by opposing the slightest leniency in this regard. As stated by the Loge de la Paix, the Lodge of Peace, in Guadeloupe's Pointe-à-Pitre: "In the colonies a distinction is made between whites and those of mixed blood. Policy essential to the regime of the American islands has refused to allow the latter—albeit far removed from their place of origin—any social ties with the colonists, who have preserved the purity of their European blood unmixed with that of the African. These distinctions are not recognized in France but here have become indispensable."

The authorities of the Grand Orient turned a blind eye. In the home country, the Lodge revealed a far more tolerant attitude, even, in 1787, encouraging the Lodge of Barbezieux to initiate members of mixed race. However, other astonishing practices were also acceptable on French soil, such as lodges made up entirely of slave traders and owners of slaving vessels. On May 21, 1787, for example, a ship called *Le Franc-Maçon* (*The Freemason*) set sail from Le Havre to the Gold Coast to load slaves. Pierre-Yves Beaurepaire has noted that the ship's departure "seems not to have aroused the slightest emotion among the Brothers." Nor would any objections be raised to Brother Mozart's incarnation, in *The Magic Flute*, of absolute evil in the person of a man of color, Monostatos.[4] Monostatos is violent, a sexual harasser, a traitor, and a coward. If Mozart's *Singspiel* is in fact a symbolically Masonic work—which has certainly not been proved—the "Moor" remains a symbol of mistrust and suspicion.

Nevertheless, a sizable number of the members of the Société des Amis des Noirs, or Society of Friends of Blacks, that Jacques Pierre Brissot (also known as Brissot de Warville) formed in 1787 were Freemasons. Essentially they belonged to three lodges: the Social

Contract, the Olympic of Perfect Esteem, and the Nine Sisters. These were also the three Lodges to which Saint-George belonged. Five years after Saint-George's initiation, the Nine Sisters would initiate Voltaire, several months before his death. It must have been difficult for Saint-George to take part in the highly elaborate initiation rites for the philosopher. Not only were Voltaire's racial prejudices still very much alive, but many of those recruited were Voltaire's loyal followers and therefore deeply contemptuous of this half-breed.

Admission to the Freemason movement worked through connections. Mozart would not rest until he saw his father admitted, as well as his teacher Haydn. In 1773, Jean-Baptiste Boullongne-Tavernier de Préninville, Saint-George's illegitimate cousin, joined the Lodge of Reunited Friends (Jean-Baptiste would, as we have seen, become Treasurer General in the Event of War after his uncle went bankrupt). Guillaume-Pierre, the composer's father, was initiated in 1778.

Despite racist opposition, it seems inevitable that Saint-George would become a Mason. In the late eighteenth century in Europe, Freemasonry and music enjoyed a symbiotic relationship. The dictionary of Freemason musicians appended to Roger Cotte's book on the subject reveals that of the Masonic composers or performers listed, a list that covers over two centuries, two-thirds were alive during this period.[5] There are a number of reasons for the close association. First was the important part music played in Masonic rituals. At the opening and closing of meetings, the so-called "columns of harmony," led by an "architect of harmony," entertained the brothers with some instrumental or choral pieces. Initially, only wind instruments were allowed in the temples, no doubt a remnant of the lodges' military legacy. For example, a brother such as the renowned violinist Rodolphe Kreutzer learned the clarinet so he could play at the lodge. Another member, a cellist by the name of Bréval, mastered the flute for the same reason, eventually even writing music for winds (notably a concerto for flute, bassoon, and orchestra, and another for clarinet and orchestra). And one of the most beautiful pages ever composed for the oboe is indisputably the second movement of the concerto for flute, oboe, bassoon, horn, and orchestra written by François Devienne, who excelled at the cello. Lodge officers thus welcomed musicians with open arms. Sometimes they were even exempted from paying the annual fee. In other cases, as soon as they had completed their apprenticeship they were excused from regular attendance (in theory, a Mason has to attend all the meetings of his lodge), provided they were available when the Worshipful Master required them.

A second reason was that this was a time when artists traveled extensively. Mozart toured all the European capitals, both Gluck and Haydn covered thousands of miles, and many Parisian musicians divided their time between the court of Versailles and those of provincial nobles. On arriving in a city—an "Orient"—the Freemason was immediately taken in hand by his brothers and invited to meetings of the local lodge. Everything he needed to know was pointed out to him: the local tariffs, how to find lodging, addresses of patrons he might visit, and so on. For instance, François Boieldieu was initiated by the Palestine Lodge founded in the Orient of St. Petersburg. It was at the home of Brother Dietrich in Strasbourg that Brother Rouget de Lisle, initiated in Charleville in the Ardennes, would compose the "Marseillaise."

Most important, Freemasonry enabled musicians to band together in solidarity against "protectors" more than willing to exploit them, and gave them the means to be recognized solely for their talent. Mozart bore a lifelong grudge against Archbishop Colloredo for forcing him to dress as a lackey. Haydn took offense, though to a lesser extent, for being subjected by Prince Esterházy to similar treatment; he was even forced to take his meals in the kitchen (although the prince did pay him handsome sums for his compositions). Both found true dignity alongside their brothers.

Freemasonry in Eastern Europe was markedly Christian and not politically or philosophically high-minded to any great extent. In France, on the other hand, Freemasonry generally attracted progressive men such as Lafayette, Benjamin Franklin, and Voltaire,

A French family with servant in Martinique

Scenes from the Lesser Antilles: preparations for the *Bal doudou*, or "Lady's Ball" REPRINTED WITH THE KIND PERMISSION OF DR. MARCEL CHATILLON

Portrait of Wolfgang
Amadeus Mozart
© ARCHIVO ICONOGRAFICO,
S.A./CORBIS

Saint-George's long-
time adversary, the
singer Sophie Arnould
COURTESY OF THE AUTHOR

Nineteenth-century portrait of the Chevalier de Saint-George

Nineteenth-century portrait of Madame de Montesson, wife of the duc d'Orléans, organizer of the period's most dazzling salon, and patron of Saint-George

Nineteenth-century view of the Théâtre Italien

A Freemason initiation ceremony

Portrait of Louis XVI by Antoine-François Callet

The legendary fencing match held in London between Saint-George
and the Chevalière d'Eon

The Garden and Cirque at the Palais-Royal

(although as we've seen he was a Mason only in the last months of his life). Progressive thinking about the arts was in the air, particularly in the musical melting pot that Paris was at the time. As Gérard Gefen has observed, the Masons represented the desire for change, the desire for a new world. Those who were the main inspiration behind the Concert des Amateurs, whose goal was to free music from its feudal bonds, were members of the "Grand Orient." The Masonic musicians applied the Encyclopedists' belief in progress. For example, they adopted the recently invented clarinet and indeed spread its use abroad through the lodges. Soon the clarinet would be thought of as the "Masonic instrument."

They also turned orchestral forms upside down. This was the golden age of the *symphonie concertante* (very similar to the *concerto grosso*, with which it is often confused), in which, as we're seen, several instruments play "solo," accompanied by the orchestra. Thus freed from the obligation to serve as accompaniment (a task left to the orchestra), the duet, trio, or quartet offers opportunities for dialogue among instruments. This approach—vigorously exploited by François Devienne, Michel Blavet, Johann Christian Bach, and Saint-George—played a leading role in the success of the Concert Spirituel and later that of the Amateurs. The *symphonie concertante* exemplifies the refusal to make a "star" of any one soloist, who for good or for ill represented a solitary, godlike figure confronting the orchestra. Indeed, it eliminated competition among the instruments—though a certain tendency toward virtuosity might reveal itself from time to time (the Italian influence had not entirely disappeared). The new orchestral formation created an easy musical cohabitation that symbolized brotherly aspirations. The music aims to please, to impart happiness and well-being; it encourages optimism, inspires the dream of a better society. The complicity among the instruments contains a message of love and shared creative instincts. We have to wait a century and a half, for the advent of jazz and its jam sessions, to rediscover the same kind of playful genius.

In Freemasonry, transmission of knowledge was paramount. The

Mason learned and taught. When an apprentice he was trained by a master, who in turn ceaselessly pursued the course of enlightenment. According to Masonic ritual, the master would until the day he died be an "apprentice in quest of light." Thus whole schools and courses of study were created. Devienne, for example, devoted part of his life to perfecting a method for learning the flute that is still used in conservatories today. The conservatories themselves first appeared in embryonic form on the eve of the Revolution under the aegis of Brother Gossec. The composer, who was initiated after his protégé Saint-George into the Reunion of the Arts Lodge in 1781, founded an institution of musical learning that introduced a heretical innovation into French education: coeducation. For the first time, girls could get an education other than that offered by the Church. Nicolas Framery, a member of the Lodge of the Olympic of Perfect Esteem and a composer and musical historian, would next take up the torch. In these days when the cause of private property was increasingly being touted as a countermeasure to absolutism, Framery attempted to take a stand for the rights of musicians. He set up the first agency for protecting author's rights, the ancestor of SACEM, the French equivalent of ASCAP in the United States.[6] From then on, no one could pirate composers' works with impunity.

The Masons' pedagogical inclinations were carried to the point of caricature in the person of the eccentric baron de Bagge. A native of Courland, then part of Poland, the baron combed the courts of Europe in the hopes of finally seeing his talents as a violinist fully recognized. De Bagge—who claimed to be a pupil of Tartini—was a true connoisseur of the violin and a very respectable performer. He thrilled audiences by picking out scales on a single string with one finger of his left hand. But his nervous tics invariably provoked hilarity, and his pretensions antagonized more than one member of the Masonic orchestra. Whether or not he truly believed his own propaganda, he accepted without demur the somewhat ambiguous compliment paid him by King Frederick II of Prussia: "My dear Baron, I have never heard anyone play the violin as you do." In the same vein are these verses written beneath one of his portraits:

> *Faithful worshiper of the god of Harmony,*
> *His impetuous zeal will not be restrained.*
> *In the violinist's art he has no peer*
> *And none would dare to imitate him.*[7]

Brother de Bagge also conducted concerts at the Lodge of the Nine Sisters. It was in this capacity that he was called on to organize the musical segment of Voltaire's initiation ceremony at the lodge and, not long afterward, the ceremony marking his death. This was a somewhat heavy responsibility, for in the controversy between the champions of Gluck and those of Piccinni, Voltaire had sided with the former. It so happened that Piccinni, a brother of the Lodge of the Nine Sisters, was also regarded as that lodge's most prestigious as well as its most senior musician. But it was out of the question to allow the least discordant note to enter Voltaire's initiation ceremony. De Bagge therefore firmly ruled out Piccinni. The latter would have a chance to take his revenge a few months later, when the philosopher's official funeral rites were held, for he conducted the orchestra. Yet he generously chose the march from his rival Gluck's opera *Alceste.*

The baron organized, at great expense, a private concert that *The Tablets of Fame of Musicians, 1785* called "one of the finest private concerts of this capital." He made it a special point of honor to train younger artists. Roger Cotte has unearthed memoirs by the singer Giuseppe Blangini in which he describes the meeting between the baron and the violinist Kreutzer, then no more than twenty years old. "The illustrious baron, who combined with his mania for music the pretension of being a highly skilled musician, told him after hearing him play: 'My friend, this is quite good, but if you want to make a name for yourself, you must attain perfection. Come and see me three times each week and I will give you lessons; the teacher will pay the

pupil—I shall give you six francs a lesson.' " Kreutzer unfailingly
turned up on each appointed day and received his lesson and the six
francs that baron de Bagge duly handed over. After three or four
months, the baron, possibly finding Kreutzer's diligence a little much
(and a little costly), solemnly told him, "Now, my friend, you know
everything that it is possible to learn. You can play everywhere." The
well-known violinist Giovanni Battista Viotti would also benefit
from—and duly be paid for—taking lessons from Brother de Bagge.[8]

Certain lodges acquired so-called "columns of harmony" that
were in effect the equivalent of an orchestra. Thus, in the Lodge of the
Nine Sisters, the baron directed a group of thirty musicians out of 258
members. The Lodge of the Versailles court, known as "Patriotism,"
had exactly the same number of musicians out of a total of 217 brothers. In the case of St. John of Scotland of the Social Contract, the lodge
of which Saint-George was a longtime member, the "column" boasted
fifty-nine musicians (out of 494 members). Besides the usual performances at the opening and closing of the lodge ceremonies and the
musical accompaniment of their *agape*s, these groups occasionally gave
concerts exclusively for members. Once or twice a year, performances
were open to the public to help the lodge finance its charitable projects.

Brother Guillaume-Pierre de Boullongne was by no means the
only patron of the arts to go bankrupt. In the late 1770s, the economic
bad news had spread to the point that no financier was untouched.
Those patrons who managed to weather it out were forced to cut back
on their largesse, with the result that the finances of the Concert des
Amateurs, still under Saint-George's direction, began to flounder
dangerously. In 1781, at the peak of its renown, the group was forced
to close. The Freemason musicians thereupon decided to take up the
torch that same year by establishing the Olympique de la Parfaite
Estime, or the "Olympique," whose founding statutes made clear its
raison d'être: "Its principal and guiding object, for the great number
of Masons who joined to create it and also for those who have since
swelled its ranks, is to establish in Paris a concert capable, in some

respects, of recompensing the loss of the Concert des Amateurs."[9] The idea was therefore to follow the model of London's Philomusicae Apolloni, which Geminiani directed, but find someone less dictatorial than Geminiani. Saint-George, who was immediately appointed to lead the orchestra, placed too much faith in individual progress and inquisitive skepticism to act as a despot over his fellow men.

The basic concept was overtly Masonic: "No one can be a member of the Society who is not or does not intend to become a Mason." One departure from the rules was, however, tolerated: "Although the most perfect equality must reign between the members of a Lodge, yet the differences of commitment make it possible to distinguish three classes among those of Olympique." Olympian Brothers were thus divided into three groups: There were 29 "administrators," for the most part financiers and aristocrats; around 450 "subscribers," who, for a fee of 120 livres, were allowed either to attend or take part in the concerts; and 35 "free associates," who were also Masons but belonged officially to another Lodge. This last category was made up exclusively of musicians invited to join the orchestra.

The Olympique consisted of an amazing social patchwork. There was an impressive number of Farmers General, bankers, and state counselors, leading members of the new *noblesse de robe,* who owed their titles to administrative or legal offices either they or their fore-bears had bought. These men rubbed shoulders with members of the great families, headed by the duc de Chartres (the future Philippe Egalité), Grand Master of the Grand Orient who in 1785 would become the duc d'Orléans, as well as the baron de Montesquieu, the prince de Broglie, and the maréchal de Noailles. But self-made men were also admitted to this august assemblage, among them the musicians Devienne, Etienne Nicolas Méhul, and Viotti, who as we have seen was one of the most renowned violinists of his day. Therefore some Olympique brothers lived in luxurious palaces—the chevalier de Roquelaure's residence, today a government building, was located next door to Guillaume-Pierre's Hôtel du Bac; others, such as Devienne, lived in the home of a grocer on the rue Saint-Honoré. Every morning Devienne, who composed music characterized by lightness and grace, was awakened by the din of carts trundling their way to the markets, the shouts of the butcher hanging his sausages and hams on the crucifix that stood at the corner of rue Saint-Honoré and rue de L'Arbre-sec, and his landlord yelling at loiterers. In the same fashion, when the first viola, a man named Alleaume, left the hall after a concert, he would embrace the second viola, the marquis de Corberon. The former would then go home to his lodging above a tobacconist's, the marquis to his sumptuous residence on the rue de Vaugirard.

Concerts could not properly be held without a sizable feminine presence. The Olympique therefore joined forces with an "adoptive lodge" made up entirely of women, the majority of them members of the nobility. There were as yet no female or mixed lodges. But lodges could create "adoptive lodges" over whom they had authority, and eventually these became federated under the authority of a grand mistress, the princesse de Lamballe. Moreover, in 1786, something rather extraordinary occurred. On the roster of the Olympic Lodge, which bore only the names of those who were truly Freemasons, appeared three "sisters": the marquise de Corberon, whose husband was also an administrator of the lodge, Sister Galoche, and Sister Légier. In theory, the Grand Orient of France was a strictly male organization, but apparently the Orléans family, a royal family whose wishes were not to be taken lightly, devoutly wished women's inclusion.

For its part, the orchestra boasted no fewer than sixty players, joined by eleven singers, and, from time to time, other "guests." Most of the great instrumentalists of the day played in it. Some were simultaneously members of the orchestra of the Opéra, such as the violinist Guénin, who played first violin at the Académie Royale but second at the Olympique. Other first instrumentalists at the Opéra were often seconds or thirds at the Olympique, evidence of that orchestra's superiority, which had, moreover, a wide range of players, such as double basses, horns, violas, bassoons, and percussion. With as many as seventy players (when joined by guest performers), the Olympique was without a doubt the first great modern orchestral group in history.

Attracting audiences and patrons were not incompatible goals. The administrators, in fact, began meeting the lodge's financial needs out of their own pockets. Some financiers sank their fortunes in it—for example, the baron d'Ogny, who at his death in 1790 left some 100,000 livres of debt. The structuring of an orchestra into a Lodge was not merely a response to the spirit of the age; it represented something entirely new, for now the recruitment of musicians was divorced from the direct largesse of patrons. Henceforth the main criteria for support were the talents of the performer and his ability, as judged by his brotherhood, to adapt to the needs of the orchestra. Thus a player like Devienne, who had long been reluctant to leave the provinces for the maze of obsequiousness that was Parisian court life, was able to flourish in his lodge orchestra. Nonetheless, royal influence remained strong. From the moment the orchestra came into being, concerts and rehearsals were held at the Palais-Royal, which the old duc d'Orléans had left to his son. The orchestra was then obliged to decamp, for Philippe de Chartres had grand ambitions for Richelieu's former home and the noise of construction made practicing or performing impossible.

In 1785 Saint-George and his influential friends got permission to move to the Tuileries, to the Salle des Gardes, which had long been the home of the Concert Spirituel. The latter, too, had fallen victim to the financial ruin of its financiers. After alterations were undertaken to make the space more suitable for performances, an inaugural concert was held on January 11, 1786. The Olympique was forthwith judged the only orchestra of outstanding quality in Paris. Very soon it attracted spectators of note, to wit, "the queen and the princes" who sometimes came "without advance notice to attend the concerts," as Brenet notes. One wonders for whose sake Marie-Antoinette made the trip to Paris? Was it for her cousin Philippe, made duc d'Orléans in 1785, whose eccentricities apparently amused her less and less, or the princesse de Lamballe, a patroness of the orchestra? Or might it have been for the sake of the orchestra's director, who twelve years before had come to Versailles to help her with her musical education? Most probably all three. The queen would regularly show up to applaud her favorite American right up to the beginning of 1789, the year that now begins to loom over this story.

The dashing Saint-George was determined that his musicians' attire honor the caliber of the audience. In the first row those administrators who were not musicians wore formal attire. As for the players, membership in a lodge allowed them to dispense with differences in dress, which in theory were obligatory. They used the clothes of noblemen: embroidered coat with lace cuffs, sword at their side—a sign of adherence to Freemasonry as well—and a plumed hat placed next to them. Performers who rented modest apartments from shopkeepers and tobacconists were as well dressed as any marquis in the audience. This meant, as Brenet says, that the orchestra "was very fine to behold and, what was more important, no less pleasant to hear. Exactly like the group at the Hôtel de Soubise [that is, the Concert des Amateurs, which Saint-George formerly directed], it was, in addition to the professionals, composed of the most skillful amateurs in Paris. Viotti would frequently direct; often, rehearsals took place in the presence of the composers."

In 1786, Joseph was forty-seven years old. Still slim, he commanded with every gesture, and was as imposing a presence as ever. But there was something different. Over the years, the man who ten years earlier had raised the Concert des Amateurs to the rank of best orchestra in Paris, and very possibly in all of Europe, had deepened musically. His compositions were more substantial and more profound. He had learned how to master harmonies and rhythmic accompaniment. Horns, oboes, and double basses brought heightened contrast to his pieces. His clarinet concerto was still played by the Concert Spirituel, and his concerto for bassoon as well was extremely popular. He was also writing for the piano. In other words, Saint-George was no longer only a violinist who happened also to write music; he was an all-around composer and an admired orchestral director able to handle even the most dense and elaborate scores by other composers.

In that last quarter of the eighteenth century, music had become more complex. Directors capable of doing justice to works they had not themselves written were rare. In those days there was no "conductor" such as we understand the term, no separate score for the orchestra director. The director had to have the scores of his sixty musicians in his head and know how to cue each player at precisely the right moment. Having the horns, trumpets, or basses "depart" at the wrong moment would be disastrous. Thus, certain wind instruments, such as horns and clarinets, had to be "prepared" with a gesture a few seconds before their actual entrance.

As Brenet notes, "the financial health of the society not only enabled it to engage well-known virtuosi but also to make special arrangements to acquire works composed expressly by illustrious musicians." After the triumph of Haydn's *Stabat Mater* at the Concert Spirituel in 1782, and then again in March 1783, every music lover in Paris was eager for more of the composer's works, many of which had been pirated. Until 1779 Haydn was bound by his patron, Esterházy, to an exclusivity clause. Compositions that managed to make it into other countries had been secretly recopied. When his contract was renewed, Haydn was able to have Esterházy's unconscionable clause waived. Thus Saint-George was dispatched to Vienna to propose to Haydn—who would himself be initiated as a Mason a few weeks later—that he write for the Olympique.[10]

In exchange for six symphonies—roughly one hour and forty minutes of music—Haydn was offered twenty-five gold louis, plus an extra five louis for publication rights. This was a princely sum, given the modest amounts Esterházy had paid him. "What a meeting that was! And what a pity that we have no written record of it!" exclaims Smidak. "It was the meeting of two worlds. For Haydn, the world from which Saint-George came must have seemed inconceivable, beyond the horizon of his imagination."[11] One was white, but a wheelwright's son and a servant (the best-known portrait of Haydn shows him in livery) who had never left a country that had virtually no colonies, and who therefore had had no contact with people of other races. The other was black, and flaunted with natural ostentation the wealth, luxury, and refinement of his milieu. Saint-George had retained his great modesty, however, and the two men had at least one point in common. On March 26, 1783, the first part of Haydn's *Stabat Mater* had been played at the Concert Spirituel, in a musical program that had also included Saint-George's clarinet concerto. Two days later, his concerto for bassoon appeared on the same program as the second part of the *Stabat Mater*. Haydn, always carefully attentive to his reputation, was aware of all this. He also knew that if Saint-George—the director of the rival orchestra—had been chosen to appear on the same program with him at the Concert Spirituel, it was because he was considered an exceptionally gifted composer. Moreover, Saint-George's work had been performed in Vienna, as well as in London, Prague, Rome, Zagreb, Potsdam (at the court of the king of Prussia), Munich, and even in Sweden—all places where Haydn's work was admired. Music smoothed over their differences.

Between concerts in Vienna and at Esterházy's *schloss,* plus a trip to Italy, Haydn would devote two years to writing his six "Paris" symphonies. Saint-George organized rehearsals and directed their first performance in late 1787. Conscious of his international reputation and proud to see that his talents were being recognized in Paris, Haydn jumped at the chance to write for a full orchestra. The number of violins the Olympique possessed (nearly forty) was, in fact, higher than the total complement of instruments in the orchestras for which he was accustomed to writing. The ten double basses, the row of horns, and the bounty of wind instruments inspired him. Symphony by symphony, his music grew more ample, more audacious, daring to stray beyond the academic framework within which, bound to an extraordinarily rigid output by his "protector," the composer had seen his music confined. (Prince Esterházy demanded that Haydn make his orchestra play a new work each Thursday.) Not since his *Sturm und Drang* period of the early 1770s had Haydn written with such freedom.

The two "animal" symphonies (opus 82 and opus 83), *The Bear* and *The Hen,* didn't get their titles until the nineteenth century. *The Queen of France* (opus 85), on the other hand, got its title when it was penned. Marie-Antoinette never tired of this symphony, the slow movement of which includes a gentle royal rebuke, for in it the playful Haydn parodies the melodic line of a fashionable French pastoral romance that the queen adored: *La Gentille et Jeune Lisette* (Sweet Young Lisette). Many critics—and some leading Freemasons—believed they detected in this second movement a spirituality that testifies to the Masonic nature of the work.

The music's success was instantaneous. "Each time, one perceives better and therefore admires more the creation of this vast genre, which, in each of its movements, so artfully draws such rich and varied developments from a single subject," wrote the *Mercure* enthusiastically. The only jarring note in this concert of praise was that the construction work being done to adapt the Salle des Gardes for use by the Olympique orchestra had not helped the acoustics. "Monsieur Haydn's symphonies, always sure in their effects, would have been even more so if the hall were more resonant and had its narrow shape allowed the director of this concert to arrange the orchestra to better advantage," deplored the journal.

No matter. Mozart had preferred to live in Paris in poverty rather than follow his father's wishes and have his works performed at the Concert des Amateurs, then directed by Saint-George. The performance of Haydn's "Paris" symphonies established beyond question that Saint-George was the director of the first great orchestra of modern times.

XI

Prima della Rivoluzione

At least one clear winner had emerged from the Quarrel of the Buffoons: the public. Long estranged from the theaters because of the academic stiltedness of the works being presented, people started to stream back, having followed the quarrel avidly and rooted for the Italian-style heroes to kick the Greek gods off the stage. Thus throughout France an urgent need arose for theaters where these eager crowds could be accommodated. The architects required for the task were picked as carefully as the musicians. For the first time, competitions were held to decide to whom to assign the various projects.

Nothing was too fine for the goddess of Music, object of passion and veneration. One was no longer building theaters, but temples. In *The Temple of Taste*, Voltaire declares: "One day you will have no more Gothic temples; your theaters will be worthy of the immortal works put on there; new squares and public markets built beneath colonnades will adorn Paris as they did ancient Rome." And indeed, the architects Oger and Bourdet in Metz, Gabriel at Versailles, Soufflot in Lyon, Victor Louis in Bordeaux, Ledoux in Besançon, Peyre and Wailly in Paris (architects of the Odéon, at that time home to the Comédie Française) all built theaters based upon classical models. Nearly all these architects had made the pilgrimage to Rome.

The Théâtre Italien, erected where the Italian performers had their stages, soon attracted large audiences eager for the operas of Grétry and his librettist Charles Favart. The building's design lent itself to all sorts of commentary. The theater turned its back on the street (soon to be named the Boulevard des Italiens), where, every day, enthusiastic crowds swarmed around the booths and rickety stages on which Harlequin, Columbine, and Punchinello played out their familiar story. The theater designers wanted the façade to face the Palais-Royal, nerve center of Parisian cultural life, an orientation that alienated the populace of the boulevards, as we can tell from the following epigram:

> *At your first glance you can tell*
> *That this new theater is quite Italian*
> *For it is arranged in such a way*
> *That passersby must show it their behinds.*[1]

The passions aroused by the Quarrel of the Buffoons had largely subsided when Christoph Willibald Gluck stepped out of the mail-coach that had brought him from Rome to Paris in the fall of 1773. French audiences had come to think of the Italian *commedia* as a little too lightweight, and were in the mood for more demanding works. Rousseau, never one to pass up an opportunity to toot his own horn, took credit for instigating—belatedly, perhaps—the Austrian composer's trip to France. In actual fact, Gluck owed his invitation solely to Marie-Antoinette, who had not forgotten him from the days when she had been archduchess of Austria and he her teacher. He had scored a resounding success at the Viennese court in 1762 with the first performances of *Orpheus and Eurydice*.

Far from underestimating French national sentiment, Gluck had studiously paved the way for his arrival by sending an article to the *Mercure* a few months earlier. In it he outlined his musical intentions: "I plan to produce music fitting for all nations and so help banish the ridiculous notion of national musicians." After making sure that this profession of faith, which was revolutionary for the time, had been well received, he set about flattering Rousseau, who since the so-called Quarrel of the King's and Queen's Corners had acquired the reputation of being able to make or break musical careers. He claimed that only he was truly capable of unraveling the secrets of the cabal. Gluck spared no effort to secure the philosopher's good graces, citing "the sublimity of his abilities and the sureness of his taste," which, he swore, had "filled him with admiration."

As regards Marie-Antoinette, Gluck would have an easier time of it. The dauphine was extremely nostalgic for her Austrian childhood, and invoked it endlessly in her letters. Moreover, she was by nature "moved by the desire to please, loving her friends with an unquestioning devotion."[2] Thus at the first performance of Gluck's *Iphigenia in Aulis* in 1774, Marie-Antoinette, now the queen of France, applauded with such uninhibited enthusiasm that her retinue of ladies in waiting felt obliged to acclaim the composer in turn. For "Chevalier" Gluck, a bright future in Paris seemed assured.

Indeed, the composer did not need to deploy his arsenal of seduction. His talent was enough to guarantee him a prime spot in the operatic landscape. When the director of the Académie Royale, Antoine Dauvergne, opened the score of the first act of *Iphigenia,* he exclaimed, "Such a work is bound to kill off all the old French operas!" Were Gluck to banish French operatic works from the repertoire, he was honor-bound to replace them. Dauvergne therefore threatened not to include *Iphigenia* in the program unless its creator promised to write operas that would replenish the repertoire. Gluck vowed he would do that, for he knew he had a recipe for success. He had managed to create a blend of French musical tradition, Italian melodic simplicity, and English sentimentality. His operas were built around three simple rules: a linear plot that could be easily grasped by the audience, an attractively written libretto, and a score that stuck closely to the dramatic action and served to enhance it.

Things clicked immediately. Intent upon winning over the Parisian audience, Gluck asked the librettist Moline (the author of the verses accompanying Mather Brown's famous portrait of Saint-George) to write a French version of the Orpheus story. It was a triumph. Rousseau attended every performance from start to finish. In the salons people hummed its arias, with *"J'ai perdu mon Euridice"* ("I have lost my Eurydice") becoming the hit of the season. Even crusty old Voltaire proclaimed his admiration for the favorite of the queen he detested. By contrast, *Alceste* had a more difficult time of it when it first opened in 1776. However, after being reworked by Gossec, that opera was successful in its turn.

Such triumphs were bound to arouse bitterness and Gluck didn't always help matters. He was capricious, tyrannical, even odious at times. In addition to everything else, he was a singing teacher. To a female singer who tried to stand up to him he cried: "Mademoiselle, I am here to produce *Iphigenia*. If you want to sing, well and good; if you don't want to, that's up to you. I shall go to the queen and tell her: It is impossible to put on my opera."[3]

One day the court watched, stupefied, as Gluck conducted an opera with a nightcap pulled down on his head, which was his way of showing how much he despised wigs. He also dared to cancel, at the last moment, a performance that Louis XVI and Marie-Antoinette, together with the court, were to honor with their presence. Such an affront would have sent any other artist to the Bastille. Not Gluck: He had the support of the queen. She found his effronteries amusing.

Nevertheless, only a few years into her reign, the "young queen" who had received such adulation from her subjects had become "the Austrian woman." Her formerly charming scorn for etiquette annoyed the highborn, while her arrogant ignorance about the state of the country and the wretchedness of her subjects soon earned her their hatred. Gluck, another Austrian after all, was seen as her henchman. Against him was pitted the gentle Italian composer Niccolò Piccinni, who despite his professed admiration for Gluck became the champion of the anti-Gluckists. Twenty-five years after the Quarrel of the Buffoons, another operatic quarrel erupted. This time the situation was nearly absurd. It was not a matter of fighting for or against a musical style. The plots of Gluck's operas were conceded to exhibit a perfectionism and excellence that the Italian's plots sometimes lacked. Indeed, the two musicians might be said to complement each other. Nonetheless, propelled by the winds of history, they became enemies. *Ritter*—"Chevalier"—Gluck was targeted for the simple reason that he was Marie-Antoinette's favorite. The right to be a foreigner, granted to Piccinni, was refused his rival. Since the king thought as the queen did and thereby absorbed part of her unpopularity, hostility to the whole regime became crystallized against the unfortunate Austrian composer.

How far had things come since the letter Rousseau sent to d'Alembert in 1757, in which he wrote that Greek and Roman bread and circuses were the surest way to keep the people from criticizing their government. Now the stage was a flimsy screen between the people's anger and its monarchy. At the worst, theater intensified the popular rage. Marie-Antoinette's blunders—her applause and silly demonstrations of partisanship—merely kindled the hatred of the anti-Gluckists. The attacks on the Viennese musician took a bitter turn. Only the truly philosophical or deeply musical would try to convince a hysterical public to distinguish between genius and chauvinism.

Yet this atmosphere of civil war had at least one positive result. Once again the public flocked to the theaters, becoming better informed, more discerning. A theatrical press developed. From their artistic criticism, gossip writers acquired a taste for a freedom hitherto unknown to them. Treason against the queen led straight to the prison cell, but who would risk throwing into the Bastille a columnist who was only doing his job when he slammed a musician—even when these critiques no longer even bothered to disguise the fact that they were political attacks?

The "theater mania" that swept across France during the last quarter of the century gave rise to notions of pre-Revolutionary inspiration. By the late 1770s, all the stage standbys—artificial orange groves, rose gardens, bushes, and vine swings—were locked away in the prop shop, where they would remain for a good hundred years, yielding their place on the stage to contemporary themes and comedies of manners. No doubt Marie-Antoinette had not understood she was lighting a fuse when she advanced the beribboned cause of the pastoral. Partly because of it, however, the nobility lost its monopoly over matters of the heart. No longer were you noble simply by birth; you became noble through the nobility of your sentiments. By focusing upon ordinary people, now permissible thanks to the fashion launched at the Petit Trianon, art could present men and women capable of experiencing and inspiring strong feeling, and young people who could legitimately rebel against the established order, beginning with the outmoded immutability of patriarchal society. As the critic Hippolyte Taine would later put it, the theater of the eighteenth century "prepared man for the world as the world prepared man for the theater."

It was at this point that Saint-George launched into opera composition. His first attempt brought him in touch with Marie-Jeanne Riccoboni, a successful novelist who fifteen years before had made a stunning debut on the decidedly masculine literary scene by writing a twelfth part to Marivaux's unfinished *Marianne*. This pastiche, which fooled many connoisseurs, gained her a notoriety that grew with the appearance of each new novel. Together with a sensibility that managed never to descend into pure mawkishness, a few moralizing formulas in the vein of the English novel reinforced her place in the literary world.

One of Madame Riccoboni's most fervent admirers was that shy artillery captain, protégé of Montalembert and sometime guest at the

Hôtel du Bac, Choderlos de Laclos. From his garrison at Besançon and later in Grenoble and Valence, the timid Laclos, who had had a few poems published in the Parisian literary gazettes, carried on a correspondence with the successful lady novelist. Soon he obtained permission to base an opera libretto on the bestseller Madame Ricoboni had published twelve years before, entitled *The Story of Ernestine, or the Misfortunes of a Young Orphan*. On the stage it would be simply *Ernestine*. The plot was hardly original. The marquis de Clémangis, madly in love with a young sixteen-year-old girl, an impoverished orphan, arranges for her to become his drawing teacher. After many twists of plot, the nobleman marries the pretty orphan and they live happily ever after. Around a story just as anemic, Beaumarchais and later Da Ponte would construct a real drama, embedded with a number of political in-jokes, at which the audience—highly vocal at the time—applauded thunderously. (But Beaumarchais did not write *The Marriage of Figaro* until 1784, seven years after *Ernestine*.) Laclos's experience was far different, at least when he first tried his hand at it. Given that he was confined to Besançon, the artistic communication between him and his composer was restricted to an exchange of letters. On receiving the text, Saint-George urgently sought the help of a writer he knew, one Desfontaines, in making a few changes. Desfontaines (whose real name was François-Guillaume Fouques) did what he could while Saint-George composed the score. Whether he improved upon Laclos's adaptation or botched it is impossible to judge, since both Laclos's original and Desfontaines's revisions have been lost.

Though the work no longer exists, the criticism of it survives. It was devastating. On July 18, 1777, a private performance given in Madame de Montesson's theater was a resounding success. Clearly the marquise and her guests were more drawn to the music of their friend Saint-George than they were to the play. But the second performance at the Théâtre Italien the next day was a near-disaster. Marie-Antoinette was partly to blame. Laclos had introduced a country bumpkin into the play, a coachman whose only function was to shout

"Halloo! Halloo!" while cracking his whip. Whenever he appeared, the queen, ever eager to be the center of attention, cried "Halloo!" and clapped her hands. And the court—including the comte d'Artois and his wife—took up the chorus, crying "Halloo!" Marie-Antoinette may have foolishly started the good-humored applause out of her friendship with Saint-George, but the effect was to send the play plunging headlong into ridicule. It did not help that another incident in a box close by was distracting the spectators. La Morlière, whom we might remember Saint-George had once roughed up at La Boëssière's fencing school, began yawning noisily enough to distract the whole audience. Unable to stand it any longer, and despite La Morlière's reputation as a swordsman, a spectator left the theater and returned with a carrot, which he proceeded to shove down the man's throat. A fight ensued and a duel was fought the next morning, in the course of which La Morlière was shot dead.

For Saint-George this was but small consolation, given that the queen idiotically hailed her coachman on leaving the theater with "To Versailles! Halloo!"[4]

During this period, as we have seen, the libretto was considered the main part of what was called the "play," as if referring to classical theater. Thus, when on the following day critics slashed the libretto to ribbons, a rout turned into a massacre. "One could hardly pick a more agreeable subject. One could hardly disfigure it in more gloomy fashion," grumbled the *Correspondance littéraire*. The baron de Grimm was scarcely kinder: "Messieurs de Laclos and Desfontaines have deemed that the basic subject, more interesting than comic, needed to be enlivened; they added a valet role that is a masterpiece of platitude and bad taste. Even Pergolesi's best effort would have been unable to produce such an outrage."

But Grimm, who by the way could be just as hard on his "protégé," Mozart, did not approve of the music much, either: "M. de Saint-George's composition, albeit ingenious and clever, often seemed to lack theatrical effect."

The *Mercure*, on the other hand, thought Saint-George had made the best possible use of his libretto. It noted that there were "some very pleasing duets, some brilliant arias, some ensemble pieces" that bespoke "a good style, with much expertise, facility, and talent." Bachaumont opined that Saint-George "must have felt that an excellent score adapted to a flat and execrable comic opera lost all its value."

Only the *Journal de Paris* forecast a bright future for the hapless *Ernestine*. However, its prediction was based solely on the quality of the music. "Several pieces of music, among them the first two dialogued duets, seem to promise true success."[5] This turned out not to be the case, for the next day Saint-George apparently did feel what Bachaumont had ascribed to him about compromising his reputation with a feeble libretto, and withdrew his play. As for Laclos, he apologized outright to Madame Riccoboni for having butchered her book. Later, after the fame of *Dangerous Liaisons*, he looked back on the failure with detachment, attributing it to the novelist's work, which, he noted, "was not cut out for the theater."

Generally speaking, however, Saint-George emerged from the experience with head held high. In the space between writing two orchestral scores, he set about composing another opera, *La Chasse* (The Hunt), together with Desfontaines, the writer who had attempted to make Laclos's mishmash into an opera. Desfontaines was a striking figure, and very representative of his day. A brilliant Jesuit, he quickly rose to become the editor of *Journal des savants*, which was enough of an achievement for him to be named the curate of Thorigny, a small domain near Fontainebleau, and then was promoted to a parish in Paris. There he became popular in philosophical circles for his encyclopedic knowledge and his tendency for debauchery. His rise would be temporarily halted by a short prison sentence, for sodomy. Voltaire took up his cause. Indeed, although he could be cruel to those who threatened to outshine him in the cafés, Voltaire was particularly generous to Desfontaines. The future author of *Treatise on*

Tolerance had difficulty believing that a mild deviance in sexual mores should lead to a dungeon. Voltaire finally obtained a pardon for the miscreant. However, Voltaire somehow assumed that Desfontaines's gratitude was owed to him *ad vitam eternam,* and that therefore he could make jokes among high society at the expense of the gay clergyman. His gibes quickly reached Desfontaines's ears. A furious polemical exchange followed in a number of magazines and journals, including the *Journal des savants.* Voltaire responded with a ferocious pamphlet entitled *Le Préservatif*—the title being a pun involving "condom"—which was not written in what one might call the best of taste. Desfontaines started a liaison with the abbé Gaumé, the priest at Taverny; together they wrote a pamphlet lambasting Voltaire, entitled *The Voltairomania.*

Voltaire's friends being the enemies of Saint-George, the latter would have been naturally drawn to the colorful Desfontaines. Although much admired, philosophical treatises did not pay the bills and Desfontaines was forced to earn his living copying musical scores. In 1776 Saint-George employed him as a copyist. Charmed by his ready wit, Joseph introduced him to Gossec, who engaged him to write a libretto. Shortly thereafter, Desfontaines became secretary to the duc des Deux-Ponts (grandfather of King Ludwig of Bavaria), at whose home Saint-George was a frequent guest, then librarian to the comte de Provence, the future Louis XVIII. His passion for the theater nearly got him led to the guillotine when in 1793 he had the hero of his last play, *The Chaste Suzanne,* say: "You are her accusers, you cannot also be her judges." The speech was singularly ill timed, the trial of Louis XVI having begun in earnest, and it was quoted in all the newspapers. Thrown into jail, Desfontaines freed himself by composing a brilliantly witty song celebrating the Commune.

The plot Desfontaines had devised for *The Hunt* followed a trend in fashion at the time: that of looking to the peasantry for those virtuous heroes who might embody humanity's grand aspirations. The painter Greuze had paved the way in 1773 with *The Broken Jug,* reinforcing it in 1777 with *The Ungrateful Son*, a painting that Diderot exalted as a symbol of the age. Desfontaines might have found a more original theme than this somewhat shopworn story. The good Mathurin is head over heels in love with Colette, the daughter of a vine-grower named Thomas. But the latter refuses to give her away, hoping to make a better match. Mathurin thereupon adopts the ruse of disguising himself as the majordomo of a certain marquis. Passing by during a hunt, the marquis takes the two lovebirds under his wing. Mathurin can marry the girl, and for good measure is taken into the marquis's service, first to help and then shortly thereafter to replace his old majordomo.

The moral of this light rustic comedy is that lovers from the lower classes experience the same torments as those from the upper classes. It was time for the crowned heads to listen to and understand the common people, who could be every bit as astute and as capable of repartee as their social betters. In short, all the ingredients were there to make *The Hunt* a triumph, even if it was not exactly a masterpiece. It was given its first performance on October 12, 1778, at the Comédie Italienne. Bachaumont wrote that it "attracted a prodigious influx of people and was tumultuous in the extreme." Indeed the comic opera was peppered with double-entendres and risqué jokes. One example is where young Rosette, Colette's sister, who spies on her sister's lovemaking while hidden behind a bush, calls out to Mathurin:

> *I am only the little sister*
> *And don't know what love is;*
> *But I too on the soft green grass*
> *Would like to receive the rose.*

And when the marquise questions the pert Colette on how she spends her time, the answer comes naturally: "Mornings I make the beds and evenings I make love." Each night such sauciness was greeted uproariously.

The *Journal de Paris* reported that the opera was "heartily applauded." Such was its success, in fact, that four days after the premiere the troupe was asked to go to Marly to play before the king, the queen, and the entire court. It was a triumph. Louis XVI issued an "express command" to his printer that the libretto be engraved. With this royal blessing, the opera had a successful run at the Comédie Italienne. Grimm sounded the only jarring note in the chorus of praise, stating that the public found "gaiety, some pleasing touches, some happy strokes, but also tedious passages, imitations, and reminiscences."

"Imitations" seems a rather surprising thing to say in a period in which everyone copied everyone else. As the Italian composer Alberto Savinio pointed out a century and a half later, Mozart's genius did not appear *ex nihilo*. Savinio's theory is that Mozart was born and grew up in a musical "garden" whose finest plants, Haydn, Gluck, and Stamitz, helped him to flourish.[6] Mozart himself explains, in a letter to his father dated June 12, 1778, how, in order to ingratiate himself with French audiences, he had included a few fashionable phrases in his Paris symphony, commissioned for the Feast of Corpus Christi on June 18. Saint-George's music was without doubt in tune with the musical vogues of his day. But he was far less likely than any other composer to outright copy works by his contemporaries, and for a very good reason. As the most prestigious orchestra director of his time, he knew that the composers who entrusted their scores to him would never forgive even the slightest plagiarism. Moreover, he was already too vulnerable because of racial prejudice to risk arousing controversy. That was something that Grimm, the minister plenipotentiary of the duke of Saxe-Gotha and a close friend of Voltaire's, knew well; he himself betrayed a hint of racism that would later become far more apparent. As for Grimm's musical proficiency, today it is taken with more than one grain of salt. It was very likely to him that Mozart was alluding when he denounced the "brutes and beasts" he found all around him in Paris. Grimm shoved Wolfgang unceremoniously into the coach for Vienna even though he was supposed to have been serving as his protector.

Two years after the success of *The Hunt*, Saint-George embarked on yet another operatic work. Intended for the Opéra, *L'Amant anonyme* (The Anonymous Lover) was an adaptation of a play by Madame de Genlis that had been well received. A few months earlier, at the instigation of Madame de Montesson, Saint-George had been made the duc d'Orléans's lieutenant of the hunt. He was thus paying tribute to his new protectors, for Félicité de Genlis, the former mistress of duc Philippe de Chartres—the duc d'Orléans's son—was none other than the niece of the marquise de Montesson. In fact, Saint-George was almost literally snatched up by the Orléans clan. In addition, the duc de Chartres was, as everyone knew, his lodge brother.

The Anonymous Lover had its premiere on March 8, 1780, probably in Madame de Montesson's elegant theater. The two-act comedy includes an overture and a finale—a general *contredanse*, or "country dance"—scored for instruments playing *con brio*. Saint-George took a sly pleasure in alternating sixteenth notes and dotted notes in his ballet music, giving the dances a light, skipping rhythm. The "ariettas," on the other hand, with their long recitatives, express deep melancholy, and that is the prevailing tone of this delicate, elegant work. Valcour, a wealthy aristocrat, is secretly in love with the beautiful Léontine, whose confidant he has become since her husband left her. Not daring to declare his love openly, he anonymously sends her flowers, presents, and passionate love letters. Léontine's heart is soon torn between Valcour's gentle, reassuring presence and the passion that she reads in her anonymous lover's letters. The dilemma is resolved when she finds out that the two are actually one and the same person. Refined and modest, Félicité de Genlis's Valcour bears little resemblance to the Valmont of Laclos's *Dangerous Liaisons*. Yet each is highly representative of the period.[7]

Four years later, Saint-George added another opera to his repertoire, *Le Droit de seigneur*. Its librettist, according to reviews, was none other than Beaumarchais himself. Today all that survives of the work is an aria published at the time by Jean-François La Harpe in his newspaper. This critic who did his utmost to stifle every instance of artistic creativity in Paris—so much so that he was dubbed "the Sepulcher"—actually did something useful for once in his life.

The early 1780s saw a noticeable decline in Saint-George's operatic output. Directing the Olympique orchestra, as well as negotiating with Haydn and the many other composers who wrote for the lodge, left him very little time to apply himself to a task as onerous as composing operas. He would also disappear more and more frequently, either on his own or to accompany his "master" and friend Philippe d'Orléans on trips that grew ever more mysterious. Nonetheless, he continued to compose songs, *romances*, bringing to this popular form innovations that would help spread his fame across Europe. Each melody could be accompanied equally well by an orchestra, piano, harp, or simple guitar. Saint-George's *romances* were performed everywhere—in the great concert halls, the salons, in the streets, even in coaches. For instance, the actress Louise Fusil, who after the Revolution traveled all over Europe with her guitar, would entertain her traveling companions by singing her friend's *romances*.

In 1787, after several years of very limited operatic production, Saint-George returned to the genre. A trip to London had undoubtedly provided inspiration. He engaged an experienced librettist named Desmaillot, who had been writing for the Italians up to that time as well as for Madame de Montesson's theater, which often put on "arietta plays." The collaboration soon resulted in *La Fille garçon* (The Girl-Boy). The heroine of the story is the poor Rosanne, whose father and elder brother have been killed in the war. To avoid losing her last son, his mother dresses him and brings him up as a girl. Given that it involved a boy in drag and for good measure contained an implied denunciation of the horrors of war, the plot created a scandal. Yet the status quo is preserved. Rosanne, the girl-boy, ends up marrying a real young lady, the young Nicette. First performed at the Comédie Italienne—like the majority of Saint-George's operas—from the start it scored a resounding success with the public. Audiences loved its mixture of seriousness and gaiety, as well as the way it thumbed its nose at the censors. Orthodox critics fulminated against what they judged to be a masterpiece of bad taste. "The subject is not well chosen," decreed the *Journal de Paris* of August 18, 1787, the day after the premiere. The *Journal général de France* grumbled about "the ease with which the so-called 'Italians' take on mediocre works and present them to the public." In the view of the critics, the opera was once again saved by the music. The many sung pieces "generated" by Saint-George were "loudly applauded," admitted the *Journal de Paris*. Its rival was of the opinion that only the music prevented the opera from being a total flop. And it added apropos of the composer: "The success he has obtained must be a highly gratifying encouragement to enrich the theater with his creations."[8]

The lowest critical blow was delivered by Jacob Heinrich Meister, coauthor with Grimm of the *Literary Correspondence*, a friend of Diderot's, and an admiring disciple of Voltaire. "This work is better written than any other by M. de Saint-George," he conceded. "And yet it also appears quite lacking in invention. This calls to mind an observation which nothing has yet gainsaid, namely that if nature has served mulattos in a particular manner by giving them a marvelous aptitude for practicing all the arts of imitation, she seems nevertheless to have denied them that flash of sentiment and genius which alone produces new ideas and original conceptions."[9]

The great minds of the French Enlightenment could no longer deny the black composer a talent that was being recognized across Europe. All that was left was to accuse him of imitation. Caught up in their pettiness, neither Grimm nor Meister took the trouble to pinpoint which work or composer might have served Saint-George as inspiration. Actually, in contrast to Rousseau, who relied heavily on assistance in writing his opera *The Village Soothsayer*, Saint-George was surely the last to turn for help to a *nègre*, the French term for "ghostwriter." His rivals, and even more so his protectors, would never have forgiven him. Of that, Voltaire's two cronies, Grimm and Meister, were very well aware.

It was in Lille, then caught up in the turmoil of revolution, that Saint-George would mount his last opera, *Guillaume tout cœur* (Big-Hearted William), the libretto and score of which are both lost. The work would next be played in Paris, during the Revolution. But he would not be there to direct it.

XII

The Chevalier and the Chevalière

In the early 1770s the house of Orléans was on the brink of breaking apart. It was not political differences that estranged the duc d'Orléans from his son Philippe, duc de Chartres. Both father and son felt equally depressed and helpless as they witnessed the financial collapse of the regime, and the discredit Louis XV was bringing down on the monarchy toward the end of his reign. Absolutism was repugnant to each duke, and both refused to take part in the installation of the new parliament, following the king's decision to exile all opposition: Their two chairs, placed within just a few yards of the royal throne, remained empty throughout the ceremony. Philippe even had the temerity to go out and get cheered by the crowd on the boulevards. Each man welcomed intellectuals and scholars to his home, and was already contemplating the reforms he believed indispensable for the country. On Philippe's advice, his father had agreed to tone down considerably the extravagant way of life of the house of Orléans. He also tried to change minds at court, insisting that the people were being crushed by poverty and could no longer tolerate the ostentatious display of royal wealth. But in vain.

Though they were open to modern ideas of liberty and justice, these princes of the blood were nonetheless still sticklers for etiquette. The duc de Chartres could not tolerate his father's infatuation with the marquise de Montesson, whom he judged to be an *arriviste* and schemer. Montesson made what she thought was a clever move by bringing to Paris her charming niece, Félicité de Genlis, to use as a pawn in the young duke's game. It came to naught: Philippe fell head over heels in love with the fascinating young woman from the provinces who, far from being her aunt's dupe, was very much her own person.

On July 28, 1773, the incident that had been brewing for months burst open. Against his son's advice, the duc d'Orléans had obtained from a wearied Louis XV permission to marry the marquise de Montesson. As hard as his son tried to accept this, he believed that any matter affecting the future of the junior branch of the royal house should have been submitted for his approval. He also did not believe the ambitious marquise's promise not to claim the title of duchesse. On the contrary, he was convinced that once again she would be able to twist his father around her little finger. During the crisis, tensions ran high, father and son communicating only through intermediaries. Excelling in this ambassadorial role was Saint-George, who was of course a lodge brother of the duc de Chartres but had also served the duc d'Orléans. He was, in addition, adept at maneuvering among the women involved, endeavoring to bring them together as much as possible. Both aunt and niece prided themselves on a particular love of the theater; therefore Saint-George pored over the repertoire to come up with plays in which they might appear together without one eclipsing the other. His efforts would be crowned by a production of Madame de Genlis's *The Anonymous Lover* in the marquise's theater. And reconciliation would be achieved in 1781, when the duc d'Orléans entrusted the keys of the Palais-Royal to his son, having chosen to lead a more retiring life.

For his part, the duc de Chartres became more and more attached to this mulatto with the golden touch. Though in 1779 Saint-George had been appointed the duc d'Orléans's lieutenant of the hunt and increasingly found favor with Madame de Montesson, he found Philippe's company highly stimulating. Philippe was indeed a charismatic figure. As tall and slim as his father was rotund and clumsy, he was a keen fencer (the old man hardly dared unsheath his épée). And he was at ease in women's company, whereas his father foundered in awkward shyness. Yet Philippe owed these very attributes in part to his father. The older duke, the son of a musician of note, had insisted that Philippe's tutor, Louis Carmontelle, give him an education that combined physical exercise with the arts and sciences. The young duke carried out to general satisfaction his duties as a prince of the blood, each day handing the king his shirt at the ceremonies of the *lever* and *coucher*. He was a good huntsman and danced elegantly. However, having reached his twentieth year, the handsome young man had still not shown the slightest interest in women. Suspecting him of homosexual tendencies, the father decided to take his son's sexual education in hand. As mentioned earlier, he summoned one of the dancers of the Opéra, Rosalie Duthé, who was only fifteen years of age but had already earned a reputation for expertise in these matters. The rewards would ensure "La Duthé's" fame and fortune.[1]

Brought by sedan to her apartments, Philippe set about making up for lost time. His father instructed a police lieutenant named Marais to make sure that the young instructress's education was bearing fruit. Marais trailed the young duke into the most famous brothels. His report is edifying: "The Duc de Chartres started at the house of La Brissaude. He entered and she presented him with the tastiest morsel at her disposal. This was Mademoiselle Lavigne, known as Durancy, who had the pleasure of leading off His Highness. . . . She found the Prince extremely crude, lacking in all delicacy and swearing like a horse-driver. Several of the young ladies found him so, and everything points to his being at bottom a libertine of the lewdest sort."

The prince soon acquired a "little house" at number 10 rue Saint-

Lazare, where, together with his friends from the nobility, he received the girls the good Madame Brissaude provided. Not long afterward he found another *séjour de volupté,* or "pleasure stay," to use the policeman's expression, at number 2 rue Blanche, which was much larger and more richly decorated. With his friend Fitz-James, the duke of Berwick, Philippe loved arranging "widows' suppers." The walls were hung with black, the only people admitted being women attired in nothing but a flimsy chemise of black lace. The policeman, Marais, was the only one to be shocked. The court, on the other hand, lapped up the reports written by this precursor of the morality brigade—of whose existence, by the way, Philippe was apparently unaware. "The excesses which the Duc de Chartres indulged in each day were regarded as actions laudable for his age and rank, as a rightful use of his time and fortune," wrote one chronicler.[2]

Nonetheless, Marais was shrewd enough to deduce that "for such a person to reform, one hopes that he might truly fall in love with a good woman who would have sufficient influence over him to oblige him to adopt the tone of a gentleman and to stop using terms that would make the basest creature blush." Such a woman would be Félicité de Genlis. Their liaison, which lasted two years, rapidly transformed the duke, at least in the manner in which he expressed himself. The libertine did not suddenly vanish. But the sexual horse-driver became a Don Juan and aesthete, to the extent of receiving in his home musicians, philosophers, and savants.

Philippe remained a close friend of Madame de Genlis after their relationship ended in 1773. He even braved interdictions and accusations by entrusting her with the education of the two sons that, according to rumor, they had had together. Her appointment to this task created a scandal, for it was the first time that a woman was engaged to act as tutor to children of royal blood. Furthermore, she had the audacity to revolutionize the young princes' education by making them take long nature walks to teach them the natural sciences, encouraging them to study physics and other sciences, and initiating them into the theater. All these things Madame de Genlis would later include in her treatises on children's education. That impenitent misogynist Rousseau must have turned in his grave.

Philippe won wide public acclaim in July of 1778 by commanding the fleet that repulsed the English navy in the Atlantic near Ouessant, an island off the Breton coast. He had also started to amuse the public with his devilish pranks and eccentricities. On a bet he rode naked on horseback all the way from Paris to Versailles. He organized banquets in the middle of Lent. And, in 1784, he was daring enough to try and travel from Paris to Orléans in a balloon, before the attempt was made to cross the Channel. He did not succeed, though he did manage to set a new altitude record of 9,000 feet. Later, without hesitating, he dove into icy waters to save the life of his jockey.

Philippe and Saint-George seemed made for each other. It couldn't have mattered less to the prince that he was lampooned for his friendship with a slave's son. He was only too delighted to enjoy the frequent company of a composer whose talent flattered him, and to be able whenever he wished to touch foils with an experienced and formidable fencer (especially when his opponent had the good taste to lose—discreetly—when the occasion demanded).

The dandy of color and the duke had yet another point in common: a fascination with England, which, in those days, was deemed a free country. In Saint-George's case, Anglomania was part of a clearly identifiable social current. Anglophiles were to be found chiefly among the new moneyed aristocracy, which envied the liberalism flourishing across the Channel and railed against tradition-bound French society. Both the duc d'Orléans and the duc de Chartres were beacons for this enlightened nobility, watching in despair as the French monarchy dug its own grave day by day with exasperating unconcern. The more Louis XVI proclaimed his hostility to "perfidious Albion," the more ostentatious the house of Orléans was in its embrace of things British. Horses, dogs, carriages, clothes, furniture—

everything Philippe surrounded himself with had to come from England. "Look at you, still dressed like a stablehand," the king would greet the duke regularly once the latter had moved to Versailles. Marie-Antoinette felt even less fondness for the England craze. The London tabloids already making the rounds mercilessly attacked her private life and accused her of the worst adulteries. A friend of England could not but agree with—perhaps even be an abettor of— these scurrilous writings. Thus the queen, formerly fascinated by her cousin, became one of his bitterest enemies.

As soon as peace was sealed with England in 1783, the duc de Chartres asked Louis XVI for permission to travel to London. He bought a house at 35 Portland Place, though it was hardly ever used. Indeed, each of his Channel crossings had to be submitted for the king's approval. After 1785 the king granted them more readily. For one thing, on his father's death Philippe had become duc d'Orléans, thus first prince of the blood. For another—for the moment, at any rate—Louis XVI was too respectful of etiquette to refuse his cousin's requests. Moreover, the new duc d'Orléans had gotten on intimate terms with the Prince of Wales, heir to the English crown. The new-found friendship would be useful in keeping the peace. The duke felt that having to make these requests was a humiliation. He would later say that he was determined to attend the Estates General "only when there was discussion of individual freedom, so that I might add my vote for a law which would ensure that when I fancied going to spend the night at Le Raincy [his country seat] I would not be sent, despite my wishes, to Villers-Cotterêts [the Orléans family château]; that when I wanted to leave for London, Rome, or Peking, nothing would stand in my way."

Saint-George's repeated absences during this period set tongues wagging. Nothing the chevalier did went unobserved. He was a fixture in the Palais-Royal gardens—newly laid out by Philippe—which had become a bustling microcosm of the whole of Paris society life, and the focus of all gossip and rumor. One such rumor was that Saint-

George was an agent of the duke, who was plotting against the king. The future Philippe Egalité was doubtless more concerned with conceiving of ways to liberalize society than with taking his cousin's place on the throne. For one thing, he was too fond of travel to appreciate the idea of being shut up in a palace. The new duc d'Orléans was certainly the focal point of the "Genlis clan" at the Palais-Royal that included, among others, Jacques Pierre Brissot, that future member of the National Convention, the duc de Lauzun, and Alexandre Cagliostro. At Bellechasse, Madame de Genlis received, rather more discreetly, Camille Desmoulins, Jérôme Pétion, Bertrand Barère, and many others who would play leading roles in the Revolution.

The suspicions regarding Saint-George came to a head early in 1787 when the duke arranged to be officially accompanied to London by his "black Don Juan," as Saint-George was still known at the Palais-Royal. Saint-George took rooms in Grenier's Hotel, one of the most luxurious establishments in the capital. In no time, he became an object of intense curiosity. Fencers, musicians, and hangers-on of all kinds swarmed into the hotel's dining room to seek him out. Saint-George was a generous host; champagne and burgundy flowed freely. His favorite haunt in London was the fencing school of Henry Angelo, who would quickly become his friend and later one of his biographers. Saint-George's reputation as a fencer had long before preceded him across the Channel. Now the leading practitioners of the art jostled for the chance to take him on. In early April, when Saint-George was parrying the thrusts of Fabien, one of the best foil experts of the day, the Prince of Wales arrived on the scene. The bull-like roars with which this mulatto punctuated his attacks amused the heir to the throne. He requested the honor of crossing swords with the man. Not surprisingly, the latter declared himself impressed by his royal adversary's grace and talent.

Saint-George thus rapidly became one of the leading personalities in London. In the evenings he was sought after for his bow, during the day for his sword. Angelo's famous fencing school was always packed when his friend was there. The price of seats for the tournaments was prohibitively expensive so that sizable purses could be given to the competitors. Despite his winnings, Saint-George's lavish ways threatened to ruin him. Ever since his own financial disaster, his father was no longer able to subsidize his son's needs. Even the duc d'Orléans himself kept a close eye on expenses. Not long after Philippe's father died, Louis XVI, strongly influenced by the queen, had curtailed his subsidy of the house of the first prince of the blood. The royal couple did agree to the duc de Chartres's inheriting the Orléans title, but they were growing less and less tolerant of Philippe's acts of bravado, which they saw as instances of rebellion against royal authority. To maintain his household would, they felt, amount to subsidizing the conspirators who, according to informants, were swarming around the duke and exercising an evil influence over him. Though part of the little court accompanying Philippe to London, Saint-George was himself continually thronged by hangers-on, genuine friends as well as parasites. "He liked people and made himself liked by all," writes La Boëssière suggestively.

In late-eighteenth-century London, sporting matches were already proving more lucrative than art. The English were huge devotees of fencing bouts or horse races, on which they could place bets. The bookmaking profession was in full swing. Meanwhile the forty-eight-year-old Saint-George, who continued to work out for several hours a week at La Boëssière's school, had lost little or none of the technique that twenty years before had so impressed the best foils of Europe. A torn Achilles tendon he had suffered a few years before while dancing forced him to economize his movements. However, he still possessed that famous "vista," and especially that speed and diabolical accuracy in "buttoning." And he still behaved like a professional. Shrewd pedagogue that he was, La Boëssière the younger observed that "when it is a question of going more deeply into an art, difficulties and faults are apt to arise of which one must explain the causes and inconveniences, in order to learn how to surmount the first and avoid the second. This was the rule of M. La Boëssière père, a rule upheld and well justified by his pupil, the celebrated Saint-George, and by all those who had the good sense to imitate him, even if they did not approach his perfection." The teacher also observes that when he "again took up his weapons," Saint-George humbly took his place in front of that forbidding practice wall and "thrust as slowly as he could in order to reestablish all the movements, and to feel them well."

When need arose, he could still be extraordinarily quick in his reactions. One evening, when he was going to a house in Greenwich to give a concert, a man wielding a pistol attacked him. The footpad barely had time to cry out when he was stunned with a blow from a stick. The speed with which this black man whirled his club, and the roar he gave when he swung it down on a skull similarly astounded three highwaymen who came to the aid of their partner in crime. Saint-George made quick work of his four attackers, putting them to flight. After which, he readjusted his clothes and his jabot, passed a powder-puff over his face, and calmly went on his way. His hosts were stupefied when he recounted his misadventure to them; it was clear the man could be as phlegmatic as any true Englishman. He laughed as he explained to them that in London, this paradise for enlightened minds, this oasis of prosperity, the streets were no safer than they were in Paris. He told his friends that eight years before he had had to fight off an identical attack near the Palais-Royal.

The story spread up and down the Thames, and Saint-George became an almost instant legend. It was at this point that Angelo himself befriended him, introducing him to a young painter from Boston named Mather Brown. Brown suggested doing a portrait of Saint-George with sword in hand, but against a background of a musical score. The evening before the final sitting, the chevalier was invited to dine with Angelo's parents. Angelo's mother asked Saint-George if he was pleased with the painter's work. "Oh, Madame, it is such a close likeness, it's frightening!" he replied. Angelo recounts this story in his memoirs. However, he does not speculate as to whether or not Saint-George was being sincere. Nevertheless, Saint-George did not bring the portrait back to Paris, preferring to present it to his host, who immediately hung it in his fencing establishment. Later Angelo had it engraved by William Ward, one of the best in London, in order to give copies to his pupils and send one to his friend. The resemblance of the print to the portrait is very close, except that the mischievous gleam so clear in the engraving is barely perceptible in the original work, which shows a somewhat melancholy Saint-George. Today, the engraving, along with copies of other representations of Saint-George, can be seen at the Bibliothèque nationale in Paris.

One of the copies was sent to La Boëssière's school. In return, Angelo received from Paris a poem about Saint-George written by La Boëssière senior, who toward the end of his life had conceived a passion for writing.

> *In arms, none ever saw his equal.*
> *A charming musician, skilled composer,*
> *Swimming, skating, riding, the hunt,*
> *All sports, in brief, seem easy for him,*
> *And in each he discovers an original style.*
> *If to combine modesty with such talents*
> *Is the* ne plus ultra *of this French Hercules,*
> *It is because his character, devoid of jealousy,*
> *Has found happiness in this brief life*
> *Only in the true friends of his heart.*

If nothing else the poem proves La Boëssière had made the right choice to live by his sword rather than his pen. It soon joined Saint-George's portrait, which was given a place of honor in Angelo's fencing school. Kept up-to-date on tales of the exploits of his former student in London, La Boëssière lost no time in spreading them to all the academies of Paris. In the French capital, where some people had by that point forgotten that the director of the best orchestra was also an unmatched swordsman, the legend of Saint-George the fencer was reborn. Once again, and for decades to come, he set the standard. "He wielded his foil like a Saint-George," wrote Balzac of Victurnien d'Esgrignon, the hero of his 1838 novel, *Le Cabinet des antiques*.[3]

In London, meanwhile, the Prince of Wales set about trying to find opponents of Saint-George's stature. His dream was to pit against each other the two most famous Frenchmen in the English capital, the chevalier de Saint-George and the chevalier d'Eon, or, more precisely, the "chevalière" d'Eon, for in 1771 Louis XV commanded that the knight henceforth use a feminine title and appear in public dressed as a woman.

Therein lies a story, of course. Charles-Geneviève-Louis-Auguste-André-Timothée d'Eon de Beaumont, born in 1728 in Tonnerre, Burgundy, was eleven years older than Saint-George, and shared the same passion for fencing. A pupil of the great Mottet, who had been Henry Angelo's teacher, he had been made an assistant fencing master in 1750. Like Saint-George he had other strengths. A doctor of law, he would also have been able to assume duties with the parliament of Paris. Instead, he led a rather different life, and by the 1750s there were all sorts of stories about the roguish adventures of a certain smooth-faced young man—a skilled lawyer and a formidable swordsman—who was so adept at disguising himself as a woman that he could fool even the keenest eye.[4] There were even rumors he was a hermaphrodite. Eon soon found his niche in the *Secret du roi*, an espionage service answerable solely to Louis XV.[5] "It was a vast network, a mesh beneath which he ensnared Europe," writes Frédéric Gaillardet, who collated and published the *Memoirs of the Chevalier d'Eon*. "When he wanted to gather information, [the king] had only to pull on a string to summon informers of all kinds. There were great ones and little ones, some out in the open and others clandestine. It was the same as with his favorites and his mistresses. Nothing was simple or open in this strange government, which was a veritable maze, a complicated labyrinth of which even the best informed never knew all the turns or egresses."[6]

Eon was twenty-seven years old when he was given his first mission in 1755. His orders were to ingratiate himself with the Czarina Elizabeth in order to negotiate a secret Franco-Russian alliance against London. War had not been officially declared, but the destruction of the French fleet made conflict with England inevitable. It was to last seven years. As it happened, the czarina was well guarded. Chancellor Bestoucheff, appointed by Prussia and England to protect Elizabeth after a number of plots and a failed palace coup, kept all intruders away. The chevalier de Valcroissant, who had been entrusted with the preceding mission at the Russian court, found himself summarily thrown into a deep dungeon. Others met a less kind fate.

Madame de Pompadour hit upon the idea of confiding this mission to a woman, reasoning that no one at the Russian court could imagine a representative of the weaker sex in the role of a secret ambassador. The chevalier d'Eon, renowned for his amazing ability to cross-dress and get away with it, was a perfect choice. And so in July 1755 a post-chaise left Paris, bound for the east. On board was one Mademoiselle Lia de Beaumont, who had brought along Montesquieu's *Spirit of Laws* to read on the long journey. The young woman was soon to enter the Czarina Elizabeth's service at the St. Petersburg court as a reader.[7] Among the books she had packed to fulfill her mission were her "mystery boxes" and invisible inks. A year later a Franco-Russian pact was signed, and the chevalier d'Eon had even managed to get hold of Peter the Great's famous last will and testament. The departure of Lia de Beaumont d'Eon was greatly mourned in St. Petersburg. The marquis de l'Hospital, the French ambassador, sent a billet-doux to Lia only minutes before she boarded the coach: "However much pleasure I would take in seeing you," he wrote ruefully, "I do not wish, my dear Lia, to have to reproach myself for a further folly. Adieu, ma belle de Beaumont."

Six years later, Louis XV sent the chevalier to London to take part in the peace negotiations. This time there was no bustled gown, no corset or coquettish beauty spot on the cheek; the individual crossing the Channel was unmistakably a man. Once again the lawyer acquitted himself so well of his task that the king bestowed on him the Croix de Saint-Louis, the highest decoration in the kingdom. With peace signed, Louis XV, who still had a mania for wanting to "duplicate" all his ambassadors with his own agents, asked the chevalier to stay on in London to keep him informed about George III's court. But Madame de Pompadour hated to see "her" people get away from her, and soon Louis had to yield to pressure and summon d'Eon back to France. Officially at least. For at the same time as that order, Louis XV discreetly dispatched him the following note, by the same messenger. It was dated October 4, 1763: "I warn you that the King has today signed, but only with his stamp not his hand, the order that you should return to France; however, I order you to remain in England, with all your papers, until such time as I shall pass on to you my further instructions." This was the *Secret du roi* in a nutshell. From that time on the chevalier led a life of amazing adventures in the English capital, forever at the mercy of La Pompadour's agents and George III's police, who tried to intercept his correspondence with Louis XV.

In London, he assiduously attended the school of the fencing master Angelo Malevolti Tremamondo, Henry Angelo's father. But first and foremost he was the friend and confidant of Queen Charlotte, whom he had met on his first journey to Russia in 1755. Soon, rumor and the London broadsheets that already wallowed in the private life of royalty depicted Eon as the queen's lover. George III fell prey to terrible doubts about the nature of the relationship between his wife and the French king's envoy. Worse, a detailed inquiry his agents had made into the chevalière's past caused him to harbor dire suspicions as to the true paternity of the Prince of Wales, the heir to the throne. Some months before he was born, in 1755, the chevalière d'Eon and the wife of the king of England had in fact met on their way to Russia. George III was not the only one who had doubts. Anybody who was anybody in London society gossiped that the Prince of Wales could only be a bastard.

The queen did her utmost to assuage her husband's fears by swearing that the chevalier was in reality a woman. A timely dispatch from Louis XV, inspired by his latest mistress, Madame du Barry, assured the British monarch that this was in fact so. Overjoyed, poor George III, who was starting to be driven out of his mind by this story, relayed the news to the London court. London society remained, however, more than a little skeptical. Spies were recruited and instructed to find out the truth, once and for all, as to Eon's sex. Bets were even made. The purses improvised by the bookmakers showed the public's intense interest in the chevalier's testicles. As for the unfortunate George III, he only sank further into a deep depression. But the crown of France had far more to worry about, for George now had serious doubts as to the worth of Louis XV's word.

There was only one thing to do in the matter, which after all involved a powerful, belligerent monarch whom jealousy was driving insane. The duc d'Aiguillon, minister of foreign affairs, ordered the chevalier d'Eon to disguise himself as a woman. The order was met with a prompt refusal. He had, the chevalier said, already risked his own skin in Russia to serve the king. "Today, to resume this disguise forever, or even for a moment, would be beyond my powers; the very idea appalls me, to the point that nothing could overcome my repugnance."[8] One might as well have asked him to take holy orders. Another dispatch followed, more diplomatic in tone: "Now an unknown man, you will become a famous woman. . . . His Majesty has given you first a lieutenant's commission, then that of captain of dragoons; today what His Majesty wishes to give you is nothing less than a commission of immortality: Will you refuse it?" The words of Louis XV's minister now seem truly clairvoyant. Reams are still being written in France today about Eon's gender. But, alas, the urging came to naught. After Louis XV's death, his successor's first task was to send Beaumarchais to London to persuade the chevalier to assume female disguise. It would take the author, an efficient agent of the *Secret du roi,* five months to make Eon capitulate, by way of substantial sums in compensation plus a few threats. Finally, on October 5, 1775, the chevalier acquiesced. After being paid a round sum, he returned to France, to Tonnerre, where he was bored to death. Then he once again left for London with Louis XVI's permission, on the sole condition that he dress as a woman.

By now the Prince of Wales was about thirty years of age and could not turn a deaf ear to the rumors over his paternity. He was often seen together with the chevalière in the London clubs. And, since fencing was his passion, he tried to get the best foils of the day to cross swords with her. Given its source, Saint-George could not ignore the proposition. A match was arranged for April 9, 1787, at Carlton House, in the presence of the heir-apparent and the most renowned French fencing masters who could be summoned for the occasion: Fabien, Beda, Rolland, Goddard. Even the "paparazzi" profession was represented: The painter Robineau immortalized the scene; an engraving made of it would later tour the European capitals. What a scene it was: The future king of England admiring his crossdressing papa mixing it up at a fencing match against a black man. In that spring of 1787, the London gentry reveled in delights that were not only decadent but positively postmodern.

Naturally, at sixty years of age, the chevalière was no longer exactly a slip of a girl. Nor did Saint-George have any overriding desire to humiliate her. He attacked sparingly, touched her chest an inch or so from the Croix de Saint-Louis that with coquettish vanity she insisted on wearing, even during fencing matches. Finally, Madame d'Eon was the first to mark her seven touches. She then displayed "enough modesty to believe in the complaisance of Monsieur de Saint-George."[9] Saint-George assured everyone that he had done everything he could to parry the chevalière's thrusts.[10] In fact, in the spectators' views, Saint-George, who was famous for attacking, seemed to content himself with defensive moves, giving his opponent the chance to take the offensive. The king's agent thus won the day over that of the duc d'Orléans. It matters little. What each competitor gained above all else was the opportunity to participate in a bizarre but highly entertaining encounter between Brother Saint-George of the Lodge of the Olympic of Perfect Esteem and Brother Eon de Beaumont of the Lodge of Tonnerre. And that was cause enough for celebration.

The high life further depleted Saint-George's finances. Not long after his match against Eon he was forced to return to Paris, "very ill-provided for," as he termed it. Back in the capital, he could once again earn a comfortable living from his music, especially as the lodgings graciously offered him by Philippe d'Orléans at the Palais-Royal allowed him to make a substantial savings each month. Thus Saint-George devoted a large portion of his time to composition. He now had a mere three months in which to write *The Girl-Boy*. In the meantime the concert halls and salons were demanding his presence.

XIII

The Palais in Revolution

The duc d'Orléans's gamble had paid off. Following construction on a monumental scale, the Palais-Royal was now indisputably the "capital of Paris," as his son, Louis Philippe, would later christen it in his memoirs. Initially the idea had simply been to mitigate the house of Orléans's fall in revenues, the result of being cut off from royal largesse. The new duc d'Orléans had therefore engaged Victor Louis, architect of the magnificent Bordeaux Opéra, to design a ring of apartments and galleries around the gardens. Rental of the living space would allow the duke to meet his needs, as well as his financial responsibilities as philanthropist and patron of the arts. Meanwhile, the shops and cafés set up beneath the arcades would bring even more activity to this already teeming quarter of the city. Thus after four years of work, elegant façades were going up in a horseshoe around the gardens, concealing the dreary walls that formerly ringed the area.

Each time he returned to the Palais-Royal, Saint-George found it even more buzzing than the time before. At first he was a little daunted by it, learning that the only way into the enclosed space was by squeezing through narrow passageways. Crowds of people, however, were once again swarming into the area. Booths had been set up, inviting passersby to gawk at curiosities like the "Prussian Giantess," who was advertised as towering seven feet, two inches tall, or "Butterlbrodt the Colossus," who weighed in at five hundred pounds. Little by little, the cafés that Philippe d'Orléans had envisioned by the dozens became meeting places for like-minded folk. The Corazza had from 1787 on been the Jacobins' rendezvous of choice, while the Café de Foy, the only establishment licensed to sell ice cream and lemonade in the gardens, was frequented by the friends of Camille Desmoulins. The Caveau became the preferred watering hole for musicians, and hardly an evening went by when the champions of Gluck and Piccinni did not meet each other face to face here. François Boïeldieu, Étienne Méhul, André Chénier, and the painter Jacques-Louis David regularly met at the Caveau before going up to the second story, home to the Society of the Arts.

However much the court might resent it, Philippe was determined to make his Palais-Royal gardens an enclosed space in which every form of discourse could find free expression. Symbols of differentiation were banned. Women were forbidden to appear wearing aprons, and soldiers could not wear uniforms. Dives like Le Pince-Cul (Pinch-Bottom) and brothels like Mademoiselle Montansier's—whose clients were recruited in the foyer of her own theater—did a roaring trade. Soon the famous Cabaret des Aveugles appeared. The musicians who played here were said to be blind, which in theory at least prevented them from witnessing the depravities going on inside.

The profound yet joyous feeling that liberty was within arm's reach was the power binding people together. They were also passionately interested in technical progress, which was deemed inseparable from that of society. An example was the popular "Café Mécanique," which worked without any visible waiters. Dishes were served by means of a dumbwaiter that popped up in the middle of each table, orders having been passed along through one of the table legs hollowed out for the purpose. Beneath the chestnut trees of the Palais-

Royal, revolution was already being waged in words and song. News-sheets were handed out. People strove for the advent of a better, more enlightened humanity. Visiting Paris from the provinces, the marquis de La Ferrières, still wet behind the ears, wrote in a letter. "One can scarcely imagine the diverse world to be found here. It is truly amazing. I have been to the circus; I have visited five or six cafés and none of Molière's plays could match the variety of sights that present themselves to the gaze: Here, one man argues for reform . . . while another reads aloud from a pamphlet; everyone talks at once; each man has his audience that listens to him with the utmost attentiveness. . . . The bookstores are filled with men who leaf through books and never buy a thing. You gasp for air the minute you walk in a café."[1]

In this forum, where as many as six thousand people thronged day and night, the arcades being lit, Saint-George's towering figure was an easy one to spot. His red coat and black breeches were designed to resemble the "Saint-Cloud costume" paraded by the duc d'Orléans's cronies. Here he met Jacques Pierre Brissot, whom the duke had recently managed to free from the Bastille, where Brissot had been imprisoned for his writings, as well as Condorcet, Mirabeau, Pétion, the abbé Grégoire, the abbé Sieyès, and Dupont de Nemours, who met regularly in the cafés to work for the cause of abolishing slavery. In 1787 they laid the foundations of the Society of Friends of Blacks. Saint-George served as an indispensable link between this group of thinkers and the duc d'Orléans, whom the king had recently exiled to the family's countryseat of Villers-Cotterêts. This was Louis XVI's way of punishing his cousin for speaking up when the Parliament of Paris had been in full session and in his royal presence arguing against the floating of a gigantic royal loan. It had been a crushing humiliation, though in the end the king had managed to impose his will. Cheered by the crowd when the parliament was dismissed, the first prince of the blood had become a symbol of resistance to authoritarianism. On one high-spirited occasion his admirers had even unharnessed his horses and drawn his carriage to the Palais-Royal. Exile only increased Philippe's popularity. "Breaking the rules of optics, the duke grows larger the farther he moves away," joked Bachaumont.[2] Before long, the pressure became such that the king shortened the distance of his exile; Philippe was confined to his estate of Le Raincy, some seven miles from the Palais-Royal.

Philippe had planted himself unequivocally in the camp of the champions of progress. From 1787 to 1788 he even seemed to serve as a highly convenient shield. What policeman would dare to harass anyone hailing the coach belonging to the head of the junior branch of the royal family? He occasionally used his authority to obtain a pardon for some writer shut up in the Bastille; this of course made him even more popular. Yet Philippe did not fit the profile of a conspirator. He refused to play the role of head of the reformers' party. At Le Raincy, he divided his time between a lovely Scotswoman, Grace Dalrymple Elliott, and the scintillating Madame de Buffon, his latest muses—making sure, sometimes having to resort to nearly vaudeville-like contortions, that the two women never crossed paths during their visits. He also did a lot of hunting. Thus his lieutenant of the hunt, Saint-George, was called upon to accompany him on numerous trips between the Palais-Royal and the princely seat. Saint-George was in a position to keep the duke informed as to what was happening in Paris.

At Versailles, Louis XVI now knew that matters were slipping beyond his control. After the downfall of Controller-General Calonne, his successor, Cardinal Loménie de Brienne, had failed miserably, appearing to be more preoccupied with treating his syphilis than with the woeful state of the royal treasury. Royalty now received precious little respect. One morning, a bill was posted on the walls of Versailles: "Palace for sale, minister to be hanged, crown for the asking." The king's first task was to gather the family together in the face of this popular rage that now threatened the throne. Against Marie-Antoinette's advice, he came to the conclusion that his cousin was more of a risk in his discreet but proximate exile, from where he could authorize every plot, than he would be in Paris, where he could be kept under close watch. On April 16, 1788, the duc d'Orléans was permitted to return to the Palais-Royal on condition that he "have nothing more to do with the whole business." Before he could go back, Philippe had to declare his allegiance in writing: "My plan being henceforth to concern myself only with what can be of use to my children . . . and not to renounce the visits of the women, nor they the habit of coming to visit me." In short, he pledged to confine himself to a purely decorative role. It was a promise extremely hard to keep. Philippe could not help being a beacon for the people of Paris. Moreover, events were gathering momentum. In July, Louis XVI was forced to recall Necker and have him make preparations for the Estates General, which had not met for 175 years.

Predictably, Philippe found sticking to his part of the bargain difficult. In October 1788 he tumbled into activism, though perhaps innocently, by hiring a new secretary—Choderlos de Laclos. Up to that time Laclos, as we might remember, had been the bane of the army chiefs, not only for his attacks on French fortifications but for the publication, in 1782, of the scandalous novel for which he remains famous. Thus he found himself being transferred from one garrison to another at the whim of his superiors. While working on the opera *Ernestine,* for example, he had been shuffled between Besançon, Grenoble, and Valence. Soon he would be stationed in La Rochelle and then, following yet another one of his broadsides against Vauban's theories, in Metz. This was the last straw as far as he was concerned. Hearing that a post on the duc d'Orléans's staff was vacant, he immediately called upon friends who were in the duke's entourage. These included Saint-George, a brother Mason (Laclos being himself a Worshipful Master). When he was considering Laclos's candidacy, the good-natured Philippe was informed by Madame de Genlis that he would have to choose between her and the author of *Dangerous Liaisons.* Characteristically, the duke did not see matters as an either/or situation and promptly took on Laclos, also managing to convince Madame de Genlis to continue in his service. Officially she let it be known that she was reluctant to upset the duke's children, who thought of her as their real mother.

Secretary and confidante each ended up demarcating their respective territories in clearer fashion and before long even came to complement each other quite admirably. The novelist-governess wielded greater influence over Philippe than did the jurists in the parliament and the intellectuals. On the surface at least, Laclos was content to let Madame de Genlis play her part. Methodical engineer that he was (around that time he came up with an extraordinary plan for numbering the streets of Paris), he would make it his business to reorganize the Orléans clan. As Talleyrand wrote later, "Laclos's ambition, his wit, his bad reputation, had given Monsieur le Duc d'Orléans the impression of a handyman whom it was good to have at one's side in dangerous circumstances." Always dressed in black—Philippe would never allow him to wear a uniform—Laclos busied himself with organizing, writing, and offering suggestions. He himself composed the *cahiers de doléances*, or petitions of complaint, drawn up by peasants under the duke's jurisdiction, penned lampoons that were published in the gazettes circulated around the Palais-Royal, and was continually urging Philippe to act more aggressively. The latter did append his signature to some of his secretary's projects; to others his support was not openly given. For instance, he did not himself sign the plan calling for the total liberalization of divorce. That was simply too risky a proposition to set before the pious Louis XVI.

The winter of 1788 was one of the severest of the century. An estimated 120,000 beggars were on the streets of Paris, out of a total population of some 550,000 inhabitants; life in the countryside was even more miserable. Philippe opened a series of soup kitchens, renting sheds in the city and sending his cooks there to prepare meals for the poor; this made him of course enormously popular. As for Saint-George, he continued to focus on his music. Given that the Olympique orchestra was also running into grave financial difficulties because of the worsening economic crisis, more and more often he played in the salons. He was frequently received by the baron de Bézenval, chief of the Swiss Guards and a member of the Olympic Lodge, who had a small orchestra directed by Nicolas Dalayrac, future composer of the imperial anthem.

It would have been impossible for this son of a slave not to see in the general demands for reform his own reflection. The groans of an exploited peasantry had reached the Palais-Royal. In the gardens, newspapers sold by the hawkers presented a vivid picture of the people's wretchedness, which also came through clearly in the petitions of complaint. Since the previous May, the Estates General had in fact been rifling through these documents, and the result was that the bourgeoisie and the enlightened members of the aristocracy were finally discovering the France to which they had hitherto turned a blind eye. "The peasant who owned his holding had to give part of his crop to the Church and pay his landlord the rent in money, pay in kind his lord's *champart*, or share of the produce, pay for labor, permissions, and sales, and had to tolerate aristocratic hunts on his lands, not counting the obligation to use the lord's oven, his mill, his olive presses," as historians François Furet and Denis Richet would write many years later.[3] Nor was this all. An aristocracy obsessed with outward signs of social rank was constantly humiliating the merchants and businessmen who believed they were fostering their country's prosperity. On one occasion, the future Madame Roland, who from time to time would go and applaud Saint-George's violin performances, was invited to dine at a château and found herself having to eat with the servants. A wealthy colonist from the Antilles named Barnave immediately sided with the Revolution when he saw an aristocrat physically turn his mother out of the box that she normally occupied at the theater. No one could have been more sensitive to social apartheid than Saint-George, who all his life had lived under the threat of ostracism, even by those people who pretended to accept him for his talents.

Necker was dismissed on July 12, 1789. The next day, counseled by Laclos, the duc d'Orléans demanded that a tax be levied on large fortunes, including those of the landowning aristocracy, and at once announced himself willing to contribute to it 100,000 livres. On July 14, Camille Desmoulins, standing atop a chair on the terrace of the Café de Foy, called on the people of the Palais-Royal to rise up and seize the Bastille; it was, he said, the only way to prevent another St. Bartholomew's Day massacre, which he was convinced Versailles was preparing. That day, Louis XVI wrote but one word in his diary: "Nothing." Three weeks later, on the night of August 4, the nobles agreed to the abolition of their privileges. And five weeks after the fall of the Bastille, the Declaration of the Rights of Man and the Citizen would be adopted. Its first article proclaimed: "Men are born and remain free and equal in rights." Saint-George set sail for London.

It might seem a little strange that Saint-George would leave Paris right at the moment when the ideas he espoused were winning the day. Did it mean that he was refusing to take sides, still being tied to Marie-Antoinette despite his friendship for the duc d'Orléans? Or, as a Freemason, was he anxious to distance himself from a conflict that was dividing his own brothers? Mirabeau was a Mason, but so was his interlocutor the marquis de Dreux-Brezé, who had tried to expel from the famous session on June 22, 1789, the representatives of the Third Estate and the lower clergy. Laclos and Brissot were Joseph's lodge brothers. But so too was the baron de Bézenval, the head of the Swiss Guards who was ordered to fire on the crowds. One rumor had it that Saint-George might be the duc d'Orléans's ambassador to the English court, his mission being to persuade it to adopt a policy of neutrality in face of the events now setting France aflame. Officially, Saint-George had gone to England "with the idea of settling there," as he confided to Henry Angelo. No sooner had he arrived in London than he went to the fencing school to cross swords with his friend. After that he made for Brighton, with Angelo still at his side. There he was to meet his friend the Prince of Wales, also of course a friend to the duc d'Orléans. Then he returned to London and once again booked a suite at

Grenier's Hotel, resuming the life he had lived there two years before, surrounded by musicians and courtiers of both sexes. "At that time Saint-George led an 'extravagant' life at Grenier's Hotel, on Jermyn Street, a hotel that was considered more fashionable than the Clarendon; he was constantly to be seen surrounded by a crowd of masters at arms, amateur fencers, and violinists," writes La Laurencie. "Everyone did their utmost to flatter and coax some favor from him. He kept an open table and entertained this 'clientele' with guineas, and with Champagne and Bordeaux," reported Odet Denys, and one wonders where the huge sums that he spent so liberally came from. Very likely one reason he was in London in the first place was to manage, or repatriate, part of the "English money" held, it was said, by the duc d'Orléans in the form of property. By dint of having crossed and recrossed the Channel so many times, the duke was rumored to have become one of the leading landowners in England. In any case, Saint-George's relative leisure enabled him to devote time to working on *Guillaume tout coeur*.[4]

On October 21, Saint-George welcomed the duke himself to London. Accompanied by Madame de Buffon and Laclos, Philippe had had to leave Paris in a hurry. The king was accusing his cousin of fomenting the rebellion of October 5 that had forced the royal family to leave Versailles for Paris. Lafayette—still loyal to the king at this point—was threatening the duke, who therefore had little choice but to flee. When he did, Mirabeau, who had hoped to set Philippe up on the throne in Louis XVI's place, roared out his disappointment and rage: "He's a eunuch who has the desire but not the potency!"

This was of course merely a figure of speech. In London Philippe was savoring the pleasures of a newfound freedom in the company of the young Agnès de Buffon and other friends. It was like 1787 all over again. Soon, however, the contagion produced by the Revolution had him looking back to the continent, and in particular to Belgium, which, like all the Low Countries, was still under Austrian control. In late October, Hendrik Van der Noot's partisans repulsed the troops of the Austrian general d'Alton. For the exiled prince this presented an irresistible opportunity. He could take advantage of his popularity as a friend of the Paris revolutionaries and set himself up at the head of a duchy of Brussels, presenting the possibility that the ruling Hapsburgs might be hounded altogether off Belgian soil. Belgian revolutionaries who had cheered the capture of the Bastille would welcome him with open arms. The Prince of Wales seemed open to the idea. All that remained was persuading the king of France. Or more precisely the queen—and Marie-Antoinette was loath to accept anyone stabbing her brother Joseph II, Emperor of Austria, in the back. The French ambassador to London was dispatched without much conviction to Paris to attempt to lift the prohibition of "Madame Veto," as the queen was called. At the same time the duke sent emissaries to Belgium to stage demonstrations in favor of his candidacy. There the cousin of the famous Anacharsis Cloots, the self-styled "Orator of the Human Race," was organizing the Orléanist party.

As for Saint-George, he abruptly left London for Lille, where he signed on with the National Guard, and was immediately conferred the rank of captain. It was imperative to stand ready to fight the Austrians, whose measures against the Belgian revolutionaries were becoming increasingly brutal. He did not stay long in Lille, returning after a few months to Paris. Here he once again frequented the salons, in particular that of Madame de Chambonas, one of his former patronesses, who had made it a point of honor to carry on in spite of the storm convulsing society. There, no doubt for the last time, he saw his friend the marquis de Champcenetz, of whom before 1789 it was said that he would get himself killed for a bon mot. (Champcenetz duly justified his reputation, joking to the prince de Salm, who was riding with him in the cart taking them both to their execution by guillotine: "Give your coachman a drink. The poor wretch isn't feeling at all well.")

In Paris, Saint-George turned up regularly at the Acts of the Apostles, a club made up essentially of "moderate" Orléanists whose newspaper was edited by Madame de Chambonas. He also soon formed an immensely affectionate relationship with the seventeen-year-old Louise Fusil (he was fifty-two), an actress and an unusually gifted singer. And he had a joyful reunion with his former fellow musician Lamothe, considered at the time the best horn player in Paris as well as one of the finest swordsmen in the kingdom. Irrepressible and talented, Louise Fusil was a mine of information. Still somewhat blind to everything going on around her, she was loyal to the king almost to the point of devotion, which gave her entree to monarchist salons. Her husband had become one of the leading figures of the Revolution and introduced her to clubs frequented by the likes of Fabre d'Eglantine, Marie-Joseph Chénier, Pierre Vergniaud, Condorcet, and David. Saint-George was constantly being asked to compose songs for her; she performed equally before both royalists and revolutionaries. And she opened up completely to Saint-George.

After this short stay in Paris, Saint-George once again embarked for London. This time he was to stay only a few weeks (time enough, however, to be the victim of another attempted robbery, as reported in the *Journal général de France* of February 23, 1790). His skills as a fencer still caused him to be much in demand. Some of the best French swordsmen then living in the English capital followed him around in the hope of fencing with him as often as possible. Then it was back to Paris again. Louise Fusil meanwhile left to sing in Belgium. Saint-George and his good friend Lamothe accompanied her to Amiens before going on to Boulogne. The massacre perpetrated by the Austrians in Antwerp and the resultant unrest forced Louise to return posthaste to France. Easter found the trio reunited in Amiens with the marquise de Chambonas. Here Saint-George gave a few concerts during Holy Week. And, of course, there were parties. It was, in fact, the marquise's birthday and one of her friends, the vicomte de Rouhaut, who had a château between Abbeville and Amiens, decided to celebrate the event. Louise Fusil describes it in her memoirs.

> It was a magnificent fête. . . . It was just at the time when Tippoo's ambassadors had aroused everyone's curiosity. [Tippoo Sahib, the

Sultan of Mysore, then fighting the English, had sent ambassadors—subjects of great curiosity—to Paris to win French support.] Some of these gentlemen organized a charming little play on the subject. They had obtained costumes that were accurate and most magnificent. M. de Vauquelin, who was famous for his knowledge of Oriental languages, told Mme de Chambonas that he had wanted to be their interpreter and introduce them. He added that these illustrious foreign visitors, having seen the most interesting sights in France, did not want to pass by the residence of one of the prettiest and most amiable ladies without being presented and offering her some rare articles from their country. . . . The play was so well conceived and acted that many people were taken in, and I was sent for in my tent so that I might see the ambassadors incognito; but I soon recognized Saint-George as the copper-colored ambassador. . . . In the evening M. de Genlis [brother-in-law of Madame de Genlis known for his culture and his debauchery] improvised a few couplets. It was a recital of the day's happenings to the aria from *Tarare* [an opera by Antonio Salieri to a libretto by Beaumarchais].

The marquise de Chambonas next played the role of the countess in *The Marriage of Figaro* and Louise that of Susanna.

This was to be one of the last grand fêtes of the French aristocracy. Again in her memoirs, Louise Fusil looked back on the period with sadness: "It was in the midst of that frivolous, idle crowd that the Revolution suddenly swooped down on that futile society, pouncing on the heads of those defenseless women like a vulture on poor doves." Still, the "dove" Louise would not hesitate to sing for the vultures, and continue to love her "black eagle," as she called Saint-George.

They returned to find Paris seething with excitement. With naive optimism, the Assemblée Générale was tackling the first sweeping reforms: creation of the so-called *départements,* or national divisions, adoption of the Civil Constitution of the Clergy, and reform of the monarchy, modeled on the English system. Philippe d'Orléans was finally able to return to Paris himself, the balance of power having swung definitively in favor of the revolutionary change. The duke, a self-proclaimed Jacobin, marched around in the mud of the huge "Festival of the Federation," held in the pouring rain on July 14, 1790. It was a chance to show himself off with his son, the future Louis Philippe, who was clad in the uniform of the National Guard. Meanwhile, Saint-George took advantage of his stay in the capital to present *Guillaume tout cœur*. He then left for Lille, moving into a house on the rue Nôtre-Dame, in the parish of Saint-Etienne.

His rank of captain of the guard left Saint-George with some leisure time, at least for a few months. He participated in fencing matches with the best swordsmen of the garrison at the Esplanade redoubt. He also presented *Guillaume tout cœur* at the opera house. Louise, who had joined him, managed to make frequent getaways to Belgium to sing. "There is but little distance from [Lille] to Tournai, which at that time belonged to Austria," she writes in her memoirs. "And before the *émigration* people often went there. There was nothing but a simple post indicating the border between the two countries. . . . The Lille theater presented concerts and plays." Up to the end of 1790, the *émigrés* who had fled Paris had still believed they were faced with what would prove a minor revolt. They even adopted a somewhat benevolent attitude toward the revolutionaries encamped on the other side of the border. "The *émigrés* were convinced that it was enough for them to appear at the gates of Paris with Condé's army to be able to enter the city, and that they would be greeted as liberators," adds Louise. Moreover, some of these *émigrés* had friends in the opposing camp; not every member of the Jacobin Club was a commoner. The duc d'Aiguillon, former minister to Louis XVI, and the prince de Broglie, future general of one of the Revolutionary armies, were both active members. Conversely, the ancient house of Orléans included some friends on the *émigrés'* side. And then, on both sides of these geographical and political divides, there were the Masons.

Saint-George tried to advance the cause of Revolution in a twelve-page brochure that he distributed as soon as he was settled in Lille. Entitled *Nous sommes donc trois? ou le Provincial à Paris* (So We Are Three? or The Provincial in Paris), it explains that his trip to Paris, where he had frequented the Jacobin Club and attended a session of the National Assembly, besides spending "some hours in the cafés," had opened his eyes to the reality of things. This revolution was not simply a duel between the progressives and those championing a return to the *ancien régime*. It was threatened by divisions within the camp of the "patriots," of which he was one. This camp, he asserted, was split into three groups. The first two consisted of those who were trying to "delay the work of the Assembly," and those who, on the contrary, wanted to go too fast and too far, led by Robespierre and Marat. "When I see this party taking all ideas to extremes, exaggerating all opinions, and preaching a bold doctrine that serves only to exalt men without enlightening them, when I see it seize every opportunity to flatter the people, defend its license, and even praise its excesses, doubts form in my mind as to its sincerity," he wrote. Enemies of virtue, factious, seditious, anarchic: Such for Saint-George were the future leaders of the Revolution. He discerned an unnatural alliance between these enemies and the royalists, aimed at eliminating those determined freely to wage a revolution. This third group, formed around the duc d'Orléans and Lafayette, was striving to avoid anathematizing the progressive aristocracy. "Thus we have one more enemy against which we must be on our guard," he warns. He exhorts "moderate" Jacobins he has known not to let themselves be carried away. "Above all, let us hold fast together, let us stay united, let us not excite ourselves over goals that do not concern us or divide our ranks for interests that are alien to us," he concludes. "We would give too much advantage to the two cliques that are waiting for the right moment to surprise us. With our side weakened by our own efforts, all that these cliques would have to do is quarrel over the right to sub-jugate us and, whichever side won the victory, our lot would still be that of slavery." This manifesto, which he signed "Saint-George, citi-zen soldier," shows unmistakably the role that he intended to play: to serve the "patriots" but also to prevent the Revolution from spinning out of control.

The situation rapidly grew tense. The adoption of the Constitu-tion and the first sale of their lands were convincing the *émigrés* that reseizing power would take far more time and effort than they had at first envisioned. In September 1789, the comte d'Artois had taken refuge in Turin, followed by a court of generally elderly nobles, all talking in loud voices and spending a great deal of money. The count claimed he was organizing a counterrevolution. No one had really been paying attention. The *émigrés* who had fled to the Low Coun-tries, the Rhineland, and Switzerland were now living there quietly, not concerning themselves to any great extent over events in Paris. Yet little by little some kind of counterrevolutionary movement was get-ting organized. First Condé, who was in the city of Worms, and then the comte d'Artois, who had just moved to Coblenz, rallied members of the impoverished petty nobility who felt they had no other choice but to try to return to France by force. Nobles and officers of the roy-alist army came forward en masse to prepare for reconquest.

Saint-George, who probably had not sensed how critical the situa-tion had become on either side of the border, went to Tournai in early June, 1791, to give a concert based on the repertoire regularly played in Lille. It turned out not to be an especially wise move. The *Moniteur universel* (no. 172) published a review of this endeavor, dated June 13: "It is reported from this city that M. Saint-George (formerly Cheva-lier), having arrived here with the intention of spending a few days and giving music lovers the pleasure of hearing him in a concert, had been secretly warned by the commandant not to show himself in pub-lic. It appears that M. Saint-George's sentiments are well-known and that they displease the French refugees, enemies of France and of liberty. Assuredly, these people have no love for music." No doubt, too, they feared that Saint-George had come to spy on them—that, at any rate, was Odet Denys's theory—or else that he had crossed the border "to rally to the Orléans cause some of the *émigrés* who were in that city at the time," as Saint-George's contemporary, the Belgian François-Joseph Fétis, affirmed.

Yet the reaction of those aristocratic refugees in Tournai was hardly violent. They had merely stored up a provision of cooked apples with which they proposed to pelt the mulatto as soon as he made his entrance.[5] Others tampered with the dish he had ordered at the restaurant where he was about to dine. Saint-George understood that it was perhaps best "not to make too long a stay there," related Louise. For the time being the atmosphere was one of hostility. A few days later, after the king was arrested at Varennes, on June 22, events would take an entirely different turn.

Back once more in Lille, Saint-George, who had definitively abandoned the "de" of his name, resumed his musical activity. *Les Annonces* of November 1791 published an article that was full of praise for the musician. "It is a long time since we have had, in our city, a concert as brilliant as that of Tuesday, All Saints' Day. Suffice it to say, to persuade our readers that this is so, that M. Saint-George conceived the concert and took it upon himself to conduct it. Here one saw a combination of the most distinguished talents and the kind of perfect ensemble which alone can delight every member of the audience. The concert began with an overture by M. Guénin [a member of the Olympic Lodge] and ended with a symphony by Paisiello. M. Granville and Mlle Guérin sang in the first section and made the chorus section extremely interesting. M. Lombart played on the cello a concerto by Pleyel, which received much applause."

For all his fame as a musician, Saint-George still took an interest in the talent of others, particularly younger performers. The same article adds: "A curious debut, which aroused much interest in the second part of the concert, was that of M. Baillé fils, who, accompanied by M.

Saint-George, played a sonata for fortepiano with a clarity, a facility, an execution, and even a sensibility not often encountered in one of such a tender age (he is at most 10 to 12 years old)." Then the final verdict: "We hope that M. Saint-George will be willing likewise to direct some of the concerts which we will be giving through next Easter, and we can give assurance in advance that the leading virtuosi of France will be heard on those occasions."

That final sentiment was wishful thinking. Saint-George was closely following the Assembly's debates concerning the treatment of blacks. Matters were in a delicate state. The colonists were giving full support to the Revolution, for it promised to free them from the regulations and excessive taxation that in their view was hampering the growth of trade. In exchange, they were banking that the new regime would help them oppose the demands of the blacks and half-castes. In August 1789, the colonial lobby founded the Massiac Club. Here so-called *monarchiens* (supporters of constitutional monarchy) sat cheek by jowl with "patriots" like Alexandre Lameth and bankers like the marquis de Laborde, who all owned plantations and slaves in the islands. Antoine Barnave, a friend of Lameth's, became the club's spokesman.

The Society of Friends of Blacks found itself somewhat in a defensive position. Only one relatively unknown deputy named Vieuville des Essarts had put forward a plan, in May 1791, calling for the gradual abolition of slavery. His speech was not even debated. Robespierre, who in this very uncertain period had a fear of sensitive questions, contented himself, hypocritically, with requesting that the word "slave" not be uttered. It was a way of postponing discussion of the whole issue. Meanwhile, the society was involved in a major struggle—that of obtaining for mulatto freedmen political rights identical to those of the whites. But here as well the assembly was proceeding with extreme caution. The slave traders of Saint-Domingue had just rebelled, threatening to secede and create an independent state in the image of the United States of America. Barnave negotiated the return of the *Grande Île* to the bosom of France with the promise that Paris would take no action regarding the rights of blacks and mulattos. Then, in a further refinement of hypocrisy, it was allowed that the assembly might study the problem should the colonial assemblies request it to do so. As it happened, these latter were made up exclusively of whites.

On Saint-Domingue, the mulattos, believing they had been swindled, were agitating. Vincent Ogé, their spokesman, organized a petition campaign. White colonials summarily executed him in the public square. The event gave the assembly a terrific jolt. In the debate that began two months after the execution, in May 1791, Barnave was defeated. The deputies nodded in agreement when Jean-Denis Lanjuinais emphasized that miscegenation had made half-castes "the children of the same mother, the brothers, the nephews, the cousins" of the colonists. And turning to his hesitant colleagues, he sneered at their claims of racial purity. "So you would not let them share your rights because their complexions are not as white as yours? I could say to several of those who voice these ridiculous pretensions: Look at yourselves in the mirror and then make up your minds."[6]

For once, Robespierre revealed himself as an early radical socialist. Supporting the ostracism of mulattos would be tantamount to throwing them into the arms of the slaves. In short, he came down on the side of their interests, though not because of any adherence to the sacrosanct principle of equal rights.

For Saint-George, there was no longer any possible doubt. Despite its faults and uncertainties, the Revolution was his new family. The king's attempted flight had caused a profound trauma among the people. Brought back to Paris, surrounded by a crowd that greeted him in stony but menacing silence, Louis XVI was suspected of having intended to flee for the purpose of organizing the army of the *émigrés* and the Austrians. On June 21—between the discovery of the king's flight and his return—the assembly issued a decree that 91,000 revolutionary volunteers be raised from the National Guard. In every city, recruiting offices opened to enlist patriots ready to defend the country against the foreign powers. Saint-George was the 244th person to sign on in Lille. His register bears the words: "Joseph Bologne St-George, aged forty-two years, native of Guadeloupe, rue Notre-Dame, parish St-Etienne, 25 July 1791."[7] Saint-George was actually fifty-two. He doubtless lied about his age to make sure of being called up. None of the fencers with whom he now crossed swords each day at the esplanade would have assumed otherwise; and he was still an extraordinary horseman.

The idea behind these battalions of volunteers, who chose their own officers, was to balance out the influence of the professional army—the troops "of the line"—that had been formed before the fall of the Bastille and whose officers had always been noblemen. The volunteer battalions bore the name of their *département* and were put under the Minister of War, who then apportioned them among the garrisons made up of the professional army. First, however, they had to be trained. The eighteen-year-old Louis Philippe of Chartres, the duc d'Orléans's son—and the future king—already commanded a regiment of the line. He pointed out that the volunteers were acquiring military spirit and discipline. "But," he added, "you have to have lived, as I did, with each of these two kinds of troops and had them under your orders to get an idea of the reciprocal irritation caused by the disparity in their organization, their regime, and their pay." The fact was that the "volunteers" earned twice as much as the professional soldiers.[8]

The baptism by fire would soon come. On September 13, 1791, Louis XVI conceded to the proposal that France would become a constitutional monarchy. In the secret messages he sent to the European courts, however, he asserted that he had been forced to accept the new constitution under duress. Threatened themselves from within, these "cousin" monarchies were hastening their preparations to march on France. Meanwhile, the king had no choice but to agree to declare war on Austria, on April 20, 1792. The government quickly decided to

take the initiative by attacking Belgium. The plan might have succeeded, Louis Philippe writes in his memoirs, "if on the one hand the
court, and on the other the generals and officers who then headed the
French armies, had sincerely wished it; but whatever their motives,
they agreed not to wish it."

There was the problem in a nutshell: This army commanded by
officers of the *ancien régime* was supposed to obey the king, and they
knew perfectly well that the king was consenting to this war under
constraint rather than giving the orders. Thus the Maréchal de
Rochambeau, commander of the army of the *département* Le Nord,
formed three corps that, embarking from Valenciennes, Lille, and
Dunkirk, would theoretically join up in Brussels. For the corps from
Lille, made up in particular of Saint-George's volunteers, the battle
ended the day it began. On April 28, General Théobald Dillon, who
had been convicted of treason, was executed by his own soldiers.
Rochambeau was relieved of his duties, and on June 16 the French
army finally crossed into Belgium. It would remain there for only two
short weeks before being ordered to withdraw. Now eminently suspect, the army of the North had to be removed far from the *émigrés* of
Tournai. The border was porous and this was clearly facilitating infil-
tration and acts of treason. Replaced by the army of the East, led by
Lafayette in person, the troops of the North would subsequently be
deployed in Lorraine.

Saint-George stayed on for a little while longer in Lille. Then he
headed to Paris, to which Louise had herself returned. For the time
being, he thought, he would be more useful in the capital.

XIV

The Republic's Black Hussar

After the turmoil he had seen in the north, Saint-George probably expected to find Paris in a state of extreme tension. In fact, what he found was a city alive with song, even more so than on grand occasions under the *ancien régime*. In the streets and cafés and in homes, revolution was being waged in refrains known as *ritournelles*. It was as though free speech, censored for so long, had been liberated by music. No fewer than 116 songs were written in 1789 (at least those we know of), 260 the next year, and 325 in 1793. The trend would continue at an accelerating pace, culminating in more than seven hundred new songs in 1794.[1] In the theaters singers sometimes changed their original text to give it a revolutionary tinge. For example, in an old opera called *Le Savetier* (The Cobbler), one of the male singers improvised a refrain:

> *The money that's hidden away will come out!*
> *How so? through promissory notes!*

The delighted audience made him repeat the refrain a dozen times.

But it was the street that afforded the broadcast stage. People never tired of celebrating in song the capture of the Bastille. For instance:

> *Marching with triumphant step*
> *Tarrum, tarrum, tarrum pom pom*
> *And to the beating of the drum*
> *The bourgeois march on the Bastille*
> *To the joyous shouting of the free!*

The royal family, beginning with Marie-Antoinette, who was harshly attacked in the revolutionary air "La Carmagnole," was an endless and increasing source of inspiration for these songs. As it grew ever more obvious that Louis XVI was aligning with foreign powers, the words became more and more venomous, a far cry from those love songs of 1789, celebrating a new and blessed alliance between the people and its king. The song dedicated to "Fat Louis, Formerly the King" was particularly cruel:

> *Poor old king, you've lost your veto,*
> *You who betrayed so good a people,*
> *Fat old Louis, you're just a zero,*
> *No Augustus in history will you be.*

The good Doctor Guillotin was exalted to the rank of saint in this music rising up from the cobblestone streets, cafés, and shops:

> *The deputy Dr. Guillotin*
> *In the art of medicine*
> *Very expert, very keen*
> *Did invent a fine machine*
> *To purge the body of the French*
> *Of all the ones with future plans,*

> *That's the guillotine, tra la,*
> *That's the guillotine.*

The "widow"—as the guillotine was known—was even celebrated to the tune of the "Marseillaise":

> *O heavenly guillotine,*
> *You shorten kings and queens,*
> *Through your influence divine*
> *We have won back our rights.*

Here we have the guillotine as divinity. Another song celebrated it to a melody taken from religious music:

> *O holy guillotine, protectress of patriots, pray for us,*
> *Holy guillotine, terror of aristocrats, protect us.*

Louis-Sébastien Mercier, that observant chronicler of street life, noted that no opportunity was lost to sing the machine's praises. "At the whim of the people, the words for everything that went into the making of the notorious instrument were set to the gayest of couplets. Facetious expressions were used to illustrate the movement of the fatal blade and the fall of the heads. Bitter irony accompanied the victims' deaths, and jokes of all kinds attended all the functions and the slightest movements of the executioner."

Despite these excesses, it was the joy of battle that provided the main theme for these popular songs, which resounded from one part of the city to the other. Toward the end of July 1792, the music faded away for a few hours, replaced by an ominous silence. Two manifestos written by the duke of Brunswick talked of destroying the capital should revolutionaries attack the king and queen. "If the least violence, the least outrage is perpetrated against Their Majesties the King, the Queen, and the royal family, threatening their preservation and liberty, they [the European powers] will draw from it an exemplary and forever memorable vengeance, by handing over the city of Paris to military measures and total subversion, and the rebels guilty of assassination to tortures which they will have well deserved." Momentarily petrified with fear, the people reacted in song, making the "Marseillaise" their national anthem.

The sounds coming from a people gaining and celebrating liberty by bursting into song delighted the heart of Saint-George; he understood the uses of music. However, for the moment he had more urgent things to do than join the chorus of general rejoicing, which in any case was interrupted by bloody prison massacres that took place in Paris in early September. In the east, European troops had crossed the borders and laid siege to Verdun. On September 2, 1792, the Paris Commune exhorted all citizens to mobilize and beat the invaders back. Five days later, a delegation of blacks and half-castes led by Julien Raimond, a mulatto from Saint-Domingue, appeared before the assembly and presented a petition offering the support of all men of color. Here is the complete text of this appeal, which is also a moving plea for equality of the races:

Legislators,

When your benevolent law of last March 24 summoned us to do our duty, we swore an oath to shed our blood for the defense of the Fatherland. [The law stipulated that "men of color and free Negroes must, as well as white colonists, enjoy equality of political rights." As a result a new election of the colonial assemblies had to be held.] This sacred oath we must uphold; like all Frenchmen, we burn with desire to defend the borders. Legislators, we are still few in number, but if you deign to look with favor on our zeal, our numbers will increase and we will form a body of considerable size.

We therefore beg you to authorize the Ministry of War to organize us as promptly as possible into a free legion, under whatever name you choose to give it.

If Nature, inexhaustible in her variety, has differentiated us by external signs, on the other hand she has made us perfectly alike by giving us as well as [all Frenchmen] a heart that burns to do battle with the enemies of the State. For myself, gentlemen, who have been chosen by my brothers to be the interpreter of their feelings, I am deprived by my age and by a particular mission from following them in the path of honor, but I shall contribute a sum of five hundred livres each year, of which here is the first third, to the cost of equipping this troop, and I shall add a similar sum for the one among them who will perform an action worthy of your praise.[2]

A wave of profound emotion swept over the assembly. These men of color to whom the Republic had given but meager support only a few months before by refusing a second time to abolish slavery were giving the deputies a magnificent lesson in generosity. Deeply moved, the president replied: "Virtue in man is independent of color and climate. The offer you are making to the fatherland of your arms and your strength to aid in the destruction of its enemies, by honoring a large part of the human race, is a service rendered to the cause of humanity as a whole. . . . Your efforts will be all the more precious in that love of liberty and equality must surely be a terrible, unquenchable passion in the children of those who, beneath a scorching sky, have groaned in the shackles of servitude. With so many men all united in pressing around the despots and their slaves, it is impossible that France will not soon become the capital of the free world."[3]

The very next day the assembly voted in favor of the formation of a corps of troops of 1,000 men of color, 200 of them cavalry. And it appointed Saint-George to head the corps as chief of brigade, or colonel, responsible for recruiting, officering, and outfitting the corps. Saint-George thus became the first black colonel in the French army. At first, his regiment was christened the "Free Cavalry Legion of the Americans and the Midi [South]" or the "American Hussars," then the

"13th regiment of Chasseurs [Riflemen and Light Cavalry]." But soon even administrative documents referred to it as the "Legion of Saint-George." A week later the corps was fully staffed.

The formation of the regiment was held up briefly by a petty conflict that Alexandre Dumas describes in his memoirs, though with a few distortions. Alexandre's father, Thomas Rétoré "Dumas" Davy de La Pailleterie, had been, as he put it, an "old" acquaintance of Saint-George. Landing in France in 1780, this mulatto from Saint-Domingue had at once been entrusted to the care of La Boëssière, "the leading fencing master of the day," as Dumas describes him, thanks to whom he made remarkable progress. The author of *The Three Musketeers* recounts that in 1787 his father, then twenty-five years old, fenced "with strength, skill and agility with Saint-George who, at forty-eight, had all the pretensions of a young man and justified all these pretensions." Saint-George played no small part in the young man's development. He had taken under his wing the little "black brother" who had knocked on La Boëssière's door; he was the same age as Saint-George had been when he first took up his foil at the master's school.

Saint-George was therefore very keen to enroll the brilliant Dumas in his legion. Lover of style that he was, he wanted all his cavalrymen to be first-class swordsmen. If we are to believe Alexandre Dumas's version of the story, as soon as the regiment was drawn up, Saint-George recruited Dumas but only appointed him to the rank of sublieutenant. As it happened, another colonel, who had just been taken on to head the Hussars of Liberty and Equality, was also eager to enlist young Dumas and the next day took him on as a lieutenant. However, Saint-George would not acknowledge defeat and, on January 10, 1793, enticed the young man away by naming him a lieutenant colonel.

In his desire to celebrate his father's achievements, Dumas the younger somewhat distorts reality. He seems determined to redeem the very parentage that he had in his early years taken such great pains to conceal. By the time he wrote his memoirs, Dumas had achieved considerable success and social recognition; his heritage would reflect this—even if it meant rewriting history at Saint-George's expense. The name Thomas Rétoré "Dumas" does indeed appear on the register of Saint-George's legion on September 15, 1792, not as sublieutenant but as a "commandant," or unit leader. There is no record of higher rank.

By mid-September Saint-George had to be everywhere at once. No sooner had he officered his regiment, which boasted some thirty commissioned and noncommissioned officers, than he was forced to abandon his legion in Paris and hurry to Lille, which was besieged by the Austrians and in danger of falling. Joseph, who was still captain of the fourth battalion of the Lille National Guard, had been recalled by his command to take part in the effort to break the enemy's hold on the city. No doubt he was all the more eager to rejoin his old unit because Louise was a virtual prisoner there. She had quit Paris shortly after the September massacres, intending to go back north to French Flanders, where several engagements awaited her. "This siege happened suddenly," she would write in her memoirs. "No one was expecting anything, when out of the blue we learned that the Austrian army was advancing along the road to Tournai." The inhabitants did not even have time to flee: The city was already encircled. Pounded for several weeks by Austrian artillery, Lille resisted, thanks essentially to the doggedness of the garrison commander, who vowed to hang anyone who spoke of surrender. In late September the troops that La Bourdonnaye had assembled at Douai descended on the Austrians, who finally raised the siege. Saint-George took part in these battles, which pitted highly motivated volunteers against the professional troops of the coalition.

Colonel Saint-George was still a man with contacts and diplomatic skills. It was he who on September 29 sent a dispatch to Deputy Lassource that was immediately read out to the convention and then printed up in the *Moniteur universel*: "I would inform you, my dear fellow citizen, that I have this moment received the news that our troops have retaken Saint-Amand as well as the camp and Maulde and that this camp is about to be set up once again."

While Saint-George was taking part in the battle of Lille, General Charles-François Dumouriez had won the critical Battle of Valmy on September 20, 1792, leading an army of euphoric volunteers who forced the occupying troops, all professional soldiers, out of their positions. The head of the Northern army then proposed, without making any preparations, to occupy the Austrian Netherlands (Belgium), massing his troops for the purpose. Nevertheless, before taking any action he had to obtain at least the tacit consent of the convention. He therefore went back to Paris. Along the way the general's path crossed that of Saint-George, who had also had to return to the capital to make final preparations for his legion and report on his action in the field.

In Paris, Saint-George immediately renewed contact with the Jacobins. On October 16 he attended a soirée held in honor of Dumouriez, "conqueror of the Austrians," by the famous actor François-Joseph Talma, "the god of the theater" and a close friend of Philippe d'Orléans as well as a member of the Jacobin club. Several of the artists who had recently been protégés of the duke were present, together with all his Jacobin friends. Suddenly Marat appeared and began to lash out at the whole human race, seeing traitors in every corner—Dumouriez, whom he accused of having counterrevolutionary views, but above all the nobles, including Jacobin nobles whom he showed no mercy, and especially Philippe d'Orléans. A few weeks before that, however, a number of these nobles had been massacred, with little attention paid to who was for and who against the Revolution. Between Saint-George and Marat the fur started to fly. According to Paul Lafond, author of a book on the singer Garat, "It was not easy to prevent the impetuous Saint-George from roughing up the fanatic—with his uncommon strength the other man would have had a bad time of it." In spite of his accommodating temperament, Saint-George must have been sorely vexed by this Parisian revolutionary who had avoided any brush with gunfire. Dumouriez would not forget the episode and remained convinced that he could count on Saint-George. Marat, for his part, would not forget either.

Back once again in Lille, Colonel Saint-George spent most of his time trying to discipline his 400 foot soldiers and 200 cavalrymen—no easy task. On November 7, the regiment had to march to the front, though preparations for its outfitting were far from complete. When it reached Amiens, recruiting and outfitting took several weeks. The convention meanwhile was having second thoughts about the anachronistic doctrine it had followed, which had recommended mixing infantry and cavalry. The foot soldiers, who slowed down the march considerably, were siphoned off from the legion and sent to the western part of the country, where later they ruthlessly brought the Vendée region into submission.

Relieved of the burden of the infantry, the regiment marched toward Laon, where on February 18 it received the order to leave and rejoin Dumouriez, who was having serious problems in the Low Countries. Given the state of his troops, Saint-George knew that would be suicidal. He therefore wrote the minister of war on February 13, 1793, that it was impossible for him to fulfill "his obligations toward the Nation." As he saw it, the wisest move would be to return to Lille. He was insistent, stressing that he could not "lead his men to the slaughter, since they had at least to be taught to know their left from their right"—obviously a minimum for a battlefield unit. The municipal authorities of Laon and Château-Thierry likewise insisted that these fighters, whose uniforms, bearing, and discipline they admired, should remain close to their cities, where they could protect the population. Several letters to this effect were dispatched to the convention.

The regiment continued to march to Lille, arriving on February 28. Like all the Revolution's forces, Saint-George's legion lacked practically everything. The soldiers' pay was late in coming and, the convention having ordered that expenses be paid in promissory notes, suppliers preferred to keep their stocks full rather than exchange their goods for paper. Only Dumouriez, still bogged down in the Low Countries campaign, had the courage to stand up to the convention. With the help of a pro-Revolutionary financier from Brussels, he was able to pay his suppliers with gold, thus avoiding total disaster.[4] Louis Philippe, who was then the general's staff officer, reported that the men were living in wretched conditions. Looting was pervasive—doubtless not the best way to export the Revolution—and desertions were multiplying. "The army administration was in such a state of confusion, in such disorder, that it could be said to be nonexistent," he notes in his memoirs. "And when you saw that as closely as I did, you could never imagine how we managed to obtain the results we did."[5] Saint-George's legion itself suffered multiple desertions. Soon a number of his soldiers were siphoned off and sent to reestablish order in the colonies. Their places were assumed by whites, who now made up the majority, although the command structure was still made up exclusively of blacks and half-castes.

Alexandre Dumas painted a glorious picture of his father's part in the campaign. "Actually placed at the head of the regiment—Saint-George, hardly eager for fire, having remained in Lille on the pretext of seeing to the organization of his troops—my father saw a wider opportunity open up before him to exhibit his courage and intelligence. The battle squadrons he himself disciplined were cited for their patriotism and their fine uniforms. Always under fire, there were few occasions at the camp of La Madeleine when his squadrons were not engaged, and wherever they engaged they left behind an honorable, often glorious, memory." The author of *The Count of Monte-Cristo* goes on to describe this northern campaign with a novelist's flair:

One day, for example, the regiment found itself in the vanguard and all of a sudden came up against a Dutch regiment hidden in the barley, which in this season and this area grew to the height of a man. The regiment's presence was revealed by the movement of a sergeant who, some fifteen paces from my father, was readying his cannon in order to fire. My father saw this movement, understood that at that distance the sergeant could not miss him, drew a pistol from its holster, and fired so quickly and accurately that before the weapon was lowered the cannoneer had been pierced through by his bullet. This pistol shot was the signal for a magnificent charge, in the course of which the Dutch regiment was slashed to pieces.

It is more likely that the reality was both less romantic and distinctly more complimentary to Saint-George. His dossier, which is in the archives of the ministry of defense, is packed with accounts from simple soldiers, noncommissioned officers from the 13th Light Cavalry Regiment, highly placed civil servants of the Republic, and even elected representatives of the districts the legion marched through. All attest to the fact that Saint-George made it a point of honor to lead his troops into battle, even pursuing the enemy farther than had been requested. His many acts of daring would later save his life.

Saint-George's legion did not stray far from the outskirts of Lille. The convention had finally come around to the black colonel's way of thinking and entrusted him with making reconnaissance forays, which resulted in a number of clashes with enemy troops. As a rule the regiment operated in split fashion: One part stayed in Lille and underwent training while Saint-George struggled to find horses, ammunition, and provisions; the other carried out cavalry operations in Belgium. There was now no point in trying to reach Holland. After several major tactical errors, Dumouriez, who had forced the authorities' hand by invading the Low Countries, was badly beaten at Neerwinden and obliged to fall back to France. From the convention's point of view it was better to wait until all the northern troops were grouped around Lille before contemplating a counterattack. Saint-George's legion therefore remained in a position of support, to prevent Dumouriez's retreat from turning into a rout.

It was a wise precaution. The first series of executions had begun in Paris and the problems of provisioning the armies were starting to give the officers, most of whom had come from the *ancien régime,* pause. On August 20, 1792, Lafayette left the country. Meanwhile Dumouriez fell into the enemy camp shortly after the death of the king on January 21, 1793. Even as he was campaigning in the northern plains, he planned to march on Paris and offer the French throne to Louis XVI's young son. The baron de Breteuil would act as regent. Young Louis Philippe de Chartres, to whom Dumouriez confided his plan, relates in his memoirs that after the Neerwinden defeat Dumouriez had established contact with the duke of Saxe-Coburg, the man who had defeated him, and concluded a secret armistice with him. He set about organizing an expedition to Paris, with the aim of freeing the royal family, then held prisoner in the Temple, and bringing the king's son back north to French Flanders, where he would be proclaimed king. At the head of his army Louis XVII would then be led back to Paris in triumph. As a former Jacobin, the traitorous general did not, however, envisage the reestablishment of the *ancien régime* exactly as before. He believed the future monarch should enforce the Constitution of 1791, favoring the new business-oriented bourgeoisie.

However, some were highly skeptical that Dumouriez's plan was a disinterested one. Among the skeptics was Antoine de Jomini, the self-styled "Newton of the military art" and later one of Napoleon's most valued advisers. "After such well-deserved disasters," he wrote, "Dumouriez could no longer flatter himself that he had escaped the vengeance of the Jacobins, who could barely forgive him his triumphs. How could anyone believe, indeed, that the desperadoes who had just cut off a good king's head would spare that of an arrogant soldier who had given them cause for complaint and whom his reversals would leave defenseless before the full weight of their attacks?"

Whatever the case, in early April, Dumouriez sent a division of four thousand men to Lille with a mission he himself describes in his memoirs as "to enter the city, have the Convention's representatives arrested as well as the chief club members, and as soon as this is done proceed to Douai and expel General Moreton." But General Miaczinsky, who commanded the division, proved to have a big mouth and confided the plan to Saint-George. He even rode up to the gates of Lille at the head of a small escort, convinced that the black colonel, a friend of Louis Philippe and someone who had a few months before had been foolhardy enough to risk defending Dumouriez against Marat, would hand over to him the keys of the city. Saint-George had shrewdly done nothing to cause him to harbor doubts in this regard. On April 1, 1793, the gates of Lille closed behind Dumouriez's right-hand man. Miaczinsky had to hand over his saber to Saint-George. Brought to Paris, he would soon lose his head.

The disarming of the elite division accompanying Miaczinsky sounded the death knell to Dumouriez's hopes. His troops, duly reprimanded by Saint-George and by General Leveneur, a member of the faded Norman gentry whose main claim to fame was for applying the ideas of the Encyclopedists to his lands at Carrouges, now turned against him. Barely escaping death by firing squad, the old hero of the Revolution left, his tail between his legs, for the Austrian camp. A few days later he went into exile in Switzerland with Louis Philippe and Madame de Genlis. The latter would never have let her boy, just twenty years old, go into battle without his "maman," as Louis Philippe called his governess.

In Paris, Dumouriez's treason sealed the victory of the Marat faction. These were the extremists, or "ultras," who spied traitors in every corner. On April 4 the convention decreed the arrest of all Bourbons, including the marquise de Montesson, who had been brave enough to stay on in Paris, and Philippe Egalité, who had never ceased to declare his support for the Revolution. The "de-Orléanization" was beginning. For months now, the ultras had been vainly seeking an excuse to bring down Philippe d'Orléans, whose only wrong in their eyes was to be a prince of the blood royal—and thus capable of representing a legitimate alternative to the Republic. The duke had never given them any cause for criticism. He had adopted the name Philippe Egalité, to the cheers of the people of Paris. Certain of his friends, like Jérôme Pétion de Villeneuve, the city's mayor, or Brissot, the friend of blacks, had sided with the Girondins. But he himself had preferred to take his seat with the Montagnards alongside Robespierre, Saint-Just, and Billaud-Varenne. He had even given up his possessions and titles, contenting himself with a modest apartment at the Palais-Royal—rechristened Palais-Egalité or Maison Egalité—and two servants (including a coachman who had stayed on in his service out of friendship). And on several occasions he had sought the "honor" of serving liberty sword in hand, either in the navy, his original "corps," or the infantry. He had even grown a mustache so as to look like the soldiers of the army of the Rhine. It was impossible for anyone to impute the slightest fault to so ardent a revolutionary. Except, that is, for Choderlos de Laclos, who, after the flight to Varennes, had foolishly demanded the fall of the king and the appointment of the duke as regent. But that personal initiative had immediately been reprimanded by the duke, who had even dismissed his imprudent secretary.

In actual fact, Laclos would be one of the first of the Orléans clan to be clapped in prison. Others would follow, among them Jacobins like Victor de Broglie, whom the convention had nevertheless offered a general's post in the Eastern army. This great friend of Saint-George would soon be led to the scaffold. In April 1793, woe betide anyone believed to be a friend of the "traitor" Egalité. The head of the American Hussars himself, Saint-George, soon became eminently suspect—especially since, considered a former "agent" of the duc d'Orléans, he had taken that absurd risk in threatening Marat to defend Dumouriez's honor. No matter that he had later played a decisive part in the traitorous general's downfall.

And so started the denunciations, each one less spontaneous than the one before it. For example:

Section Mauconseil (permanent assembly),

On this day April 29, 1793 year II at 8 o'clock in the morning, there came before our Revolutionary Committee and Committee of Public Safety the citizens Louis-Philippe-Joseph-Sébastien Bambiboucingy known as Narcisse, lieutenant of the 13th Chasseurs, and Louis-Joseph Azor, known as Ferrand, adjutant to the said regiment, who declared to us that the citizen formerly called the Chevalier de St-Georges, their commander-in-chief, had almost never been seen in their corps since he was appointed chief and further declared that he had never carried out any review of the said corps, and also declared that the said St-Georges was an intimate of M. Dumouriez, former general, traitor to the Nation.[6]

Neither his lieutenants nor the Committee of Public Safety could be unaware that, as a captain in the Lille National Guard, Saint-George had been urgently recalled to his original posting, from which he had not had time to resign. The battle to raise the siege of Lille temporarily took precedence over the formation of his legion. As for his "friendship" with Dumouriez, it had actually been extremely valuable, enabling him to learn of the plot the general was hatching and frustrate it.

Another denunciation followed a few days later. On May 4, a certain citizen Maillard denounced to the Committee of Public Safety "the suspicious appearance of enrollments in the Legion of Saint-George." As a result, the executive council instructed that patriot to "obstruct everything that this corps might undertake against the interests of the Republic."

The police were also hard at work. They pointed out number 148 of Maison Egalité (the former Palais-Royal) where a "counterrevolutionary club" had met that was "frequented by Dumouriez, Miaczinsky, Saint-George, and numerous aristocrats." This nest of "counterrevolutionaries" was in fact merely one of the Jacobins' meeting-places where Saint-George, Philippe d'Orléans, and a few noble patriots like Victor de Broglie or Alexandre Beauharnais were wont to get together. Marat and Desmoulins often showed up as well. But in those paranoia-driven days it was enough to have been in a suspect's company in times past to be guilty today.

Following a formula that has proved effective since that time, the attack on Saint-George began with the dispatch of political agents. The agent assigned to the task, one Dufrenne, was not overscrupulous in distinguishing gossip from fact. He opened his report by stating, "Saint-George is a man to be watched"—which, after all, was what the man was being paid to do. And he went on: "Crippled with debts, he took it into his head to raise a corps; this was allowed him, I believe, and paid for to the tune of 300,000 livres by the Nation to provide for the outfitting of his soldiers, who in spite of that still had huge requirements! I am convinced that he did not devote more than 100,000 livres to the needs of this corps; the remainder went to pay the debts of M. Saint-George, who lives in blatant luxury and, it is said, has more than thirty horses in his stables, several of which cost 3,000 livres apiece. What a scandal!"[7]

This cry of reproach would have been more plausible had it not relied so heavily on the "it is said" disclaimer that this professional denunciator felt obliged to use. In fact, Saint-George, who never skimped on either his friendships or his confidences, probably did regale his comrades in arms with tales about the luxurious Hôtel du Bac, where, once upon a time, his father did keep a large stable of very fine horses. Now his past and his stories about it were being turned against him. Dufrenne also tried to pit the soldiers (probably living in wretched conditions) against their colonel. It mattered little that the testimonies concerning Saint-George depicted a man more inclined to ruin himself to help others than to enrich himself. He was presumed guilty simply because he was "a man to be watched."

Nearly six decades later, Alexandre Dumas turned the situation to his (or his father's) advantage. Once again, he sought to burnish the senior Dumas's legend by tarnishing Saint-George's. In fact, in Dumas's mind Saint-George's great sin seems to have been that he stayed in everyone's memory—in particular, that of Balzac—because of his fencing skills, and because of the fact that a Republican regiment had been named for him, something that General Dumas, despite his long military career, would never achieve. The great novelist had been only four years old when his father died, in 1806, and thus was unable to recall much about him. Nor is there any document or testimony to support his story. Dumas embroidered Dufrenne's report in an effort to show that Saint-George had been brought before the revolutionary tribunal for "making deals" in order to buy expensive horses, though the government had provided him with "remounts." According to Dumas, "As Saint-George's accounts were very badly kept, he saw fit to shift all the blame onto my father, saying that Lieutenant-Colonel Dumas had been given responsibility for the regiment's remounts." Vexed and humiliated, Dumas therefore purportedly decided to "fight it out to the death with his former colonel." But, lo and behold, "Saint-George, good fellow that he was, when he had a pistol or a sword in his hand liked to choose his duels. . . . My father thus went to meet Saint-George three times without finding him; then he came back three more times and left his card." According to Dumas, however, in the end it was Saint-George who, upon finding the card, went to Dumas's house, found him lying sick, and threw himself on the bed: "What's all this?" he said. "So you wanted to kill me? Dumas kill Saint-George? Not possible. You're my son, aren't you? When Saint-George is dead, who but you could take his place? Come on then, quick, get up! Give me something to eat and let's have no more of this nonsense."

The anecdote illustrates, no doubt quite faithfully, the kind of banter the two men indulged in. There is no question but that Saint-George who, according to La Boëssière, "adored young people," treated Dumas like a son. In 1780, the forty-year-old Saint-George had taken the eighteen-year-old youth of mixed race under his wing when the lad first pushed open the door of La Boëssière's school. Both men were also very tall; they could in fact have been taken for father and son.

It seems fairly clear that Dumas conjured up this story of a duel merely to establish that his father was skilled enough to compete with the legendary Saint-George. The idea of a fight to the death between the two most famous black soldiers in continental France was a highly romantic one. It was a scene that could only have taken root in the fertile imagination of the creator of the swashbuckling d'Artagnan. At the time these "facts" were said to have taken place, all duly dated in Alexandre Dumas's memoir, his father was leading a detachment in the Alps. As for Saint-George, he was engaged, as we shall see, in a fight against adversaries far more devious and dangerous than the Austrians.

After Dufrenne had submitted his report, Colonel Saint-George was summoned to Paris on May 11 and ordered to explain his actions before the revolutionary tribunal. His duty sheets proved convincing; he came away cleared of all suspicion. In the atmosphere that reigned at the time, such a release seemed miraculous. And, under the Terror, miracles didn't happen twice. The colonel's enemies refused to be mollified, however. On June 25 a new report emerged, written by a second commission member sent by Marat's crew. This individual, named Beaumé, attacked Saint-George's military record. "Desertions continued to take place," he wrote. "Saint-George's hussars, yesterday four at least, have gone over to the enemy, equipment and all." This was indeed shocking. But desertion plagued all the Revolutionary armies. In his book on the French Revolution, Albert Mathiez notes that on December 1, 1792, the French army consisted of some 400,000 men. By February 1, 1793, they numbered no more than 228,000.[8] In particular, according to Mathiez, "the Belgian army was perhaps more sorely tried than the rest. 'There is a certain battalion of volunteers,' Dubois-Cranc said on February 7, 'which has not even a hundred men left.' Some companies had only five. Those who remained were poor devils or professionals who looted and marauded and were not noted for their discipline, even if they still acquitted themselves bravely."

It so happened that Saint-George's hussars—who were, by the way, attached to the Belgian army—played an exceedingly onerous role in that war. Armed with only sabers and pistols, they had to gallop across enemy positions to harass the regiments of the line, popping up where least expected, such as by attacking the enemy's rear or flanks when it believed danger was coming toward them head-on, and then vanishing. The role was tailor-made for a horseman and swordsman of Saint-George's abilities. But these riders who moved in small bands of a few dozen men and acted like commando units also presented ideal targets, far from their billets and continually vulnerable to ambush, or of being stranded because of an exhausted horse. This meant that Beaumé must have been unusually keen-sighted to distinguish those who did not return after a long day spent riding into enemy lines because they had deserted from those who did not return because they had been killed. His arguments did not convince the convention any more than Dufrenne's had swayed the revolutionary tribunal only a few weeks before. On July 1, the convention's executive committee confirmed Colonel Saint-George in his rank of brigade chief. It was miracle number two.

In Paris during that summer of 1793, the revolutionaries saw the ground giving way under their feet. "The Republic," wrote Barère at the time of the mass uprising of August 23, "is now nothing but a huge city under siege." Lyon had been captured by the Royalists, Toulon had fallen to the English, Condé and Valenciennes had been seized by the Prussians, Saumur and Nantes by the Vendeans. This meant the revolutionary tribunal could ill afford to show a clemency that would appear suspicious—a paltry sixty-six death sentences emerging from 260 "trials." Marat's assassination rang out like a thunderclap. It showed the Revolution's leaders, already steeped in paranoia, that the enemy was no longer content to attack the borders;

it was within. The guillotine was lying in wait. The Girondins were among the first to be led to the scaffold, with Brissot and Madame Roland, both friends of Saint-George, first in line. "O Liberty! What crimes are committed in thy name," cried the woman whom the great historian Michelet, as we have seen, would call "the wonder of the Revolution," as she mounted the steps to the guillotine. Pétion, another intimate of the duc d'Orléans and of de Genlis, the duke's former captain of guards, was later found to have committed suicide.

On September 5, 1793, a new law on "suspects" was promulgated. "Denunciation, which was deemed dishonorable under the *ancien régime*, became a virtue and a duty," Furet and Richet would later point out.[9] At this time Louise Fusil was staying in Boulogne, sheltered from the fighting and its dangers, yet a stone's throw from Lille. In her memoirs she would describe the anger of a certain Joseph Lebon, who had been dispatched from Paris to arrest suspects:

"What, no list of suspects?" he repeated. One of the members of the committee (a wigmaker from Gascony), who was terrified of what would happen to them as a result, assured the citizen representative that there had been a mistake, that he had had the list in his hands, that he was going to look for it at the town hall and that he would bring it himself to his lodging. . . . The wigmaker closeted himself with another member of the committee, and they hastily drew up a list containing all the names they could remember.[10]

On September 25, and as a result of this highly unusual legislation, Colonel Saint-George was stripped of his command by order of Minister of War Bouchotte. At first Saint-George tried to wait patiently to learn of the reasons for his dismissal, but day after day the eagerly awaited mail delivery brought him no news. Unable to contain his impatience, he sent a letter to Bouchotte dated October 29 from Château-Thierry, requesting an explanation:

Citizen Minister,

Until now I have waited with submission in the hope that you would be kind enough to inform me of the causes that may have merited my suspension; I can no longer remain in this cruel uncertainty; I have nothing in the world with which to reproach myself; everywhere I have given proofs of my good citizenship and my republican sentiments, which are innate in me. Do me the kindness, Citizen Minister, to put me in a position to justify the false charges that have been brought against me, and to prove to you that your good faith has been abused.

I beg for this justice in the name of humanity; it is the due of every French republican.

With assurances of the most perfect citizenship, I remain,

> Your fellow citizen,
>
> Saint-George, chief of brigade[11]

An experienced bureaucrat, Bouchotte replied with a refusal, but also pointing out that the decision had come from a level higher than his own: "I can give you no other response, save that the Executive Council has judged this measure necessary in the circumstances." Clearly, the minister could not admit the inadmissible, namely that the only reproach that could be leveled against the man was that he had been an intimate of the duc d'Orléans. Nonetheless, the conscientious apparatchik could not disguise his obvious unease in the face of Saint-George's vibrant profession of revolutionary faith: "You may write me all the reasons that you believe capable of making the Council reconsider its decision, and I shall submit them."

A few days later, by order of Representative Le Jeune, Saint-George was arrested and imprisoned in the house of detention of Hondainville, near the town of Clermont-sur-Oise.

XV

Singing to Victory

Saint-George had most certainly not chosen the easiest path when, past fifty years of age, he took up arms to defend the Revolution. While he was fighting in Flanders his "brother musicians," as he called them, had been devoting their talents to the cause. During that winter of 1793–94, while one of the greatest composers and instrumentalists of his day was huddled in a freezing prison cell, the men he had directed not long before were being showered with praise.

The revolutionary leaders had not been slow to grasp the many ways in which music could help their cause. For example, Dubouchet, a member of the convention, declared from the tribune on Nivôse 26 of year II (January 17, 1794): "Nothing better serves to galvanize republican souls than hymns and songs."[1] During the first months of the Revolution, the theaters suddenly became enormously popular. New ones opened in every quarter of the city. The *Journal des théâtres* of November 4, 1791, even claimed that "theaters have become almost as plentiful as clubs."[2] Old plays were dusted off and new operas joined the repertory, notably those by Luigi Cherubini and Nicolas Dalayrac. The librettos of these new works sang the praises of a blessed era now within reach, an era when concord and prosperity would finally reign throughout the land.

Stages turned into outright political platforms. The salon of the Palais-Royal theater, presided over by Mademoiselle Montansier, regularly received Danton and Robespierre, while the theater itself featured a number of pro-Revolution plays. Top billing went to the great Talma, the "god of the theater," who after having been adored by *ancien régime* audiences was now fully committed to the revolutionary cause. Jean-Baptiste Drouet was entrusted with management of the Théâtre Molière. It was a reward for services rendered the Republic. Formerly Drouet had been the postmaster for the city of Varennes, and then had recognized Louis XVI huddled in the corner of a coach passing by, leading to the king's eventual recapture. Soon rechristened the Théâtre des Sans-Culottes, its repertoire consisted almost solely of plays celebrating Jacobin fervor.

Conversely, the law of January 13, 1791, abolishing every and all forms of censorship allowed the monarchists to stage plays on their favorite themes, albeit for a brief time. Here the public served as censor. For example, when Méhul and Hoffman set to music an old libretto by Metastasio, Gluck's former poet, entitled *Hadrian, Emperor of Rome*, the audience erupted in outrage. The opera celebrated an emperor's triumph over a rebellious city; the public was convinced Hadrian represented Joseph II, the Austrian emperor who was threatening to march his army straight into Paris. Two lines in particular provoked fury among those in the pit:

> *Rule, Caesar! And may your noble brow*
> *Grow accustomed to the sacred laurel.*

Eventually the Paris Commune, proprietors of the Opéra, decided to withdraw the work, ostensibly for financial reasons. Asked to explain matters, the playwright Fabre d'Eglantine argued that it was the commune's job to make up the Opéra's deficits, and that therefore it was acting perfectly within its rights to ban a work that might result in "the failure of the enterprise whose employees it would still be obliged to pay." Méhul quickly adapted to the requirements of these new, and already apparently quite powerful, economic laws.

On the other hand, the commune wholeheartedly supported Gossec's *L'Offrande à la liberté* (Offering to Liberty), libretto by François-Marie Chénier, which had its first performance on October 2, 1792. The opera was essentially one long dramatic crescendo, leading to the climactic singing of the "Marseillaise." The first act, lugubrious in tone, is set during the waning years of the monarchy. After a few bars of a popular romance by Dalayrac (and polished up by Gossec) comes a thunderous cry—"Liberty!"—from the chorus. Dancers and children dressed in white appear on stage and begin to worship before Liberty's statue, then light fires at the foot of the altar on which the statue sits. Next, a soloist sings the first couplets of the "*Chant de guerre de l'armée du Rhin*" ("War Song for the Army of the Rhine"), the original title of the "Marseillaise." The entire chorus explodes with "*Aux armes, citoyens!*"—"To arms, citizens!"

The opera was revolutionary spectacle on the grandest possible scale, and it set the stage for others. Any compositions that didn't follow its themes, even those that were meant to be merely entertaining but were judged (for whatever reason) "dissident," didn't last long. Again, at first there was no need for the new authorities to impose censorship; the public was doing the job for them. Spectators did not hesitate to boo loudly any reference, however small, that might appear sympathetic to the monarchy. Meanwhile, the classics were revised to suit contemporary tastes. Molière's *Tartuffe* and Corneille's *Horace* and *Le Cid* were adapted to evince greater revolutionary purity. Even Rousseau's *Le Devin du village* (The Village Soothsayer) was made to positively glow with patriotic fervor. And of course original works extolled the greatness of the Revolution, such as Méhul's *Départ des patriotes* (The Patriots' Departure) or the *Offering to Liberty* described above, or glorified exploits, such as the lifting of the siege of Lille. The Opéra was becoming "the veritable primary school of the citizen," as the *Feuille du salut public* (Public Safety Leaflet) proclaimed on October 5, 1793.

Composers who had been the darlings of the *ancien régime* didn't balk at writing music for the new government. Grétry, Méhul, Kreutzer, and Gossec offer examples. Similarly, Marie-Antoinette's favorite librettists, such as Moline, the poet for Gluck's *Orpheus*—and for Saint-George's work as well—or Desfontaines, the librettist for Saint-George's *The Hunt*, happily wrote works that were steeped in revolutionary spirit. Nevertheless, those who sold out their talent purely to ingratiate themselves with the authorities were the exception. Far more numerous were those musicians who, having prayed for a freer world in their Masonic Lodge meetings, supported the new regime's ideals. In the Revolution's early days, Gossec, the uncontested musical leader of Paris during Saint-George's absence, spoke for the whole corps of musicians when he said, "It is the public that feeds us. Therefore it is for the public that we must work." (By 1797, the public finally tired of these propaganda-like plays, which even the regime's dignitaries shunned. In 1799, the administrators of the Opéra wrote the Central Office of the Canton of Paris: "Every time we stage patriotic subjects, the public and the censors, the people's magistrates as well as the highest authorities all seem to flee from a place where, at least to set an example, they should congregate. Every man makes fine phrases about his patriotism, in the papers or on the tribune, but no one risks three francs to prove it.")

The revolutionary period witnessed an operatic explosion: seventy-six new operas in 1790 and more than fifty per year for the next five years. One out of two of these new works celebrated revolutionary virtues and fervor, and in the main it was the huge, quasi-religious revolutionary "Masses" that provided the greatest vehicles for musical talent. To quote the *Journal des théâtres et des fêtes nationales* (August 18, 1794): "Of all the institutions which the revolutionary genre has produced, that of national festivals is without question one of those most worthy of attracting the attention of republicans." In his September 1791 *Report on Public Education,* Talleyrand had emphasized the importance of spectacles, festivals, the arts, and music "as means of education."[3] Three years later, on May 7, 1794, Robespierre harangued the convention: "There is, however, one kind of institution that must be considered an essential part of public education. . . . I refer to national festivals." Not much later, Boissy d'Anglas, a deputy from the Ardèche region, theorized on the significance of festivals for the Revolution: "National festivals have for their adornment the happiest sensations of the soul; thus in recalling to mankind the first emotions of childhood, that is, those that are the purest, those that are accompanied by innocence, naiveté, confidence, and good faith, they will help to soften and bring to perfection the morals of the peoples, and give the nations that moral sensibility that must exist among them and be reflected in their actions as in those of individuals." Thanks to festivals, the people would enjoy a second childhood.

The Revolution soon mastered the art of burying its dead, for it offered the best opportunity for holding them up as models for the living. The death of Mirabeau, struck down in his cups on April 2, 1791, set the stage for what Michelet later called "along with Napoleon's, the most immense and popular funeral the world has ever witnessed." The ceremony was punctuated by the drumbeat from Gossec's *Marche lugubre,* "a long lament based on the development of a short rhythmic idea, supported by the somber beating of drums."[4] All the great revolutionary occasions from that time forward were accompanied by that impressive march. Shortly afterward, the transfer of Voltaire's ashes to the Panthéon would provide just as imposing a ceremony. Gossec wrote the music, Marie-Joseph Chénier the words of the hymns, while David prepared a grandiose *mise en scène.* "There were many people in the cortege, men and women attired in all varieties of antique dress who walked in front of, beside, and behind the triumphal chariot."[5] The huge chariot itself, drawn by twelve white horses, was surmounted by a statue of Immortality, placing a crown of stars on Voltaire's head.

Other obsequies were celebrated with the same pomp—with, again, backdrops and sets by David, words by Chénier, and music by Gossec: those of Lepeletier de Saint-Fargeau, who was assassinated after voting in favor of Louis XVI's execution, those of Marat, those celebrating the transfer of Rousseau's ashes to the Panthéon, and finally the funeral of General Lazare Louis Hoche. The instigation behind them all was the search for the Revolution's martyrs and saints. The same need pervaded the grandiose "festivals" held to celebrate victories. One example was held in the Savoie region on October 14, 1792, marking the enemy's retreat into the Alps, during which the "Marseillaise" was sung for the first time at a grand event; another celebrated the capture of Toulon; and finally there was the so-called "Festival of Victories."

Indeed, the deification of the Revolution required the skills of many musicians and stage designers. In 1790 when the "Festival of the Federation" was held (with Philippe d'Orléans attending), the Fourteenth of July became the Republic's great annual gathering. Inevitably it had to be celebrated with increasing pomp, year by year, with the result that the owner of the largest fireworks factory made a fortune. Again homage had to be paid—with music and vast crowds—to the deities of the Revolution: Liberty was honored magnificently on April 5, 1792; Law on June 3 of that same year; and Unity and Indivisibility on August 10, 1793, when the crowd sang Gossec's "Hymn to Nature."

Two festivals in particular illustrated the new republican spirit. The first was the "Festival of Reason." "Reason" had been proclaimed the national religion on November 7, 1793. The ceremony instituting it, which took place three days later, used as a backdrop Notre-Dame Cathedral, renamed the "Temple of Reason and Liberty." An enormous artificial mountain was erected for the occasion in the cathedral's nave. Atop it stood a small round temple, bearing the dedication "To Philosophy." Around it were busts of Reason's priests, such as Voltaire and Rousseau. During the ceremony a woman representing Liberty emerged from the temple, clad in white and wearing the red Phrygian cap, to receive the homage of republicans in the form of a hymn, again composed by Gossec, with words by Chénier:

> *Descend, O Liberty, daughter of Nature,*
> *The people have won back their immortal power;*
> *Above the pompous remains of ancient imposture*
> *Their hands will raise your altar.*

Whereupon the "Marseillaise" rang out, followed by a *symphonie concertante* for eleven wind instruments (not including orchestra), Gossec's funeral march, and an overture by Méhul.

The second of these gigantic mystical ceremonies was the "Festival of the Supreme Being," which Robespierre had conceived of to combat godlessness that might lead to anarchy. Several hundred musicians and a chorus consisting of nearly 2,500 singers were assembled on Prairial 20 (June 8), 1794, to celebrate "the Idea of the Supreme Being and the Immortality of the Soul," which, according to Robespierre, "is social and republican." The staging, supervised down to the last detail by David, was spectacular, and took place in a number of locales. At the Tuileries gardens, Robespierre, acting as high priest, set fire to a papier-mâché statue representing Atheism supported by Ambition, Egoism, Discord, and False Modesty. Once burnt, the monster Atheism was replaced by a gigantic statue of Wisdom while the choir sang the "Hymn to the Supreme Being" (again by Gossec). Unfortunately, David had not foreseen that the flames consuming the hated allegories would flicker so dangerously close to Wisdom. Her statue, which was meant to be dazzlingly white, looked as black as soot to the spectators. It was a disturbing omen. At the ceremony held on the Champ-de-Mars, David had designed a mountain of rocks and grottoes, covered with luxuriant greenery. Members of the convention had to clamber up the thing. Once they had reached the top, an enormous choir directed by Gossec and Sarrette sang out the "Marseillaise," followed by other hymns.

The period of these "mystical operas" ended in pure tragedy. On Thermidor 10 (July 28), 1794, less than two months after the Festival of the Supreme Being, Robespierre was sent to the guillotine. The final curtain fell. As *La France musicale* put it, "The Revolution is a great lyric drama, with stage design by David, words by Chénier, and music by Gossec."

The Belgian Gossec, Saint-George's old friend, protector, and teacher, was certainly not the only composer capable of setting the Revolution to music, though he was unmatched when it came to exhortative volume. While Saint-George was languishing in prison, his friends and former employees were being sought after as never before. François Giroust, a member of the Olympique orchestra (though he belonged to another lodge), composed a hymn to the glory of the night of August 4, 1794: *J'ai tout perdu et je m'en fous* ("I've lost everything and I don't give a damn"). But things could have turned out worse; he managed to get a job as concierge at Versailles, where he died in 1799. Etienne Nicolas Méhul, whom Saint-George had brought into the Olympique orchestra in 1786, became a musical star of the Revolution with his *Chant du départ* (Song of Departure), which elementary schoolchildren in France were taught for a century and a half. He would also write a *Chant du retour* (Song of Return), though it is much less well known. These two hymns, alas, have completely eclipsed the output of this precursor of the great symphonic composers. Dalayrac, who was famous during the *ancien régime* for his gossamer-like compositions, also contributed to the revolutionary hymn genre with *Les Canons* and *Réponse au salpêtre*. Saltpeter, the raw material of gunpowder, inspired a few dozen revolutionary songs and hymns. For instance Luigi Cherubini, another musician whom Saint-George had brought into the Olympique orchestra, composed a work entitled *Republican Saltpeter*.

He also wrote no fewer than eleven works for revolutionary festivals, among them the very affecting hymn played at the funeral of Maréchal Hoche. Cherubini, the object of Mozart's hatred shortly before, lagged far behind Gossec's record output, which came to no fewer than forty-four large-scale works. But Gossec is a special case, having been both a staunch monarchist and then an ardent supporter of the Revolution. Cherubini seems in hindsight to have been a sort of musical Talleyrand. Born under the reign of Louis XV, he would die six years before the revolution of 1848 at the age of eighty-two. In the meantime he served the Revolution, the Empire, the Restoration, and the July monarchy, composing for example the coronation masses of Louis XVIII and Charles X. He might have turned out to be one of the bards of the 1848 Revolution had he lived a few years longer.

In his defense, it should be said that with the possible exception of David, who was harassed for a time after the fall of Robespierre, artists showed an extraordinary talent for sensing which way the wind was shifting. One example was Saint-George's beloved Louise Fusil, who professed an inordinate love for the royal family yet performed in every revolutionary festival. Giroust remained deeply royalist. And those who idolized Robespierre and composed hymns and odes to the Supreme Being at his demand were later the first to celebrate the fall of the "tyrant." Gossec was unashamedly able to compose a song entitled "Hymn to Humanity in Memory of Thermidor the Ninth." Méhul and Chénier likewise would compose music celebrating the day of Robespierre's arrest:

> *Hail, Nine Thermidor, day of deliverance!*
> *Thou comest to purify a soil drenched in blood.*

But what would the Revolution have been without the "Marseillaise"? There was no festival, big or small, and no commemorative occasion in which it was not the high point. Within a very short period of time after its composition in 1792 it became for the Revolution what the *Te*

Deum had been for the monarchy. Its composer, Claude Joseph Rouget de Lisle, was a Mason, as was Saint-George, and like him had joined the army to defend France. In his work *Roland à Roncevaux,* an opera celebrating the great French hero of the middle ages, de Lisle would set to music Horace's famous line, "It is sweet and honorable to die for one's country" (*Dulce et decorum est pro patria mori*). However, this refined composer, who could write works far different from his war songs, proved a poor soldier. The comte d'Aumale, who commanded his Besançon regiment, had him transferred, noting that "Rouget de Lisle has very little to recommend him. He has no self-discipline and his superior requests with as much justification as insistence that he be employed in another brigade."[6] Rouget de Lisle was sent to Strasbourg, where instead of spending his time in his garrison he attended Masonic meetings organized by baron de Dietrich, the city's mayor, a monarchist but also a fervent patriot. At Dietrich's request, Rouget de Lisle composed his "War Song for the Army of the Rhine" in the euphoria of the night of April 24–25, 1792. The battle hymn was played by the municipal band the next day. A soldier named Mireur went to Marseille a few days later to arrange for the troops there to march northward. Mireur took part in a colossal drinking bout at a tavern called Chez David. When he was asked for a song, he got up on the table and began the "War Song for the Army of the Rhine." The next day the volunteers of the Marseille battalion each had a copy of the song. The "Marseillaise" was born.

Propelled by this battalion from the south, the hymn spread like wildfire throughout all the armies. "It was like a lightning bolt," Michelet relates. "Everyone was caught up in it." One general, for instance, asked the convention for "a reinforcement of one thousand men and a copy of the 'Marseillaise.' " Another wrote, "I've won: The 'Marseillaise' was serving with me." Before turning traitor, Dumouriez himself gave his soldiers this order of the day: "Close up your ranks, lower your bayonets, sing the 'Marseillaise' hymn, and you'll win the day!" An officer who had fought for the Austrians in the

1792 campaign recalls in his memoirs: "The French who had been advancing on us for some hours saluted the enemy by singing over and over the terrifying hymn called the 'Marseillaise.' To describe the effect of that hymn when it is sung by thousands of voices is humanly impossible!"[7]

In a cruel irony of fate, Rouget de Lisle, who was in large measure a symbol of the Revolution, was devoured by it. A *monarchien,* that is, one favoring constitutional monarchy, he, like Saint-George, fell victim to the so-called *loi des suspects,* or law of suspects, of September 1793 and was thrown into jail in Paris. Every morning, like so many others he listened as the names on the list of those destined for the Widow—the guillotine—were read out, one by one. His turn at last arrived on July 28, or Thermidor 9. But that day it was Robespierre who climbed into the cart. De Lisle was spared.

In their own ways, both Rouget de Lisle and Saint-George were examples of the vagaries of the world, going from glory to a desperate fight to evade the guillotine. De Lisle had celebrated the fight for a new world. In addition to his musical contributions—contributions that were themselves revolutionary to the world of musical creation—Saint-George had been a symbol of what men of color could conquer with their sword in hand. Before 1789, his talent had eclipsed that of friends who would later become more famous than he. He could easily have been anointed a musician-hero by the Republic. The man who had essentially invented orchestration for more than eighty musicians would doubtless have loved directing those gigantic revolutionary orchestras (at the "Festival of the Federation" it consisted of three hundred brass and three hundred percussion instruments) and choirs (the 2,500-member chorus for the "Festival of the Supreme Being"). Instead, Saint-George chose to take up arms. Throughout this whole period his output was fairly modest. He did manage to direct concerts between two battles in Lille, in particular *Guillaume tout cœur.* Nonetheless, he had generally permitted his musical talents to lie fallow. His only output at this time seems to have been a few melodies and songs, which were published in 1793 by the *Journal de guitare*.

It did not take long for rumors of Robespierre's fall to reach Saint-George's prison cell at Hondainville; he began to hope for an end to the nightmare. The end of the Terror aroused renewed courage on the part of those who had previously hesitated to help him. Thus on August 18, only three weeks after Robespierre's demise, several municipal officers of Château-Thierry, now renamed Egalité-sur-Marne, signed a petition in favor of the black colonel:

> We, citizens living in the commune of Egalité-sur-Marne, do certify that on every occasion when we have been in the company of General [*sic*] Saint-Georges, who was relieved of his duties by a measure of [the Committee for] General Security, we never knew him to make any unpatriotic speeches or actions. We certify on the contrary that during his stay in this commune he has shown himself to be a good and courageous republican, that he candidly mourned that his courage was rendered inactive and evinced the keenest desire to measure his strength against that of our oppressors and their slaves.

Gradually, other friends also began to raise their heads and orchestrate efforts to try to free him from the Republic's dungeons. Instead of petitioning, they addressed a letter to the Ninth Committee for the Organization and Movement of Land Armies, officially asking to know the precise reasons for Colonel Saint-George's suspension and imprisonment. It was a clever move. On October 6, the head of the committee, one L.-A. Pille, answered them in writing that when the defunct Executive Council had sentenced Saint-George, it "did not make known the reasons which had determined it." This amounted to admitting that Saint-George had been incarcerated groundlessly, as in the days of the old *lettres de cachet*, the orders under the king's private seal allowing for imprisonment without trial.

There was more to come. One item in Saint-George's file clearly showed that an *affaire* had been trumped up against the impetuous colonel. This was a letter from one Latuellière, commander of the revolutionary army at Egalité-sur-Marne, testifying that "inspired by a love for the public weal" he had handed over to the authorities "the chief elements of the denunciation of Saint-George," received "from the mouths of several citizens unknown to him." Having done his civic duty as an informer, the officer had nevertheless worried about the truthfulness of his own accusations. And in fact he felt obliged to state that they "had no certain foundation." Admitting that he had been "led into error," Latuellière therefore courageously retracted his denunciation "in its totality."

On October 24 the Committee for General Security and Surveillance of the convention was forced to acknowledge that the accusations leveled against Saint-George were baseless: "The Committee decrees that Colonel Joseph Bologne-St-Georges, held in the house of detention of Hondainville, near Clermont-sur-Oise, will be forthwith set at liberty and that the seals will be lifted in all the places where they have been affixed, on condition that he conform to the laws of August 20 and September 9, 1793."

And so he was freed. To see once more the light of day after eleven months of confinement (in his letters he himself states he was jailed for eighteen months) was not enough for the tenacious Saint-George, who had had to combat jealousy, pettiness, and racial prejudice all his life. To fight was second nature to him. No sooner had he celebrated his release with his friends, including the faithful Lamothe—his partner in fencing and in music—than he began the battle for his rehabilitation. His first order of business was to draw up a dossier designed to expunge from the records the injustice done him. He was determined that the authorities restore his command over his beloved American hussars. To this end he wrote "to the Citizen Representatives of the People, composing the Committee of Public Safety":

Citizens,

With confidence in your justice, I claim a reparation surely due me because of the persecutions of which I have been the victim. My devotion to the Revolution is known to the whole Republic. Since 1789 I have never ceased to speak out in the most energetic manner. Our country might perhaps have found it difficult to escape the direst misfortunes without the zeal with which I strove to prevent the fortress of Lille from falling to the forces of Cobourg and Dumouriez. The latter's Memoirs give you, Citizen Representatives, the measure of the service which I rendered my country in that disastrous period. Despite this, I was arrested shortly afterward by Bouchotte and later incarcerated, by order of Representative Le Jeune, for eighteen months. Rescued from so many ill-deserved persecutions, I find myself at last returned to an era in which shining Justice cannot be refused me, and the most fervent of all my desires is to continue to serve my country, to sacrifice to it the last drop of my blood.

I would therefore beg you, Citizen Representatives, to give orders for my reintegration into the regiment which I used to command and which at this time is leaderless.

I am sending you the documents justifying my request, which you will surely welcome because you are just and because the oppressed, persecuted Innocent is certain to find support and justice with you.

Greetings and fraternity,
Saint-George.[8]

The dossier attached to this request consists of a series of papers chosen to demonstrate his patriotism and his valor as a soldier. The first is an extract from the enrollment register of Lille, showing that Saint-George was among the first volunteers to enlist in 1791. Next, and most important, is a certificate from the municipal government testifying that the head of the "American hussars" had journeyed to Lille in order to warn the city of Dumouriez's treason. This official text, signed by Lefebvre d'Hénin, mayor of Lille, states that "citizen Saint-George, colonel of the 13th regiment of cavalry *chasseurs*, has shown patriotic sentiments in all circumstances, and especially when he came to announce the treachery of Dumouriez." With regard to the denunciations stating that the half-caste colonel had welcomed royalists into his regiment, the mayor and municipal officers likewise stated that the regiment was "composed of good patriots."

His former comrades in arms joined in the effort, thirteen regimental officers declaring: "It is both just and the duty of true Republicans to attest to their sorrow at losing so stalwart a citizen as Saint-George, in whom they have seen nothing but a good leader perfectly fulfilling his patriotic duties, animated by the purest of intentions, and possessing to the highest degree the love of his comrades of the 13th regiment." "We ardently hope," they concluded, "that the suspicions which have been raised against his intentions will disappear when his conduct is closely examined, and that such a good man, who can only have made enemies through error, can be returned to his post to defend the Republic."

Finally, Jean-François Target, the modest sergeant who had been promoted to colonel to take Saint-George's place, offered his decisive support in a moving and heartfelt letter to Saint-George dated March 18, 1795. Target proposed nothing less than to give the commander of the American hussars back his place:

My friend,

Since I have had the misfortune to be the passive and involuntary instrument of the injustice that has been done you, it is my honor and my duty to make genuine reparations. When, after you, I took command of the regiment you formed, I did not know you. But having owed that honor solely to your disgrace, I do not think I can make myself more deserving of the post which I filled in your absence than by arranging for it to be returned to the one to whom it should always have belonged.

I therefore swear to you, on my word as a man of good faith, that my keenest desire is to return into your hands a command which should never have been taken from you, and if I have rendered a few feeble services to the regiment and to my Fatherland, the only reward I crave is the honor to serve under your orders in whatever rank that may be.

I shall regard that circumstance as the happiest of my life, if you consent to regard Target as the best and the sincerest of your friends.

Target.

On May 12 the Committee of Public Safety met to examine the Saint-George "case." Again, it was commissioner Pille who presented the report summarizing the dossier and its conclusions:

The Committee will no doubt decide to decree the reintegration of citizen Saint-George, against whom there exists no note in the offices, who appears to have been suspended without grounds, and concerning whom, to the contrary, the Committee has some flattering testimonies as to his bravery and civic-mindedness that were given by his companions in arms, attesting that they have seen citizen Saint-George in particular present himself to the enemy and command not only his chasseurs but also an entire column purely for the pleasure of serving the Republic, and in an action in which, because of his very rank, he could have dispensed with appearing, since there were but fifty men in his corps.

Thus Saint-George was morally rehabilitated in the eyes of the Republic for the wrongs perpetrated against him by the men of the Terror—but also, in the eyes of history, for the willful mischaracterization that he was posthumously subjected to by Alexandre Dumas. True to its word, the next day the Committee of Public Safety restored the command of the Saint-George Legion to its founder and namesake.

One battle was won. Now another, longer struggle loomed. Although on paper Saint-George was reinstated with full honors, his arrival in the north of France was not so eagerly awaited. His foes were not, however, Austrian bayonets; they were the elements of a bureaucracy that had been formed by coups d'état and atrocities, that had become hardened to all interests and prerogatives but its own. It happened that Saint-George had been replaced twice as head of the regiment during his time in prison: first by Target, then by a certain Bouquet. The former had not been altogether shunted aside but simply put in the supernumerary position of "auxiliary" colonel. "There are now three chiefs of brigade for only one corps," declared a report to the Committee of Public Safety. The Target case was settled with dispatch: The Committee, only too happy to have the pretext handed to it by his moving letter to Saint-George, simply ousted him from the regiment. Bouquet pointed out, not unreasonably, that the Committee of Public Safety had never officially relieved him of his command. He therefore continued to behave as if he was still leading the 13th *Chasseurs*. Saint-George stayed on for a few weeks in Paris to rekindle something of his love of life and stock his kit in minimum fashion. Every day he sent orders to his regiment, whereupon Bouquet promptly shot back with a counterorder. Bouquet even boasted about this in a letter he sent the Committee on July 28: "I did not believe I could be derelict in the exercise of my duties without an order informing me I should do otherwise, so that it often happened, and indeed still happens every day, that an order given by the one is contradicted by the other." And he sharply accused his rival of still not once presenting himself before the corps, "which he has not seen for two years."

The criticism hit home. Colonel Saint-George made at once for Valenciennes, where the American hussars were stationed. Bouquet protested and made a legalistic attack, refusing to yield his position to his rival on the grounds that the latter should have appeared in the month following his assignment. The Valenciennes municipal government came to Saint-George's aid, even casting doubts on Bouquet because of the "royalist tendencies" it said the regiment had demonstrated under his command. Bouquet was out.

On September 1, 1795, the 13th *Chasseurs*, present at full strength, stood at attention in the middle of the parade ground of Valenciennes. The previous night, General Kermorvan, the regional commander, had given orders for all brass to be polished, uniforms cleaned, and the soldiers bathed and shaved. Saint-George marched forward, a solitary figure in the center of the vast square, martial and elegant as ever in his red uniform, his boots gleaming. Standing up to his full height, he seemed to dominate the awaiting troop. When he came and stood in front of the general, the latter returned his salute and then, with a few words, officially installed him at the head of his legion of Saint-George.

Meanwhile, a few hundred yards from this scene, Bouquet had slipped into a building to write an incendiary letter to the Ninth Committee, the one that had previously relieved Saint-George of his command. He complained roundly that this "abuse of authority" shown by General Kermorvan with the complicity of the municipality of Valenciennes was "contrary to law, contrary to the order of the army of Fructidor 2, contrary to the public interest, to that of the regiment in particular, destructive of discipline."

Matters didn't end there. For weeks on end Bouquet badgered the government. In the end he managed to convince these civilians, who up to now had been unable to agree on appointing a single brigade chief, to unite against one soldier's show of strength. Bouquet's stubbornness had paid off. Gradually the idea dawned on the Committee of Public Safety that General Kermorvan might have exceeded his rights in appointing a commander. Therefore it was decided once again to relieve Saint-George of his command, with the request "that he no longer remain in the regiment." Nevertheless, the colonel could hope for handsome compensation. On October 19, Commissioner Pille asked that the "American" be appointed to head the 11th Regiment of Dragoons, replacing Colonel Neuilly, who was retiring. Saint-George would find himself at the head of an elite regiment made up of cavalrymen.

Then the political situation changed yet again. After Robespierre's demise on Thermidor 9, a number of Republicans who had fled the Terror started to trickle back. Life in Paris began anew. People were less afraid to enjoy themselves—they went to see light comedies and organized dances. Gradually, as well, a few aristocrats with decidedly weaker Republican convictions also wended their way back. The new government welcomed them warmly, particularly those who were experienced military men who might prove extremely valuable to an army singularly lacking in competent leadership. Officers with aristocratic names replaced those who had won their gold braid in the battles against the coalition.

Rivalries sprang up. Among this influx of people were true-blue monarchists who had fled with the *émigrés*. Homesickness—in addition to the often wretched conditions of exile—had been too much for them. Some of those returning didn't even attempt to conceal their royalist convictions, and their presence in ever larger numbers was starting to destabilize the government. There were rumors of plots, murmurings that these men now encamped within the city walls should be disarmed before they did any harm.

In the end, the fears proved justified. In Lyon and Marseille the "White Terror" struck. A rebellion broke out in Dreux in early October and a white flag was hoisted over a number of buildings. This was the signal for the Paris uprising. On October 5 (Vendémiaire 13) several thousand royalists tried to seize power in the capital. The Committee of Public Safety ordered the prisons emptied and battalions to be formed of the men who had been thrown into jail after Thermidor 9. A final pitched battle took place on the steps of Saint-Roch, directly beneath the windows of the townhouse that had formerly belonged to

Philippe-Guillaume Tavernier de Boullongne, who had been guillotined two years earlier. After hours of fighting, General Napoleon Bonaparte finally destroyed the "whites," making him the savior of the Republic.

The Law of Brumaire 3, year IV (October 25, 1795), which followed, fell like a guillotine blade. To rid the army of all those royalists who had been infiltrating it for some months, and who had almost succeeded in overthrowing the Republic, the law stipulated that any officer who had not been in active service on April 5, 1795, was immediately suspended. At that point Saint-George had still been struggling to draw up his rehabilitation file so that he could take up arms for the Republic. All those efforts were rendered useless. On October 30, five days after the law was adopted, the Committee of Public Safety, now in possession of Pille's proposal to give the black colonel a prestigious command, called a halt to matters: "In light of article 15 of the law of the 3rd day of this month discharging citizen Saint-George, there are no grounds for further deliberation in the matter."

XVI

Coda

Spring 1797. It seemed to Louise Fusil as if the air in the gardens of the Palais-Royal had never been more fragrant and soft. Sitting on her favorite bench, she and a female friend were discussing something she had read in the magazine lying open on her lap. Like the season, the political atmosphere within this enclosed world—from which she had hardly been able to tear herself away since being forced to hurry back from Lille—had calmed. The *Directoire* had succeeded in assuaging people's fears; the nouveaux riches (yes, even the Revolution had produced its share) were now strolling beneath the chestnut trees, showing off the latest fashions. After years of turmoil, the Revolution was engaging in a little healthy fun. Louise had survived the tough years as best she could. The painter David had often asked her to appear as a vestal virgin in his grandiose stagings. And she had been the only woman admitted to the "Club of Midnight to Two A.M." a group of veteran songwriters who, when sober, might ask her to perform some of their compositions. But after a few glasses, the charming Louise would be begged to sing some racy refrains in that innocent way that so aroused the old men.

Like everyone else, her home had been subject to nightly raids when the sans-culottes had ransacked each room from top to bottom, searching for incriminating objects or papers. One day, after the contents of her closets and desk had been strewn on the floor, the men had overlooked the score of some royalist song. Despite being married to an eminent sans-culotte—a collaborator of Collot d'Herbois and one of the pacifiers of the Vendée—the sentimental Louise had remained firmly loyal to the monarchy.

She often spoke of Saint-George to her friends and asked around for news of him. No one seemed to know anything. Eventually Louise convinced herself that "that hothead" Joseph, as she called him, was hidden away somewhere in a corner of France or back in the islands. Most likely, he was with his old friend Lamothe. Then, after a while, she gave up hope. "For quite a long time I believed them dead and I mourned them with all my heart," she confides in her memoirs.

Suddenly her gaze fell on the bench a few yards from the one on which she was sitting. "At first I hadn't noticed the two people who had sat down opposite me. When I looked up I recognized them and cried out as if I had seen two ghosts; it was Lamothe and Saint-George." As spontaneous as ever, Saint-George rushed over to his friend and launched into a popular vaudeville song:

> *Ah, here at last I find you! I thought you had been hanged,*
> *In the past two years what has become of you?*

Louise answered: "No, I didn't exactly think you'd been hanged, but I was sure you were dead and I took you for ghosts."

"So we are," came the reply, "because we've returned from far away."[1]

Louise asked her two friends to explain. After the Committee of Public Safety and then the *Directoire* had each refused to give him back his command, Saint-George had accepted the suggestion of Deputy Raimond—who had been the inspiration behind the Legion of Saint-George—to accompany him to Saint-Domingue. The *Directoire* government had in fact given a civil committee the task of reestablishing Republican order on the island. Three of its four members were of European origin. Most likely Raimond had intended to alter the balance of power somewhat by engaging Saint-George's services. Saint-George was a famous figure on the island; the people there took great pride in his achievements in Paris. Moreover, his talents as a fencer and soldier—together with those of Lamothe—might prove useful to the commissioners.

During the preceding year, Toussaint-Louverture, a freed slave—who had himself owned three slaves up until abolition—had succeeded in repulsing English and Spanish attacks on the island because of his exceptional gifts as war commander and organizer. His troops, however, were ragged and poorly armed. Guns seldom arrived from France in a fit state to function; when the powder was delivered, there was no cardboard for making cartridges and vice versa. And yet this ragtag army of 5,000 had managed to defeat much larger and better-equipped forces, supported by the best navy in the world. Toussaint had been made general and now enjoyed a warm relationship with Governor Etienne de Laveaux, who had also fought against slavery.

The white colonists, who had offered to deliver up the French part of the Great Isle to the English in order to maintain slavery, were defeated. Now the problem was with the half-castes. Even before the Revolution, these had possessed small landholdings on which they could grow food crops, or worked as artisans or traders. And they had owned slaves. Thus they were highly unappreciative of the convention's decision to abolish slavery. What is more, proud of their white blood, they loathed Governor Laveaux, who intended to put all humanity on an equal footing, blacks and those of mixed race in particular.

On March 20, two months before the *Directoire*'s committee arrived, a rebellion broke out in Cap François. The victorious mulattos threw Laveaux into jail and set up one of their own as commander of the town. At first Toussaint had tried persuasion:

> Brothers and friends,
>
> It is with the utmost regret and the keenest pain that we have learned of the arguments and quarrels that prevail among you.
>
> What? Surrounded by enemies on all sides and crushed by all kinds of difficulties for four years, would you still want to cause fresh troubles, starting civil war? To cut each other's throats like scoundrels: Now there's a fine state of affairs! . . .
>
> You asked for liberty and equality and France has granted them to you; she has given you a governor and you refuse to recognize him. By failing in your duty to the governor you are failing France. What will the mother country say when she learns of your irregular conduct toward her representative?

It was a waste of breath. A half-caste named André Rigaud had just seized power on the southern part of the island when the commissioners, accompanied by Saint-George, hove into sight of Saint-Domingue in the spring of 1796. Rigaud hurriedly set up an authoritarian regime over the entire part of the island under his control. Governor Laveaux himself was placed under arrest. The defenseless black population took to the streets to try to defend its freedom. The intervention of Toussaint-Louverture, at the head of two battalions and eight hundred cavalrymen, prevented a bloodbath and made it possible for the situation to be reversed. When he welcomed the commissioners, together with Saint-George and Lamothe, who had seen from far off the flames engulfing the town, Toussaint-Louverture already seemed the very embodiment of the "black Spartacus" that the abbé Raynal had prophesied would "avenge the outrages done to his race."

Rigaud took refuge in the western part of the island, where, however, he agreed to let the commissioners visit and inspect certain areas. Saint-George and his friends discovered to their horror that the mulatto had set up a dictatorial regime in which half-caste soldiers held all the administrative posts. The few whites that remained in the territories he had conquered suffered the same fate as the blacks: the slavery that he, Rigaud, had reestablished. The prison of Les Cayes alone held nine hundred prisoners in unspeakable conditions; with the exception of two mulattos, all the prisoners were white or black. Rigaud argued that "these places of correction were used to punish farmers who left their fields to become brigands." The delegates did not believe a word of this, having found out that the "farmers" in question were in fact slaves. They set them free, replying sardonically: "There are now no bonds for those who wish to live a life of idleness."

No sooner had the Republic's representatives turned their backs than Rigaud's men once again seized power. Whites and blacks were massacred by the dozens in the streets of Les Cayes. The envoys from Paris had either to flee or be killed themselves. Edouard, a black aide-de-camp to the general in command of the regular army, addressed the all-black platoon that was about to shoot him: "My friends, my brothers, I have returned from France to make known to you the generous Frenchmen who have given you liberty, and now you are cutting their throats to serve new masters! Yes, kill me, so that I am not a witness to your ingratitude."[2] Rigaud instituted a new form of slavery. Blacks were assigned to small farms that, in theory, they were responsible for running, but from which they could not escape on pain of being thrown into a dungeon or summarily executed. All authority over these parcels of land, all the production and negotiating of the sugarcane, lay with the mulattos.

Meanwhile Toussaint's overriding problem was to fight the English, who were again threatening to invade the French part of Saint-Domingue. He was forced to let Rigaud set up his rule over the entire western part of the island. Saint-George, who, according to a rumor that made the rounds in Paris, had witnessed these uprisings and even narrowly escaped being hanged, set sail for France. Most probably he left the island at the beginning of 1797 on the *Watigny*, one of the only vessels fast enough to risk running the English blockade. Aboard the ship were two of Toussaint-Louverture's sons. On August 17, 1796, the *Directoire* had in fact promoted the "black Spartacus" to the rank of division general and proposed that his sons be brought to the capital, there "to receive instruction and education at the government's expense."[3] In February 1797, the ship reached the French coast. Six years later Toussaint, captured as a result of being betrayed by Bonaparte's troops, would perish in a dank cell in the fortress of Joux, in the Jura Mountains in France. And Napoleon would reestablish slavery following an unbelievably savage repression.

Despite his emotion at being reunited with Louise, Saint-George was still brave enough to crack a joke—albeit a bitter one—about his stay in the Antilles: *"Ils ne m'ont pas pendu mais perdu*—they didn't hang me but they lost me; for since my time there I've been looking for myself everywhere and have not found myself."[4] The massacres of blacks and whites by men of mixed race had deeply affected him, especially as his own escape had been so narrow. It called into question, yet once again, his whole identity. Did referring to himself as "Creole" really mean anything? Who was he? What was he? His mother's son or his father's? Musician or soldier?

Nonetheless, Saint-George had preserved intact that pride that drove him to demand reparation for the wrong that had been done him. The very fact that he had been invited to accompany a Republican mission to the islands suggested that he was no longer in disgrace with those governing France; the *Directoire* had felt sure enough of itself to abrogate the draconian law depriving Saint-George of his command. On April 25, 1797, the demoted colonel therefore believed he could finally, and definitively, obtain justice. He wrote Jean-François Rewbell, a member of the *Directoire*:

I have consistently demonstrated my devotion to the Revolution, I have served it since the beginning of the war, with an indefatigable zeal that persecutions have been unable to diminish. I have no other resource than that of being reintegrated into my rank. I turn to you with confidence, citizen director, and I would beg of your justice the position of chief of brigade of which I was deprived by virtue of an article that is no longer in force since it has been rescinded by a later law.

George

One notes the simplicity of his signature, as though by omitting the "Saint" in his name he was giving further testimony to his revolutionary ardor. There is something sad about this. Times had changed. Anything harking back to the spirit of '89 had fallen out of fashion. He was now living in a time when once again royalist dandies—the ultra-fashionable *merveilleuses,* and the so-called *incroyables* or the "incredible ones"—thronged the streets of Paris. By proclaiming his Revolutionary convictions, Saint-George was proving only that he was out of step with the times. In actual fact it was precisely to reintroduce the nobility that the *Directoire* had repealed the law that had ousted Saint-George. Rewbell would not even bother to reply to the petition. Saint-George would never regain his rank.

When Saint-George had admitted that he had "no other resource" than to seek a command, he was without doubt alluding to his financial situation. His uncle and cousin, both Farmers General in their day, had been guillotined; no one knew what had become of his father. In his heyday Saint-George had lived surrounded by luxury and splendor. Hoarding wealth, however, was not in his character, as La Boëssière knew: "Despising wealth for himself, what he possessed belonged to his friends. Liberal and kind, he denied himself the better to assuage the unfortunate. I myself have known some old men whom he helped and cared for in the most touching manner, as far as his means would allow him."[5]

Now he had to work in order to live. Perhaps that was all to the good; once again he was forced to concentrate upon music. Musical clubs were staging a comeback. One such club, called the Circle of Harmony, took up residence in Philippe d'Orléans's old apartments in the Palais-Royal; Saint-George was admitted after undergoing the demanding "purifying" test. Music was not the only activity in this "magnificent locale," as the *Mercure* described it. People played billiards, backgammon, and chess, danced and read the papers. In short, life was almost as it had been before the Revolution. Except that in Saint-George's case, the intervening years had taken their toll. Still, the atmosphere and setting worked their magic, and before long the direction of the orchestra was entrusted to him. Only a few days after that he gave proof that the passing years and their trials had in no way impaired his talent. According to the *Mercure*, he was still "the famous Saint-George," and his musical direction left "nothing to be desired as to choice of pieces or superiority of execution."[6]

Because of his reduced means he was obliged to take a relatively modest apartment some distance from the Palais-Royal, at 13 rue Boucherat (near what is today the place de la République). Many of the nobles who came back to Paris after the years of turmoil found it hard to forgive their former friend for fighting on the Republican side, and therefore could hardly be counted upon to help him recapture his former lifestyle.

And yet here he was, once again one of the most prominent men in Paris. As much at ease as ever on horseback, and displaying amazing physical stamina, he still impressed everyone around him with his elegance. On July 22, 1798, a crowd swarmed into the Parc Monceau where André-Jacques Garnerin was about to attempt a balloon trip with a female companion. Soon, as Alfred Marquiset relates, "people saw the beautiful young nymph of the air appear accompanied by Saint-George, who offered her his arm and made several tours of the enclosure amidst enthusiastic applause." It was to be his last flamboyant performance.

A few months later, he felt a sharp pain in his lower abdomen. No doubt just the onset of old age, he told himself. But the pain became more acute, even crippling. Every day he found the trip from the rue Boucherat to the Palais-Royal more and more exhausting. Nicolas Duhamel, a captain of Saint-George's legion, and someone with whom Saint-George had remained in close touch, grew worried and brought him to his apartment on the rue de Chartres, next to the Louvre. Thus he was back in the neighborhood of his childhood, a few dozen yards from his friend La Boëssière's fencing school and the Palais-Royal. He didn't want to leave it again. His bladder ravaged by an ulcer, he waited for the end.

The eighteenth century was nearing its close. Returning from Egypt, Napoleon was sailing ever closer to the French coast. Ahead were the coup d'état he would stage, in a few weeks' time, against the Republic; the bloody suppression he would order against Toussaint-Louverture's humanist government in Saint-Domingue; the wars he would unleash throughout Europe; and the slavery he would reestablish in the islands, where it would remain in force for another half-century.

On June 10, 1799, the eyelids of the chevalier de Saint-George closed on the Age of Enlightenment.

Blackout

Napoleon Bonaparte reinstated slavery on May 20, 1802, having drowned Toussaint-Louverture's young Haitian democracy in a sea of blood. This was a second death for "the black Mozart," as Saint-George was called in the years immediately following his death. Once again blacks and people of color were deemed incapable of serious artistic endeavor. Those who by their example or their works furnished proof to the contrary were dismissed or banished from thought. Pushed from his pedestal by Napoleon's empire, thrown into oblivion by the smugly complacent culture of Restoration France, Saint-George, one of the truly great spirits of the Enlightenment, entered obscurity and remained there for nearly two centuries.

The time has come to perform and listen to Saint-George's music again, and thus to begin a process of rehabilitation.

NOTES

I. Nanon

1. Based upon documents housed in the Centre des archives d'outre-mer (CAOM), located in Aix-en-Provence, France, Dossier Series E37.

2. There is some doubt as to whether this individual actually existed. "Monsieur Platon" was first described in Roger de Beauvoir's 1840 novel, *Le Chevalier de Saint-George*. De Beauvoir claimed to have relied entirely upon oral testimony in writing his novel, which lends credibility to those passages related to the character.

3. See Gaston Bourgeois, *"Le Chevalier de Saint-George, inexactitudes commises par ses biographes"* ("The Chevalier de Saint-George: Mistakes His Biographers Have Made"), *Bulletin de la Société d'histoire de la Guadeloupe*, 1964, p. 6 and following.

4. See Lucien Abenon, *La Guadeloupe de 1671 à 1759: Etude politique, économique, et sociale*, vol. I (Editions L'Harmattan, 1993).

5. From documents housed in the Archives nationales, Paris, Collection C7A11. Cited in Abenon, op. cit., vol. II, p. 139.

6. Archives nationales, Dossier C8 55, Op. 79. Cited in Abenon, op. cit.

7. Archives nationales, Dossier C8A.

8. See Gabriel Entiope, *Nègres, danse, et résistance: La Caraïbe aux XVIIIe et XIXe siècles* (Editions L'Harmattan, 1996).

9. Ibid.

10. Archives nationales, Dossier C7A11, p. 110. Also quoted in Abenon, op. cit. Entiope, op. cit.

11. Odet Denys, *Qui était le chevalier de Saint-George?* (Who Was the Chevalier de Saint-George?) (Paris: Le Pavillon-Roger Maria, 1972).

12. See Eric Saugera, *Bordeaux, port négrier* (Karthala, 1995).

13. See Olivier Pétré-Grenouilleau, *Nantes au temps de la traité des noirs* (Nantes During the Age of Slavery) (Paris: Hachette-littérature, 1998).

14. See Alejo Carpentier, *Le Siècle des lumières* (Paris: Folio Publishers—Hachette, 1995).

II. The Child and the Slaves

1. Roger de Beauvoir, op. cit., Chapter 6.

2. Denys, op. cit.

3. Argument offered by Gaston Bourgeois in *Bulletin de la Société d'histoire de la Guadeloupe*, op. cit.

4. Entiope, op. cit.

5. Ibid.

6. Denys, op. cit.

7. Abenon, op. cit., vol. II.

8. Jean-Baptiste du Tertre, *Histoire générale des Antilles habitées par les français, 1667–71* (reprinted by Les Horizons Caraïbes, Fort de France, 1973).

III. Race and the Enlightenment

1. Abenon, op. cit., vol. I.

2. Denys, op. cit.

3. Figures quoted by Victor Schoelcher in *Vie de Toussaint-Louverture* (Karthala, 1982).

4. De Beauvoir, op. cit. The novelist avers that the description of this property and its personnel was based on actual testimony.

5. Denys, op. cit.

6. See Pierre Pluchon, *Nègres et juifs au XVIIIième siècle* (Blacks and Jews in the Eighteenth Century) (Tallandier, 1984).

7. Ibid.

8. Entiope, op. cit.

9. Marie-Jean Antoine Nicolas Condorcet (Marquis de), *Réflexions sur l'esclavage des nègres*, 1781.

10. Voltaire (François Marie Arouet), *Essai sur les moeurs et l'esprit des nations* (An Essay on Universal History, and the Manners and Spirit of Nations), 1756.

11. Pierre Pluchon records a large number of these paintings, op. cit.

12. Jacques-Vincent Delacroix, *Peinture du siècle*, Paris, published in 1777.

13. Pluchon, op. cit.

14. Chevalier de Boufflers, *Lettres d'Afrique à Madame de Sabran* (Arles, France: Actes Sud, 1998), p. 60.

IV. An American in Paris

1. Caix de Saint Aymour, *Une Famille d'artistes et de financiers aux XVIIième et XVIIIième siècles* (Henri Laurens, 1876).

2. *Almanach royal de 1748*, Archives nationales, Section 18C.

3. Archives nationales, *Minutier central* XX, Section 596.

4. De Beauvoir, op. cit.

5. Fétis's chief claim to fame is his biography of musicians, included in the *Biographie universelle Michaud*, published in 1812. Joseph Michaud, the general editor, was born in 1767 and had known Saint-George, whose life is described in vol. XXXIX.

6. See Jacques Hillairet, *Connaissance du vieux Paris* (Princesse Publishing, 1956).

7. Jean-Nicholas Dufort de Cheverny, *Mémoires*, vol. I.

8. Inquest report of Judge Nicolas Maillard, King's Counsel, Centre des archives d'outre-mer (CAOM), Dossier E37, series G1.

9. The detail is duly noted in Judge Maillard's report.

10. Ibid.

11. CAOM, Dossier E7.

12. May be consulted in the Bibliothèque historique des armées, Fort Vincennes, France.

13. Gérard Gefen, "*Joseph Boulogne, chevalier de Saint-George.*" *Harmonie*, March 1983.

14. Archives nationales, *Répertoire* G7.

15. Alfred Marquiset, *"Le Don Juan noir." La Nouvelle Revue*, September 1919.

16. Henry Angelo, *Angelo's Pic Nic* (London, 1905).

V. The Foil and the Bow

1. Angelo, op. cit.

2. Emil Smidak, *Joseph Boulogne, nommé chevalier de Saint-George* (Joseph Boulogne, called Chevalier de Saint-George) (Lucerne, Switzerland: Fondation Avenira, 1996).

3. De Beauvoir, op. cit.

4. Madame de Genlis, *Mémoires* (Paris: Ladvocat, 1825).

5. This aspect of Saint-George's life has been studied by the genealogist Boisserie de Masmontet, who is cited by Gaston Bourgeois, *Bulletin de la Société d'histoire de la Guadeloupe,* op. cit.

6. L. Petit de Bachaumont is quoted by Denys, op. cit.

7. Archives nationales, *Minutier central des notaires, succession Bernard, conseiller d'état,* ET/LXXXVIII/1278.

8. Archives départementales de la Seine. "Tavernier de Boullongne" file.

9. This description relies in large measure on the wording contributed by the late Bruno Pons to the plaque on the rue du Bac in Paris, erected in 1990 by the Délégation artistique de la ville de Paris and the Société d'histoire et d'archéologie du 7e arrondissement.

10. Bruno Pons, op. cit.

11. Angelo, op. cit., pp. 398–99.

VI. "Quarreling Buffoons"

1. Johann-Melchior, baron de Grimm's letter was published in 1752. *Correspondance littéraire, philosophique, et critique,* a collection of his letters, was published posthumously between 1877 and 1882. See also baron de Grimm, *Historical and Literary Memoirs and Anecdotes* (London: Henry Colburn, 1815).

2. Jean-le-Rond d'Alembert, *De la Liberté de la musique,* in *Oeuvres,* vol. 1, p. 514. Note that d'Alembert's musical knowledge was universally recognized.

3. Louis Striffling, *Esquisse d'une histoire du goût musical en France* (Outline for a History of Musical Taste in France) (Librairie Delagrave, 1912).

4. Ibid.

5. Ancelet, *Observations sur la musique, les musiciens, et les instruments* (Amsterdam, 1757).

6. *Letters of Mozart and His Family*, translated by Emily Anderson, third edition (New York: W. W. Norton and Company, 1989). Letter by Mozart dated May 1, 1778, written to his father in Salzburg.

7. Ancelet, op. cit.

8. *Letters of Mozart,* op. cit.

9. Wanda Landowska, *Musique ancienne* (Paris: Mercure de France, 1909).

10. *Le Point,* May 10, 1997.

11. Jean-Benjamin de la Borde, *Essai sur la musique* (Paris, 1780). Quoted by Smidak, op. cit.

12. Biographical note by Wendy Thomson, *Oxford Encyclopedic Dictionary of Music, French Edition* (French & European Publishing, 1988).

VII. The "Famous" Saint-George

1. De Beauvoir, op. cit.

2. Reported by Michel Brenet, *Les Concerts en France sous l'ancien régime* (Paris: Fischbacher, 1900).

3. Gérard Gefen, *Les Musiciens et la franc-maçonnerie* (Paris: Fayard, 1993).

4. Brenet, op. cit.

5. Martha Rioux and Jean-Yves Patte, *Le Concert spirituel* (Paris: Le Monde de la musique, 1997).

6. Ibid.

7. Brenet, op. cit.

8. Striffling, op. cit.

9. Brenet, op. cit.

10. Barry S. Brook, editor, *The Symphony, 1720–1840,* reference volume (New York: Garland, 1986).

11. Arthur Pougin, *Viotti et l'école moderne de violon* (Paris: Fischbacher, 1924).

12. Smidak, op. cit.

13. In particular by La Borde, op. cit.

14. Félix Clément, *Les Musiciens célèbres depuis le XVIième siècle jusqu' à nos jours*, 1878.

VIII. The Salon Man

1. Madame de Genlis, *Mémoires*, op. cit., vol. II.

2. Dufort de Cheverny, op. cit.

3. As noted in Georges Poisson, *Choderlos de Laclos; ou, L'Obstination* (Paris: Grasset, 1985).

4. Denys, op. cit.

5. Madame Roland, *Mémoires* (Paris: Mercure de France, 1986).

6. Didier Thirion, *La Vie privée des financiers au XVIIIième siècle* (Paris: Plon, 1895).

7. Ibid.

8. *Letters of Mozart*, op. cit., no. 278.

9. Thirion, op. cit.

10. Roger de Beauvoir also supports this argument.

11. Madame de Genlis, *Mémoires*, op. cit.

12. De Beauvoir, op. cit.

13. Elisabeth Vigée-Lebrun, *Souvenirs* (Paris), *"Des femmes,"* 1984. For an English translation, see *The Memoirs of Elisabeth Vigée-Lebrun*, translated by Lionel Strachey (New York: George Braziller, 1989).

14. Marquiset, op. cit.

IX. The Voltaire of Music

1. Smidak, op. cit.

2. *Harmonie*, op. cit.

3. Letter reproduced in Grimm's literary correspondence, op. cit.

4. The quotations that follow are taken from Vigée-Lebrun, *Souvenirs*, op. cit.

5. The poem celebrating Gustave Dugazon also honors Saint-George's paternity: "Brilliant, sensitive, and always ravishing / He is noble, kind, and tender / But one would expect no less / Given from whom he is descended." See *La Nouvelle Revue*, September 1919.

6. Baron de Grimm, op. cit.

7. Pierre Constant, *Histoire du Concert spirituel* (Paris: Société française de musicologie, published with the support of CNRS [Centre nationale de recherche scientifique], Heugel, 1975).

8. These quartets figure in two volumes of a rare discography. The first is a vinyl LP recorded in 1970 by Columbia Records, at the initiative of the Afro-American Music Opportunities Association (AAMOA), whose objective was to promote the work of black musicians. Only the first of these six pieces is included on the record, which presents different facets of Saint-George's talents. The Juilliard Quartet, which performs the piece, was considered one of the finest—if not the finest—of the day. The other volume was recorded in 1974 by the Jean-Noël Mollard String Quartet, and has just been reissued as a compact disk by Arion. Although the acoustic quality leaves something to be desired, these six quartets—performed beautifully—give a powerful sense of Saint-George's "youthful" works.

9. I'm referring to the recording made by Bernard Thomas and Jean-Jacques Kantoro in 1974, with Arion Records.

X. Toward a More Perfect Society

1. We owe this "scoop" to Alain Le Bihan, a historian of the Freemasons, who was able to consult the archives of the Social Contract Lodge. Le Bihan, to whom I am very grateful, is the author of *Francs-maçons parisiens du Grand Orient de France à la fin du XVIIIième siècle,* which was published in 1966 by the Bibliothèque nationale under the auspices of its commission to study the economic and social history of the French Revolution. Bihan's work covers all the Freemasons of the period as well as their lodges.

2. Alain Le Bihan, in Daniel Ligou, *Dictionnaire universel de la franc-maçonnerie* (Paris: Presses universitaires de France, 1998).

3. Pierre-Yves Beaurepaire, *Franc-maçonnerie et cosmopolitisme au siècle des Lumières,* published—bravely—by the Grand Orient de France (Editions maçonniques de France, 1998).

4. This supposedly "Masonic" opera (and in this regard see Gérard Gefen's superb book, *Les Musiciens et la franc-maçonnerie* [Paris: Fayard, 1993])

also gives us the Queen of the Night as a source of evil. At best, Pamina seems to indicate that woman can help free man of the evil with which he is born only by following him along the path to wisdom.

5. Roger Cotte, *La Music maçonnique* (Paris: Editions du Borrégo, 1991).

6. Gefen, op. cit.

7. Cotte, op. cit.

8. Pougin, op. cit.

9. Bibliothèque nationale, Masonic Collection, Cabinet des manuscrits.

10. This is the thesis of Barry S. Brook and H. Barbadette (in *Le Ménestrel*, January 1871). Cited by Smidak, op. cit. Gérard Gefen advances the same argument; Gefen, op. cit.

11. Smidak, op. cit.

XI. *Prima della Rivoluzione*

1. Hillairet, op. cit.

2. Gustave Desnoiresterres, *Gluck et Piccinni* (Paris: Didier et Cie, 1872).

3. Ibid.

4. Marquiset, *La Nouvelle Revue*, 1919, op. cit.

5. Smidak, op. cit.

6. Alberto Savinio, *La Boîte à musique* (Paris: Fayard, 1989).

7. Smidak, op. cit. We should point out that the score and libretto, which were thought to have disappeared, were found intact at the Bibliothèque nationale (collection of the Conservatoire de Paris).

8. *Journal de Paris*, August 18, 1787, and *Journal général de France*, Thursday, August 23, 1787.

9. Grimm and Meister, *Correspondance littéraire*, vol. XV.

XII. *The Chevalier and the Chevalière*

1. André Castelot, *Philippe Egalité, le prince rouge* (Paris: Sfelt, 1950).

2. Quoted by Castelot, ibid.

3. Text edited and annotated by Nadine Satiat. The reference note leaves no doubt as to the identity of the said Saint-George: "The Chevalier de Saint-George was born in Guadeloupe, the natural son of a highly placed civil servant and an exceedingly handsome black slave. Outstandingly talented

in sports, notably fencing, he was a member of the corps of musketeers and became a society figure before the Revolution. He was also an excellent violinist."

4. André Frank, *D'Eon, chevalier et chevalière, suivi de sa confession* was written in 1796 but not published until 1953 by Amiot-Dupont, Paris. The cover shows an engraving of the match with Saint-George.

5. See Gilles Perrault, *Secret du roi*, three volumes (Paris: Fayard, 1996, 1997, 1998). Available in paperback from LGF.

6. Chevalier d'Eon, *Mémoires,* edited by Frédéric Gaillardet (Paris: Ladvocat, 1836; reprinted by Grasset in 1935).

7. Frank, op. cit.

8. Chevalier d'Eon, *Mémoires,* op. cit.

9. Captain Telfer, *The Strange Career of the Chevalier d'Eon de Beaumont* (London, 1885). Quoted by Smidak, op. cit. For more on the Chevalier d'Eon, see Gary Kates, *Monsieur d'Eon Is a Woman* (New York: Basic Books, 1985).

10. Angelo, op. cit.

XIII. The Palais in Revolution

1. The letter by the marquis de La Ferrières was reprinted in *Lettres d'aristocrates,* published by P. de Vaissière.

2. Bachaumont, op. cit.

3. François Furet and Denis Richet, *La Révolution française* (Paris: Hachette, 1965).

4. Gefen, cited in *Harmonie,* op. cit.

5. Marquiset, op. cit.

6. Furet and Richet, op. cit.

7. Archives administratives du ministère de la Guerre, municipalité de Lille (Administrative Archives of the Ministry of War, City of Lille). *Extrait du registre aux inscriptions des citoyens qui se sont offerts à marcher les premiers en exécution du décret de l'Assemblée nationale du 21 juin 1791* (Extract from the register of citizens who volunteered to march first in the execution of a decree made by the National Assembly and dated June 21, 1791). Cited by Lionel de La Laurencie in *L'Ecole française de violon de Lully à Viotti.*

8. Louis-Philippe, *Mémoires.* Cited by Smidak, op. cit.

XIV. The Republic's Black Hussar

1. Figures cited by Adélaïde de Place, *La Vie musicale en France au temps de la Révolution* (Paris: Fayard, 1989).

2. P. Descaves, *Historique du 13eme régiment de chasseurs* (Béziers, 1891).

3. Denys, op. cit.

4. Antoine de Jomini, *Les Guerres de la Révolution,* originally published in 1810 (Paris: Hachette, 1998, reprint).

5. Louis-Philippe, *Mémoires,* cited by Smidak, op. cit.

6. Marquiset, *La Nouvelle Revue,* op. cit.

7. Document quoted by La Laurencie, op. cit.

8. Albert Mathiez, *La Révolution française,* vol. II (Paris: Denoël, 1985).

9. Furet and Richet, op. cit.

10. Ibid.

11. Archives of the Ministry of Defense. Dossier Saint-George, number 2065, reads as follows: "At Château-Thierry, the 9th day of the 1st decade of the 2nd month of the year II of the French Republic."

XV. Singing to Victory

1. Gefen, op. cit.

2. Citation from de Place, op. cit.

3. Ibid.

4. Ibid.

5. Nicolas Ruault, *Gazette d'un Parisien sous la Révolution* (Paris, 1975).

6. Louis Garros, *Rouget de Lisle et La Marseillaise* (Paris: Librairie Plon,1936).

7. Ibid.

8. Letter found in the archives of the Ministry of War at the beginning of the last century by La Laurencie but that can no longer be found in Saint-George's file.

XVI. Coda

1. Louise Fusil, *Souvenirs d'une actrice* (Paris, 1841).

2. Schoelcher, op. cit.

3. Ibid.
4. This is according to Odet Denys, op. cit.
5. Ibid.
6. *Mercure français,* no. 20, Sunday, April 6, 1797.

For a complete list of
Saint-George's compositions, please visit
www.saint-george.fr.st/

DISCOGRAPHY

Le Mozart Noir
Ensemble: Tafelmusik Orchestra
Performer: Linda Melsted, Geneviève Gilardeau
Label: Cbc Enterprises; Audio CD (March 18, 2003)

Monsieur de Saint-George: Le Nègre des lumières
Ensemble: Orchestre de la Suisse italienne
Performer: Hana Kotkova, Hans Liviabella, et al.
Label: Forlane—#16792; Audio CD (April 17, 2001)

Chevalier de Saint-Georges: Violin Concertos
Ensemble: Cologne Chamber Orchestra
Conductor: Helmut Muller-Bruhl
Performer: Takako Nishizaki
Label: Naxos—#8555040; Audio CD (May 15, 2001)

Boulogne: String Quartets
Label: Arion—#55425; Audio CD (July 10, 2001)

J. Boulogne Chevalier de Saint-Georges: Symphonies & Violin Concertos CD 1

Performer: Miroslav Vilimec

Label: Avenira—#9985; Audio CD (July 25, 2000)

J. Boulogne Chevalier de Saint-Georges: Violin Concertos—CD 2

Performer: Miroslav Vilimec

Label: Avenira—#9986; Audio CD (July 25, 2000)

J. Boulogne Chevalier de Saint-Georges: Symphonies and Violin Concertos—CD 3

Performer: Miroslav Vilimec

Label: Avenira—#9987; Audio CD (July 25, 2000)

J. Boulogne Chevalier de Saint-Georges: Symphonies and Violin Concertos, CD 4

Performer: Miroslav Vilimec

Label: Avenira—#9988; Audio CD (September 19, 2000)

J. Boulogne Chevalier de Saint-Georges: Symphonies and Violin Concertos, Vol. 5

Ensemble: Radio Symphony-Orchestra Pilsen

Conductor: Frantisek Preisler, Jr.

Performer: Miroslav Vilimec

Label: Avenira—#9989; Audio CD (September 19, 2000)

Saint-Georges: Violin Concerto with Oboe Obbligato in C Major, Opus 5, No. 1; Symphony Concertante for two violins in G Major, No. 13; Symphony in D Major, Opus 11, No. 2; excerpts from the opera L'Amant anonyme *(Léontine's first and second arias)*

Ensemble: Les Archets de Paris

Performer: Christophe Grindel, Christophe Guiot, Laurent Philipp; Odile Rhino, soprano

Label: Les Archets de Paris Records (2000)

Saint-Georges: Concerto in G Major for violin and orchestra; Symphony in G, Opus 11/2; Symphony in D, Opus 11, No. 2
Ensemble: Orchestre de Chambre de Versailles
Conductor: Bernard Wahl
Performer: Anne-Claude Villars
Label: Arion—#55434; Audio CD (January 26, 1999)

Saint-Georges: Sonatas for violin and harpsichord
Performer: Brigitte Haudebourg, Jean-Jacques Kantorow
Label:Arion—#55445; Audio CD (June 15, 1999)

Violin Concertos by Black Composers of the 18th and 19th Centuries, including Saint-Georges: Violin Concerto in A Major, Opus 5, No. 2
Ensemble: Orchestre de chambre Encore (Daniel Hege, conductor)
Performer: Rachel Barton
Label: Cédille—#35; Audio CD (November 1, 1999)

Vachon, Saint-Georges, Cambini: Quatuors à Cordes, including Saint-Georges: String Quartet in G Minor, Opus 14, No. 6
Ensemble: Les Adieux Quartet
Performer: Hajo Bab, Ursula Bundies, et al.
Label: Valois—#4761; Audio CD (March 11, 1996)

Saint-Georges: Concertos pour violins
Conductor: Bernard Thomas
Performer: Jean-Jacques Kantorow
Label: Arion—#68093; Audio CD (August 12, 1993)

Forthcoming Releases

First Series of Quartets
Ensemble: Antarès Quartet
Label: A et A

Complete Quartets
Ensemble: Wallonia Quartet
Label: Forlane

Complete Symphonies concertantes for Violin
Label: Naxos

Recordings of Historical Importance
(in chronological order)

Les Caquets, staccato rondo for violin
The Bibliothèque nationale de France in Paris has two copies; the record library at Radio-France also has a copy.
Performer: Marius Casadesus
Label: Polydor (1936)

Symphonie concertante in G Major, No. 13; Symphony in G Major, Opus 11, No. 1; aria from the opera Ernestine
Ensemble: London Symphony Orchestra
Conductor: Paul Freeman
Performer: Faye Robinson, soprano
Producer: Dominique-René de Lerma
Label: Columbia Records (1970)

String Quartet No. 1
Ensemble: Juilliard String Quartet
Producer: Dominique-René de Lerma
Label: Columbia Records (1970)

String Quartet in C Minor, No. 3; String Quartet in C Minor, No. 4; String Quartet in G Minor, No. 5; String Quartet in D Major, No. 6
Ensemble: Jean-Noël Mollard String Quartet
Label: Arion (1974)

SUGGESTED READING

Anderson, M. S. *War and Society in Europe of the Old Regime, 1618–1789*. New York: St. Martin's Press, and Leicester: Leicester University Press, 1988; revised edition, Montreal, Quebec, and Buffalo, N.Y.: McGill-Queens University Press, 1998.

Badinter, Elisabeth. *Emilie, Emilie: L'Ambition féminine au XVIIIième siècle*. Paris: Flammarion, 1983.

Black, Jeremy, and Roy Porter, editors. *A Dictionary of Eighteenth-Century World History*. Oxford and Cambridge, Mass.: Blackwell, 1994; as *Dictionary of Eighteenth-Century History*, London: Penguin, 2001.

Braudel, Fernand. *Civilization and Capitalism, 15th–18th Century*, 3 vols., translated by Siân Reynolds. London: Fontana, and New York: Harper & Row, 1979–84 (original French edition, 1967–79); see especially vol. 2, *The Wheels of Commerce*, 1979.

Brown, Bruce Alan. *Gluck and the French Theatre in Vienna*. Oxford: Clarendon Press, and New York: Oxford University Press, 1991.

Bullock, Steven C. *Revolutionary Brotherhood: Freemasonry and the Transformation of the American Social Order, 1730–1840.* Chapel Hill: University of North Carolina Press, 1996.

Burke, Edmund. *Reflections on the Revolution in France.* London: Dodsley, 1790; edited by Conor Cruise O'Brien, Baltimore: Penguin Books, 1968.

Castle, Egerton. *Schools and Masters of Fencing: From the Middle Ages to the Eighteenth Century.* New York: Dover Publications, 2003.

Charlton, David. *Grétry and the Growth of Opéra-Comique.* Cambridge and New York: Cambridge University Press, 1986.

Le Code noir; ou, Recueil des règlements rendus jusqu'à présent concernant le gouvernement, l'administration de la justice, la police, la discipline, et la commerce des Nègres dans les colonies françaises et les conseils et compagnies établies à ce sujet. Paris: Prault, 1767.

Cohen, Richard A. *By the Sword: A History of Gladiators, Musketeers, Samurai, Swashbucklers, and Olympic Champions.* New York: Random House, 2002.

Debien, Gabriel. *Les Esclaves aux Antilles françaises, XVIIième–XVIIIième siècles.* Basse-Terre: Société d'Histoire de la Guadeloupe, and Fort-de-France: Société d'Histoire de la Martinique, 1974.

Diderot, Denis. *Political Writings,* translated and edited by John Hope Mason and Robert Wokler. Cambridge and New York: Cambridge University Press, 1992.

Forrest, Alan I. *The Soldiers of the French Revolution.* Durham, N.C.: Duke University Press, 1990.

Furet, François. *Interpreting the French Revolution.* Cambridge and New York: Cambridge University Press, and Paris: Editions de la Maison des Sciences de l'Homme, 1981 (original French edition, 1978).

Gaugler, William M. *The History of Fencing: Foundations of Modern European Swordplay.* Bangor, Me: Laureate Press, 1998.

Gay, Peter. *The Enlightenment: An Interpretation,* 2 vols. London: Weidenfeld and Nicolson, 1966; New York: Knopf, 1966–69.

Goodman, Dena. *The Republic of Letters: A Cultural History of the French Enlightenment.* Ithaca, N.Y.: Cornell University Press, 1994.

Gordon, Daniel. *Citizens Without Sovereignty: Equality and Sociability in French Thought, 1670–1789.* Princeton: Princeton University Press, 1994.

Grétry, André Ernest Modeste. *Mémoires; ou, Essais sur la musique,* 3 vols. Paris: Chez l'Auteur, 1789; reprint, New York: Da Capo Press, 1971.

Hampson, Norman. *The Enlightenment.* London: Penguin, 1968. As *A Cultural History of the Enlightenment.* New York: Pantheon, 1968.

Jacob, Margaret C. *The Radical Enlightenment: Pantheists, Freemasons, and Republicans.* London and Boston: Allen and Unwin, 1981.

Lynn, John A. *The Bayonets of the Republic: Motivation and Tactics in the Army of Revolutionary France, 1791–1794.* Urbana: University of Illinois Press, 1984.

Moreau de Saint-Méry, M. L. E. *A Civilization That Perished: The Last Years of White Colonial Rule in Haiti,* translated and edited by Ivor D. Spencer. Lanham, Md., and London: University Press of America, 1985 (original French edition, 1798).

Porter, Roy. *The Creation of the Modern World: The Untold Story of the British Enlightenment.* New York: Norton, 2001.

Roberts, John Morris. *The Mythology of the Secret Societies.* New York: Scribner, and London: Secker and Warburg, 1972.

Scott, Samuel F. *From Yorktown to Valmy: The Transformation of the French Army in an Age of Revolution.* Niwot: University Press of Colorado, 1998.

Weisberger, Richard William. *Speculative Freemasonry and the Enlightenment: A Study of the Craft in London, Paris, Prague, and Vienna.* Boulder, Colo.: East European Monographs, and New York: Columbia University Press, 1993.

Wellesz, Egon, and Frederick William Sternfeld, editors. *The Age of Enlightenment, 1745–1790.* London and New York: Oxford University Press, 1973.

Yolton, John W., et al., *The Blackwell Companion to the Enlightenment.* Oxford and Cambridge, Mass.: Blackwell, 1992.

INDEX

Index

Index

Index